C000173802

Alone I Made the Signs of My Way

Raili Ojala-Signell

"Raili, have you ever looked in the mirror, when you sign?" Pastor for the deaf Eino Savisaari asked me this question at my first sign language course in 1973.

Raili Ojala-Signell: Alone I Made the Signs of My Way
© Raili Ojala-Signell
🕊 © Anita Ojala
ISBN 978-952-80-0930-6
Book designer Eeva-Liisa Bahnaan
Published by BoD – Books on Demand, Helsinki, Finland
Printed by BoD – Books on Demand, Norderstedt, Germany
1. edition
Helsinki 2019

remember

I remember if I do remember
at least I should be reminded to remember
otherwise I would not remember
it would be so good, if I remembered
what I should remember
but who is it to tell me that I should remember even that
when I hardly can remember
what I should remember
I would not mind otherwise, but it would be good
if I remembered why it was good to remember
but I just cannot remember
how it was when I remembered
all the important things to remember
in order to have remembrances to share
for others to remember

Author's notes

Because I wrote my stories over a twelve-year period, between 2000 and 2012, some of them repeat events which have already been mentioned in previous stories. My Finnish memoirs received some criticism for this repetition. I have taken note of these repetitions in this English translation by mentioning them each time they occur. As my stories are their own entities and were originally intended to stand on their own this kind of repetition was partly necessary.

In some of my stories I have used capital letters to show that a deaf or deafblind person is signing that expression or that it is a gloss of sign language. This type of transcription of sign language has been used in sign language dictionary and research work in many countries because sign language as a visual language could not be written. From this way of noting the difference between sign languages and spoken languages, I have wanted to show that sign language has its own grammar and word order, but that, of course, the full richness of sign language is missing from this type of notation, since it fails to take account of all the facial expressions, the use of the hands to show, for instance, how big or how fast etc. something is, the way in which space is used too in relation to expressing where and when everything takes place. I do hope the readers of my book are aware, or will become aware, of how rich sign languages are in their ways of expression and that it is in no way my intention to suggest that the language of deaf and deafblind people is poorer than that of spoken languages.

Raili Ojala-Signell

Table of contents

Prologue

"I am not deaf, but not quite hearing either. I feel that both these worlds live happily and strongly in me. Of course I am also much else besides these elements, which makes me the Raili that I am." – This is how one could describe the stories of Raili Ojala-Signell on her experiences as a hearing child of deaf parents. Vivid mini short stories offer insightful flashes and door openings to a world that is not so well known: where she was born and where she has lived multi-dimensionally and colourfully all her life with her family, work, training, advocacy, and in her leisure activities. These stories include a strong positive suggestion and above all belief that ignorance and prejudice against deafness, sign language, and sign language culture can easily and surprisingly be made to vanish.

The stories, intriguingly, include insights, which change fluidly within one story and from one story to the next. Insights into a deaf, and a deaf blind individual, a hearing child of deaf parents, representatives of the hearing majority, and a worker in the field of deafness appear in the stories along with their experiences, often in a humorous way. These views make it easy for the reader to become absorbed in the situations, ambiences, and emotions in the stories. With their help the reader can also identify with the experiences and even with the identities depicted.

Regarding identity and difference of experience, it is interesting to note that the experiences of hearing children of deaf parents and of deaf children do not differ much in the end. As a deaf child of deaf parents it was easy for me to dive into the world of the writer and experience it, so that I did not think of the differences between our two groups at all. These differences are minimal after all, maybe more like shades of difference, although one would imagine that the world of sounds would be the most decisive area of difference. I was once in a while thrilled that I could, through these stories, return to scenery, situations, and people that I have not encountered since I was a child. Joy, happiness, grief, and sadness seized me in their turn, when I re-lived these stories.

The stories seem to have a certain basic structure, which at the end is condensed into some kind of solution, surprise, discovery, or clever explanation. But the end can also be left completely open to make the reader ponder more deeply; for instance, how things could have been totally otherwise. Some stories seem almost to be paintings or visual prints of a happening or a passing moment, which the reader can follow like a spectator of a short film in which they can submerge themselves.

Raili Ojala-Signell's stories gently portray how deaf culture is much more than not hearing sounds or the so-called inability to hear, or that living as a deaf person might be only a very painful process in the path of life. These stories convey a whole way of life and its traditions, into which the writer has merged herself like any member of a linguistic and cultural group. For me, joyful and surprising were descriptions which were connected with sounds because they were so unbelievable and unimaginable as expressions from the world of deaf people I know.

The stories include positive life experiences as well as sad incidents, which are part of life, solemn experiences, prejudices, and people in doubt, all of which one can survive as a whole and stronger person. The deaf community offers the means for this survival, means born from the lives of people living in the community, which one can easily identify with. These are beautifully included in these stories.

Any person interested in deaf culture and sign language, or a professional who has long worked in the sign language field, can benefit from this book. I believe that this book also can be meaningful to the children of deaf parents and their families. For the families, these stories can bring light into the wide field of deafness and reveal the fact that the whole community is so very many-sided. The book is a welcome addition to the literature which is still scarce in this field, and also to the rich tradition of storytelling in the deaf community.

Markku Jokinen
Executive Director, the Finnish Association of the Deaf
President, the European Union for the Deaf
Honorary President of the World Federation of the Deaf

How I became me

I was not asked
if I wanted to
alternatives
were not given

born hearing
genes from my parents
ran in the family
deafness

a step not yet taken
words not yet uttered
but already producing
signs with my fat hands

relatives were sighing
grandmothers moaned
cannot be deaf, too
poor little one

hearing ears
open eyes
sharpness of two
the adult world demanded

a hearing person
wanted to talk
to my parents and
then I was needed

difficult words
adult matters
for a child to perceive
and convey

beautiful language
richness of expression
whole deaf culture
suckled from mother's milk

interpreter mediating
thoughts, feelings
something even
left unsaid

impartial, objective
honest, exact
not taking
any sides

too much to ask
when feelings lie
always on the side
of the weaker

did I choose
to work in this field
or did I simply take
the road signed to me

two languages
two cultures
between two worlds
I have been a bridge

but what am I
not deaf
not completely hearing
will I stay as a bridge

I
Deaf world

Sounds in silence

I was born in a silent world. I have grown up and been raised in silence. In silence I have also carried out my life career. At least this is the generally prevailing understanding of the deaf world, which is considered to be a silent world. Spiritual work among deaf people still carries the title The Silent Congregation.

Because deaf people cannot, through hearing, control the level, nuance and clarity of the voice they produce, they cannot judge or estimate what kind of voice is appropriate for each situation. The majority of deaf people have never heard, and that is why they cannot even imagine what kinds of sounds all their actions produce as a side-effect. Thus, the deaf world where I grew up is far from being silent and soundless.

Our silent house, from the hearing people's viewpoint, was unbelievably full of sounds my parents produced unintentionally and without even knowing that they produced them. My father reading his morning paper before leaving for work was pain to my hearing ears. Rustle and crackle – my father was turning the pages of *Keskisuomalainen*, our local morning paper when slurping his morning coffee in the kitchen. Opening the paper, turning the pages and finally folding it together could wake me up when I was sleeping in the living room around the corner. Or it was mother who woke me up when she had got up early to make coffee and pack lunch for father. She might have decided to do the dishes, which were left by the sink in the evening. The crashing of pots and lids, the clink of dishes and the running of water disturbed my sleep. Sometimes I had to get up, dash into the kitchen and just look at mother, who understood from one blink, if not totally to stop her morning work, at least to quieten down her clinking and banging.

For older deaf people, being a hearing person has even represented being clever and knowing it all. Through hearing, one has the possibility of fully participating, receiving and picking up information from the environment without any attempt and strain. How badly we hearing people have been using this gift of hearing! It was often very difficult for my parents to understand how we children could have the radio and TV on simply as background sound and did not listen to what was being said in the news. When my parents saw a photo or film in the news which interested them in what was for them a silent TV before captioning started, they wanted to know what had happened somewhere. It was difficult for them to understand that I could sit there in front of the TV without constantly picking up news of what was happening in the world. Very often it was impossible to interpret the news item for them because it had slipped by so fast. I should have been concentrating on listening in order to be able to convey the information.

My parents used their voices to talk to their hearing discussion partners. My mother's voice was deaflike, but pleasantly clear so that even a stranger could understand it. My mother connected easily even with total strangers. My father's speech was very difficult to understand and his voice was strong and even coarse. But that did not bother my father. He was not shy in speaking to total strangers. If this stranger did not understand right away what father was saying, he added more volume. If the matter was not clear even after that, my father used any and all other means to enliven the message.

My father was a great pantomime actor. He could gesticulate, move, and make facial expressions so vividly that his whole posture changed into this person whom he wanted to describe. If the facial expressions, gestures and pointing did not get the partner to understand, he took to drawing and writing to help out.

So my parents never had communication difficulties even with unknown hearing people who often had difficulties in understanding my father's speech. Sometimes my father forgot and left his speech and voice accidentally on even when he was speaking to us children, when we could safely show him "to turn the voice off, key-sign on the throat", in order to turn off the strong sound. This home sign could never be used with other deaf people, although their strong voice production often hurt my ears.

Most often deaf people do not have the faintest idea how much sound they produce while they are moving and doing something. At the get-together weekends of we hearing children of deaf parents, we had many good laughs, when imitating the unintentional sounds our own parents or deaf people we knew had produced. What groaning, sighing and panting is connected with bowing down, tying their shoe laces, putting their clothes on, when air is pushed out from their lungs due to that effort. This is also very typical of the only deaf amateur dancer in Finland whose jumps, movements, moving of hands and the effort of a dance movement are followed by panting, huffing, fizzling, whooshing and groaning.

And signing in itself is not always quiet. You can hear slapping, when a hand hits hard on bare skin. Clanging and clinking can also be produced by the buttons, laces and jewellery in clothing when they hit each other or the surface of the table.

When I was living at home, I often commented on the matters connected with sound production to my parents. Never did I dare to start a discussion on the sounds connected with love making and how much they scared and confused me as a child.

I am convinced that if I opened up my window at the moment, I could hear the humming of the wind in the branches of my backyard pine, singing of sparrows in the hedges and the metal hook hitting the top of the flagpole. Total silence might be an unknown concept to me.

Sounds – difficulties in being a hearing person

As I have grown up and worked among deaf people, I have daily seen what all deaf people are missing in this world of sounds dominated by we hearing people. Participation, access to information and interaction between people is mainly based on hearing and receiving and interpretation of all kinds of sounds. Words, sentences and the whole world of information flashes by the eyes of deaf people in the speed of lightning without them getting any grasp or clarity about it. Still nowadays, only a fraction of information, programmes and interaction between people is available for deaf people in a visual form, as a picture, text or sign language.

All of this I have myself both experienced and understood. Through my own work I have tried to improve the situation. But how to get deaf people to understand that hearing people do not have it all so well and easy either?

On a September weekend in 2001 I participated in the 50th anniversary conference of the WFD in Rome. I returned home from there all worn out and complaining about how difficult it is for we hearing people to live in a world full of sounds. I got to experience the hardship of being a hearing person even during the conference, as the mobile phones of the participants sitting in the audience kept ringing with every possible ringing tone or peep announcing the arrival of a text message. The deaf participants did not have a clue about this disturbance.

The music the orchestra played during the banquet dinner was really getting on my nerves. The music must have been intended to entertain the few hearing people as background music. Deaf people did not even know that music was being played, although the volume once in a while was wrecking the nerves of the hearing banquet guests. At other tables, lively discussions went on without problems in spite of this background music because the hearing people in those tables knew sign language. I had been stupid enough to volunteer as an interpreter in a table where there were four "stone hearing" people sitting with two deaf and two hearing people who were using sign language. It was impossible to try to hear what people were saying at the other end of the table during the saxophone solos. My throat started hurting, when I tried to interpret the lively discussion at our table. A couple of Italians were trying to convince the orchestra to reduce the volume a bit, without much success.

When the dances the deaf way actually began, the hearing people were in a hurry to leave the restaurant. The pounding of the basses and increased volume in order for the deaf people to feel the rhythm would have made our ears ring and heads ache.

In good company with good food and drink, the evening continued till the wee hours. We were in no hurry as it was possible to sleep late the next morning. The following day was Sunday. We had only self-directed sightseeing in Rome on the programme without a tight schedule. Or at least that was what my roommate Liz and I thought. It was past three o'clock in the morning when we finally fell asleep.

I woke up in the pitch dark hotel room to the nerve-wracking peeping sound of an alarm clock. How can anyone bear that kind of sound from one morning to another and wake up to the new day with a positive mind? The metallic ringing went straight into my nerve centre. Groaning and moaning started on Liz' side of the room. With a fast movement she got the sound to stop. I checked the time on my mobile phone: 6.15! Liz had forgotten to turn the alarm off for this day after early mornings for interpreting. We went back to sleep.

Then an uneven, but heavy banging started in the hallway. Many participants were leaving in the early morning hours from the hotel. Some deaf person had overslept and had not come to breakfast as agreed with his mates. His travelling companion was pounding the door in despair with his fists. The doorbell was just a buzzer which was no use for deaf people. At some point the pounding stopped and silence fell into the hallway. Back to sleep I went.

Our hotel seemed to be quite a popular place for having conferences.

Hotel guests streamed in and out every day. Under our hotel room window there was a construction site. On weekdays the workers had started their work at seven, but we had not paid much attention to that. We had to make it to breakfast before eight and the transportation bus to the Vatican right after that. Who could have guessed that in a Catholic country people would work also on Sundays? The clang of hammers, the loud talking of the working men and the clatter of wooden planks started to creep into our room through the open balcony door.

I must have fallen back into quite a deep sleep because it took a while before I realised that my mobile phone was ringing. I pulled out my earplugs, when answering the phone drowsily.

– Good morning, darling! Did you have a nice evening? my husband asks calling me from Järvenpää, waking me up at eight o'clock on a Sunday morning after the banquet.

I was whispering, when I replied and told him that Liz was still asleep and it was too early in the morning in Rome. Silence returned to the room.

At this point someone else would have given up, but I nestled my head back into my pillow and tried to get back to sleep. Hardly had my anger vanished, when a new sound attack was directed at the room. The telephone cried out next to my ear. I grabbed the receiver, which was giving me the free line sound. New ringing. Still no one on the line. Soon a rustling of keys could be heard at the door. I jumped out of my bed and dashed to the door. I almost got the door open, when the cleaning woman opened it first. She saw my angry face, apologised and slunk away fast. It was then that I realised that the doorbell was connected to the telephone. I must have expressed a few swear words when I reacted to this disturbance. Can a hotel guest not sleep later than eight in a hotel on a Sunday morning?

Hardly had I got back to my bed and between the sheets again, when a real morning concert started: all the church bells in the churches nearby began to peal, deep and devout. It was 8.30! Catholics were getting ready for their Sunday morning mass. I have always loved the soothing sound of church bells, but that morning the ringing was the last straw for me. I gave up and started dressing for breakfast.

During breakfast I tried to explain to the deaf people from different parts of the world who were sitting at my table how difficult it is to live as a hearing person in this world full of sound, where one cannot even get a

23

good night's sleep. They did not take me seriously. The sources of sounds are usually developed by hearing people to satisfy their own needs. Deaf people have for years expressed their wish to get all auditory information in a visual form.

Dances at the Deaf Club

I was a child of the small Säynätsalo Deaf Club. Säynätsalo town had grown around a plywood factory. Adolf Marttila was the first deaf carpenter engaged to work in the factory. He smoothed the way for other deaf people through his skills and conscientiousness. Little by little the deaf community in Säynätsalo started to grow. Every time there was a deaf friend or acquaintance around who needed work, a deaf factory worker took him to see his boss or to the factory office, and usually a job was offered. Later on, deaf people even from Jyväskylä, a nearby city some 20 kilometres away, worked in the Säynätsalo factory. Deaf workers were considered good workers because they did not take unnecessary breaks and dutifully fulfilled every task assigned to them. Usually the deaf workers had been placed in different units of the factory, so there was not much opportunity to stop and sign with a fellow deaf worker, only by passing them accidentally.

The Säynätsalo Deaf Club was founded after a row between some deaf people in Jyväskylä and after that the Säynätsalo deaf people did not want to join the activities of the Deaf Club in Jyväskylä. At its largest, there were some thirty members in this small Deaf Club. Besides the annual meeting, which was obligatory, the Deaf Club organised at least a Mothers' Day Party and a Christmas Party. Once in a rare while an opportunity came up to have a visitor from the Deaf Association and that was when the enlightenment days or lectures were organised. During the summer picnics were organised on a camp site owned by the Säynätsalo Lutheran church.

There were not that many organised activities in the Deaf Club, but being a member of it was very important both for the deaf parents and their hearing children. We hearing children used to have the honour of presenting a signed song, poem or a play in the Deaf Club parties. But the best thing was to be together with the other hearing children, play together and run around the school corridors without anyone ever telling us not to be so loud. Our sounds did not disturb our deaf parents.

Usually at the end of every party with a planned programme, there was time for dancing. At that time, music and loud speakers were not known among deaf people. The dances were organised without music, they were silent dances. When the formal programme was over, all the tables and chairs were pushed aside. The person in charge of the programme blinked the lights a few times to get the attention of the participants. Standing on the stage he proudly presented the announcement that the first dancing piece would be a TANGO. Men circled around and asked the ladies for a dance. Tango was danced for some time without music but with the tango rhythm. The internal rhythm and familiar tango steps glided them along the dancing floor. That is, until the person in charge thought that it had been enough time for a tango. Lights were flashed and an announcement came that the next piece would be a WALTZ. This continued for the next hour and a half until it was time to say goodbye and go home.

The leave-taking rituals of deaf people are another story. First leave-taking, thanks for seeing one another, agreeing where they would meet the next time and other things that needed to be agreed upon were happening in the banquet room. In the vestibule the last important issues were being discussed, so getting your coat on could take some time. It was difficult to get out of the door because there always was something more to tell, when it still was light and warm inside. The lit yard of the building also needed to be taken advantage of before the darkness would make it difficult, if not impossible, to continue the discussion. Those who were going in the same direction still made a stop at each lamp-post to exchange a word or two. Leave-taking, moving from the hall through the vestibule to the yard and beyond might well take another hour and a half. This was very difficult to understand for those hearing people who had been assigned to the vestibule or to closing the doors, when an occasion reserved for deaf people might go on at least one extra hour beyond the scheduled time.

Once we were sitting on the porch of our cabin together with our cabin neighbour Hermanni, when the subject of deafness came up. Hermanni started to tell about his own experience. Once when he still was young and wild, he had been spending a Saturday evening with his friend. They had stopped by a few bars to have something to drink. That was when his friend remembered this good dancing place nearby. Hermanni had difficulty keeping up with his friend because he was so drunk, when his friend started climbing up the stairs of a building in Elizabeth Street. They entered a room where everyone was dancing, where their heels were tapping the floor. His friend joined the dancers right away as he knew the system because he had been there before. Hermanni stood by the door, tried to clear his head by shaking it. All of the sudden he froze with fear. He realised that all those people were dancing, but he could not hear the music! He thought that he had become deaf. He kept shaking his head and could not wait for his friend to return. When he finally did after dancing a couple of times, Hermanni shared his anxiety with him. No, no he might not be deaf after all because he still could hear and understand what his friend was telling him – that they were at the dances organised by the Helsinki Deaf Club!

Wake-up the deaf way

In the old days people used to wake up to the roosters' call. Deaf people instead have always needed some sort of a light signal for waking up. Lately when I have been waking up automatically, when the sunrise has lit the whole room, I have started to ponder about how deaf people used to wake up in the old days, when it was still dark and when there was no electrical equipment available.

But a human being is a thinking and creative creature who has always tried to solve the problems he has faced in his everyday life through his own inventions. I have become acquainted with stories about different kinds of inventions, which the most handy and skillful deaf people have come up with to get their own attention and make their waking up easier. Someone tied a string around his big toe when lying in bed. Through a very complicated system this string was attached to the roller blind in the window where there was also a burning lens at the end. When the sun rose, its rays burned up the string of the roller blind from the burning lens. This caused the roller screen to roll up and pull the sleeper up with the string. Somebody else had tied a string to a chair and hung it out through the mail box opening in the door. That functioned as a doorbell. When someone wanted to enter and attract the attention of the deaf person inside, he just pulled the string and got the chair to move and catch the deaf person's attention.

My father had built a primitive alarm-clock with a light signal from our old table-lamp to which he had attached a switch. When going to bed he just had to adjust the alarm-switch of the alarm-clock in the right position. When it went off and started to turn around, it hit the light switch and the light went on. Nowadays these kinds of equipment for deaf people are manufactured industrially with both light and vibration available. There are even complete alarm-centres where all the voice activities of the household can be connected, to be produced either by light or vibration, such as the doorbell, ringing of the telephone, alarm-clock, baby crying and fire alarm.

Many times hearing people question how a deaf mother can wake up when her baby is crying. Before the above-mentioned equipment, the deaf mother did not have any other option than to take the baby to sleep beside her during the night. This way she certainly would wake up to her kicking and restlessness. When we had meetings for the hearing children of deaf parents, we often also discussed those times, when a hearing child had to cry all alone and in vain in the night without anyone waking up and coming to soothe the baby. Modern technology has come to the rescue even in this regard. Nowadays the parents can put a microphone by the baby's bed and a light or vibrating alarm in the other room where they are, so that they can instantly react to the baby's crying.

Early waking up for deaf people, when they have been leaving to go somewhere or when travelling in a group, has always brought some worry, heartache and needed special arrangements beforehand. Some people have not dared to go to sleep at all the night before in order not to miss the bus or the plane in the very early morning hours. I have all kinds of experiences of the special arrangements necessary for a whole deaf group to be up and ready to go when agreed. Explanations and special information have been needed for the hotel reception people in order for them to understand that the normal wake-up call by phone certainly is not enough in this case. During congresses and seminars for the deaf we have had to ask for a special individual service for deaf people from the hotel reception so that they agree and understand that the person on duty has to go up into the deaf person's hotel room with the master key to wake up the deaf guest.

Various stories have been heard about how this request has been carried out and how a deaf person has woken up too late by himself and found a piece of paper under the door which says: *It is 6 AM. Wake up!* Or when a deaf person has gone angrily to the reception to complain that he has missed his early flight and received a friendly reply that the wake-up call was certainly made at 6 AM as asked, or that the person on duty had knocked on the door, but there had been no reply. In customer service too much attention might be given to the intimacy rights of the guests and that is why it has often been difficult to break these rules. When it is a question of a deaf customer, it is not enough that the person on duty comes into the hotel room with the master key and stands by the bed, but touching of the sleeping customer is also required, which is often very difficult for hearing people. One also has to make sure that the deaf person really wakes up to the touching, not to just turn over and fall back to sleep again.

When travelling with deaf people as an interpreter and a group leader, I have been in different kinds of situations, when we have had to get our group together for leaving early in the morning. It has happened more than once that at the end of the evening I have ended up getting all the room keys of the participants from my group so that I can get up even earlier than them and have a tour around their rooms, waking them up or making sure that they are up. Most of the time they have been up already and we have got on our way soon after having breakfast. Once I had some difficulties when we were in the United States and one of the group had been too afraid of American criminals and had put the chain-lock on after giving me his room key. I was able to open the door, but did not get close enough to wake him up from his sound and deep sleep. The situation was even more complicated because the bed was situated behind the door, I only could see his toes from under the blanket. We did not want to take extreme measures right away, which might have caused extra expense. We went out, collected small rocks and other little things to throw at him. He must have had a heap of stones on his bed, when we finally got a hit to his toe. Of course, he was ashamed of his thoughtlessness in the situation, but our group got their journey started a little bit later that morning. Luckily we did not have a plane to catch, only another city and sights waiting for us that day.

Another experience of waking up the deaf way, which I will never forget, happened to me in Leksand, Sweden, when I paid my first visit to the Folk High School for the Deaf there. It was our first morning there. We did not need to be up very early, but woke up to a horrible noise and pounding from the room next door at five o'clock in the morning. The pounding and even hammering continued and did not stop. The whole building seemed to be shaking and it felt like someone was hammering the walls somewhere in the house. Later that day we were shown this magnificent new invention to get the deaf students to wake up for their morning lectures. Under a wooden bed a wooden hammer was placed, which was connected to the alarm-clock. When the alarm went off, the hammer started pounding the bottom of the bed so hard that the whole bed started shaking. Next door to our room someone had already left the day before and forgotten to turn off the unnecessary alarm, which went off and woke us up too early, needlessly, driving us almost mad with the sound.

But there are also deaf people who have a well-functioning alarm-clock inside their body. My colleague at work, a good friend of mine, has this kind of well-trimmed and trustworthy inner clock in her body. She travels a lot in her work and many times to places where the time-difference is huge. When she arrives in a new country and goes to bed the first evening, she adjusts her inner clock to the time of that country and gives a wake-up order to that clock for a particular time. And her clock has not yet failed her.

Nowadays deaf people who travel a great deal also carry their vibration alarm-clock with them during their travels. We here in Finland have not got as far in providing services for deaf people as they have in the United States where their ADA-legislation demands that all hotel receptions have to have all the technical equipment a deaf customer needs when staying at their hotel. After registration the deaf customer receives an alarm-clock with vibration and in addition to that also a doorbell and flashing fire alarm. In the hotel lobby there should be at least one text telephone. The deaf customer pays the same rate for the hotel services as a hearing customer and that is why he is entitled to these special services in adapted form because of equal rights.

"Own best friend for many years"

Both my mother and father went to the School for the Deaf in Oulu. They were even in the same class. From their school days they have many good friends, some classmates, and some schoolmates who had been in the school at the same time as them. One of these schoolmates was Aino, who actually was my deaf Aunt Lahja's classmate and even a godmother to one of my cousins. Aino is married to Toivo and they have three hearing children.

For me as a little girl Aino was a very gorgeous looking woman. Every time they were on their way south they stopped overnight at our place and I could not wait till it was evening and time to go to bed because that was the moment, when I could see it again – Aino's huge bra! It was something to wonder at for a little girl like me. I had never seen anything so huge. I did not have any idea of cup sizes then, but hers were something extra.

Aino was good at keeping her own side up. I guess that also has another word, called boasting, but for Aino it had become an art of her very own. In a way, she was very heartfelt, she took people under her wing and acted as if she owned them. Later in my life I met Aino again somewhere and she always remembered to tell me that my parents were "her own best friends for many years". If I remember it correctly, my parents did not quite feel the same way. When I had a working trip to her town, I could almost feel Aino's disappointment when I met her, because I had not informed her about my coming, nor to mention that I had booked a hotel room and not asked to stay with them. I should have, because my parents were her "own best friends for many years".

Once again, Aino and Toivo had stopped at our house on their way down south to visit their daughter. This time they did not stay overnight, only stopped to have a cup of coffee and a short rest. They had a brand new car, which Aino had bought her husband for his birthday. At the coffee table Aino kept on telling us what a wonderful car they had, how she had bought it and how much it had cost. I am sure we also heard how well their children were doing both in school and in work life and what smart kids they had. That could not have been called much of a discussion, Aino only needed an audience and also demanded everyone's attention. We did not have much to add to her stories. If any one of us tried to convert the theme into something else, Aino had the skill to turn even that subject to her advantage, boasting about herself and her family.

It started to be time for them to continue their trip. We thanked them for stopping by and saw them out to the veranda. I guess we had not been sufficiently interested in and overwhelmed by Toivo's new car, since when Aino got outside and noticed our old Saab standing in front of the shed, she signed in a matter-of-fact way:

– I HAVE HEARD – SAAB NOT A GOOD CAR!

"You have gained weight!"

When I was 17, I spent a year in the United States as an exchange student. I guess I did not move around much during that year, when even getting to school was organised by my American sister driving me in a car. Once in a while I did try to walk home from school along the sides of the busy highway or on the green berms by the streets because there were no sidewalks and I had an urge to get some exercise. This custom of mine raised some curiosity in the neighbourhood.

All the new tastes I experienced were so fascinating that I took seconds more than often. The American desserts, especially, were so lovely and tempting: fruit and berry pies and different kinds of puddings. In my family the main meal was eaten quite late because everyone needed to be at home for dinner. That was one reason why my young body started saving all the extra calories.

After only half a year, because of this American effective diet, all my clothes which I had brought from home started giving signs of being a size or two too small. Because the weights and scales were different from those ones I was used to, I did not quite seem to understand by how much I had actually gained weight during that year. The truth was certainly revealed to me, when I returned home: I had gained ten extra kilos.

It was time for me to learn to live with the new me, with my new figure. Meeting deaf people in my home town did not make my life any easier. Some 100 deaf people live in Jyväskylä city and its suburbs, most of whom I had known for a long time. It was painful for me to participate in any Deaf Club activities after I had returned back home from the States as every deaf person I met remembered to tell me:
– OH, YOU HAVE GAINED SO MUCH WEIGHT!
– SO MUCH BIGGER NOW THAN BEFORE!
– BEFORE YOU WERE NORMAL, NOW TOO FAT!
What could I tell them in return? I had some vicious thoughts in my mind after those comments, such as:
– There are also mirrors in America, did you know that?
– Just try to imagine how many clothes I have had to give up because I do not fit into them anymore?
– Oh really, I have not yet noticed it myself!
But my way was to reply with a joke about the situation to get it over with and to show that overweight was no problem to me. Every person

certainly enjoys ten extra kilos for sure; it makes every fat person look even more attractive.

But I did not leave it at that, it bothered me that much. I did try to understand the background and reasoning behind the different ways of thinking deaf people had. What actually was it that made them blurt it all out always so directly and bluntly so that someone always got hurt? I did find many explanations for and an understanding of their behaviour. Deaf people had lived, and in most parts of the world still lived, in the hearing world without actually getting enough information about all that was being discussed around them. When the closest people to a deaf child do not use sign language, the deaf child never learns to understand what the proper behaviour is in each situation, what kinds of norms and rules guide communication and contact between people. Usually these kinds of behavioural rules do not exist in a written form, but they are learned in communication situations within families and with other people in the community. When deaf people have never been told what is proper and what is not in their own language, they often are put in an awkward situation because of their straightforward comments when they are in a hearing environment. Once in a while in an interpreting situation there happens to be a culturally competent interpreter who has internalised the deaf culture and knows that the intention is not to hurt, and knows how to express it in the spoken language so that the hearing person does not get hurt.

I collected similar examples from people around me where deaf people had been hurting their friends with their blunt comments, and I gave a talk about it at the Jyväskylä Deaf Club. I had hardly got started with my examples, when a deaf unmarried lady over 50 years of age asked for the floor and said that deaf people should stop asking her if she had found a husband yet. She said that whenever she was going somewhere out of town, on a trip or a deaf gathering somewhere else, every time she got back to her own deaf community there were questions like:

– DID YOU FIND A HUSBAND THERE?

– WAS THERE ANYONE WHO GOT YOU EVEN INTERESTED?

– YOU STILL DID NOT MANAGE TO GET MARRIED, ALTHOUGH YOU WERE GONE FOR TWO WEEKS?

She said that she was so sick and tired of these kinds of comments, as if there was nothing else in her life that mattered except finding a husband.

In my lecture I tried to highlight the idea that before anyone expressed their opinion to someone about something that seemed so obvious and eye-striking to them, one should first always try to think how that other person might feel after what had been said. There is so much that one can leave unsaid or keep themselves. You do not need to say everything aloud, or to express it in signs.

Not too long a time had passed after the lecture I had given, which people really appreciated at that time, when one of my colleagues from work was visiting my parents' house. She was over thirty at that time. She had beautiful, white, even teeth. We were sitting by a coffee-table, when my mother expressed her polite opinion to my colleague:

– YOU MUST HAVE FALSE TEETH FOR SURE?

The VIP person in my life

Sister Aune came into my life when I was eleven. At that time deaconess Aune Ihalainen started her work as deaconess for the deaf and blind with the Jyväskylä Lutheran church. In the 60's there were not many hearing people, not to mention professionals, who knew sign language and understood issues concerning deaf people. Sister Aune became a VIP in the lives of deaf people and their families in the Jyväskylä region.

From the very beginning Aune was completely different from other adult people who used sign language. She also existed for we children. It was very usual that deaf parents took all the attention of the adult hearing person who knew sign language for themselves and their own important matters. Such mediators who knew their language were not too many and not often at hand. The hearing worker who knew sign language had the key to information and to conveying it so that even a deaf person could understand it.

We children followed our parents to different kinds of events for deaf people till we were in our teens. Other workers for the deaf used to tap us on the head and ask:

– How are you doing?

But they seldom had time to stop and listen to our news. Sister Aune was different. First she listened to what our parents had in their hearts, after that she dared to turn her back on our parents, to her real clients. She signed WAIT with her hand and had a moment to share our small sorrows or joys. Aune understood, comforted, encouraged, advised, and guided us, but above all, she had hearing ears to listen to us.

I was too old to participate in the camps Aune organised for hearing children of deaf parents in her region. Many years afterwards the hearing children from my home region were still talking about those camps and how much fun they had had there with Aune as the camp leader. I took Aune as my own, as my friend. On my way home from school, when I passed the University street in Jyväskylä where Aune lived and still had her office in her home, I was brave enough to go and ring her doorbell. If there was a client there, she let me into her lovely living room to wait my turn. I had time to admire and wonder at all the beautiful things she had on the walls and on the shelves. Aune had brought tusks of a wild boar, lovely woven baskets and African sculptures from her travels. I felt so important, when she had time to sit with me for a moment over a cup of coffee. Very often there was no reply to my ringing of the doorbell. Aune was out running errands and interpreting for her clients at the hospital, at a doctor's appointment or some other office.

Afterwards I have heard how incredibly long working days Aune was doing then. Many days were prolonged till late at night with a deaf client at the emergency room or queuing up for a doctor's appointment. She often did not have time even to have lunch. Deaf people from far away knew about her services and came to Jyväskylä to get help from her in sign language. At that time there was no one to draw the line to her working hours. Workers who knew sign language were only a handful in the whole country.

Our friendship has started from me being the active partner. I took Aune as my friend. The contact with her has continued all these years. Often Aune introduces me to new people by telling them how I stopped by her door with red cheeks and full of energy, I biked ten kilometres one way to school from Kinkomaa to Jyväskylä every day and showed up at her doorstep and needed someone to listen to me.

My exchange year in the States made us even closer. It was wonderful to get Aune's reports and the news of my home deaf community. Aune is a letter writer like me. She keeps in touch with an unbelievable number of people by writing letters. Her letters are not just anything. Usually she comments on the thoughts and questions her friend has written to her in the letter. Next she writes her piece of news and adds good life guidance, tips and quotes from the Bible or other wise sages. Aune always writes her letters by hand. She does not even have a typewriter. Her four page handwritten letter is starting to be quite a rarity these days. On her letter-writing days, she produces close to a dozen of these kind of handwritten letters.

Time almost stopped for deaf people in Jyväskylä, when over 40 years ago, Aune first started her long sick-leave and after that early retirement. People thought that no one could ever fill Aune's place. No one knew how to serve, listen to and be of help like Aune did. Of course a new worker was found for the position, and she earned her place in her own way and style. When Aune left Jyväskylä, it was an end to one major period in the work for deaf people in Central Finland.

Leaving work was a new beginning for Aune. Thus far she had been married to her work and to the deaf people in her region. When she went to Lapland to do some volunteer work for a Christian organisation in their holiday place, she met the man of her life, Olavi. Her letters from Lapland started to have a new colour in them, which at first I could not figure out. After Aune returned home the reason was clarified. At Easter they got engaged and at Whitsunday time Aune's and Olavi's wedding was celebrated in Vesala, the course centre owned by the Jyväskylä church. After that her life changed completely. Aune left Jyväskylä and moved to Vammala into a new home as a newlywed bride, wife and companion to a staid man Olavi from Satakunta. She kept only her name sign, which comes from her maiden name Ihalainen (HAPPY) even after she became Mrs. Kulmala. She spent close to twenty years in this role before Olavi died.

Celebrating Aune's birthdays marked the start of our hilarious group called *The Foundation for Overexhausted Workers in the Field of Sensory Impairments*. Like any other foundation, we too have our official and unofficial meetings and telephone conferences and keep the minutes from them. From the original group of four we have grown into ten members, who are more or less honorary or deservedly overexhausted. Every fifth year since Aune's 50th birthday we have organised gatherings, which have developed our creative thinking, when we have tried to surprise the birthday girl in a new way. A weekend or a day spent together laughing has strengthened stomach muscles and prolonged our life expectancy by few years. We have kept the minutes from the get-togethers and also funny and punchy scrapbooks for each birthday pal, which tell about the journey we have travelled together.

My friend Aune has been in my life sharing all kinds of feelings and life situations. When a big sorrow or small joy has hit me, it has been Aune I have wanted to share it with. I have not yet had any feeling or incident, which Aune has not been able to reflect and respond to, understand and support. She has a special skill for finding the right kind of words for every situation. She always has time to listen to her friends. Aune does not show her friendship only by letters or by being a telephone call away. If needed, she jumps on a train and comes to you to share your loss or big sorrow. This I experienced, when my husband had a brain haemorrhage and was for weeks in a critical condition in hospital. Aune moved to live with me to give me support, to listen to me, to take care of my everyday life and to go to the hospital with me the first few most difficult times.

I could write a novel about Aune, her different sides and hobbies, moments I have spent with her. Close to her heart is the Finnish Deaf Mission, keeping in contact with her godchildren in Africa and helping them. Aune is the mainstay of the Vammala mission circle to support deaf godchildren in Africa. Thousands of euros are collected every year at the mission market in one day. In the autumn Aune picks by hand over 100 litres of lingonberries from the forest, most of which she sells for the mission's work. For Aune, the forest and its fruit are the biggest joy in life, something she always praises in her letters. Aune has serious pain in her back, she has osteoarthritis in her hands and has arthroplasty in her right shoulder, so considering all of this, her hard work for the good of others is even more exceptional.

Aune has been more than a friend to me. She has been my hearing grandmother, wise old woman, whom I have been able to turn to, to ask for advice during the difficult moments in my life. She has been my supervisor when I have had my difficulties in my deaf work. She has been a good partner during trips and outings. Aune has always been the see-er and doer, source and light of inspiration. She is a piece of the history of work among deaf people in Finland. But for me, Aune has mostly been the most important person in my life.

My mother wearing a bow on her dress at the Jyväskylä Deaf Club in the 1940s.

Members of the Jyväskylä Deaf Sports Club, my mother in the middle row, second from the left.

At the Jyväskylä Deaf Club in 1951, Little-Raili with a white frilled collar between her mother and father.

Dean Lauri Paunu in the third row, at an event of the Säynätsalo Deaf Club.

Mother receives an award for her work as secretary at the 10th Anniversary of the Säynätsalo Deaf Club.

My father on the left in the sign choir of the Säynätsalo Deaf Club, Uncle Antero in the middle.

At the outing of the Deaf Club, brother Risto with binoculars around his neck.

Little-Raili mimicking at the Midsummer Party of deaf people.

Mimicry continues at my grandmother's farmyard.

Showing determination already in 1952 on the rocks by the Määttänen house.

Aune in discussion with deafblind Saara Tikkanen.

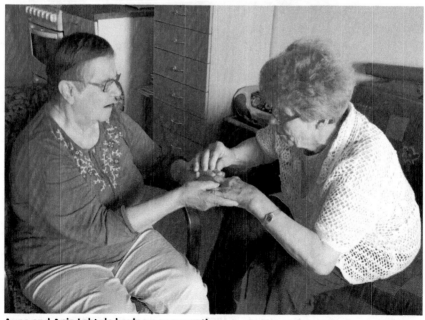
Aune and Anja Lehtola having a conversation.

With Aune at the Hoikka Course Centre in 1977.

The overexhausted workers at Aune's 80th birthday party in Vammala.

II
Me and us

Ifs and buts

IF my grandma Edla had decided to stay in the States after all
like her two brothers did,
she would never have met the young man from the village nearby,
grandpa Jaakko

IF grandmother Lyydia had remained as a servant girl
for the Russian family,
the four deaf children of the Lehtola family would not have been born

IF the first boyfriend of my mother Terttu had not died of tuberculosis,
she never would have got interested in her classmate
Eero Ojala from Pohjanmaa

IF my older brother had not received a ladleful of every talent,
I might have received more than a spoonful of everything

IF my parents had not been deaf,
I might never have got an interest in sign language
or met any deaf people

IF I had not gone to the secondary school,
which seemed too big an expense for my family,
would my life been a different one behind a country store counter
as the wife of the local taxi driver

IF I had not got interested in applying for a scholarship
with my classmates,
I would have graduated from high school only a year older
than my fellow students

IF I had after all studied to become a crafts teacher,
I would have trained quite a few classes
in the intriguing world of handcrafts

IF I had not had the opportunity to spend a year
in a hearing family in America,
I would probably not have found my way to the deaf world
and the richness of sign language

IF I had after all begun my studies in a language institute
to become an interpreter or translator,
I would have made it into this natural profession of mine much earlier

IF I had not taken my first job before finishing
my social work degree at university,
I would probably still be working in the field of social work

IF I had been selected for that social worker position
I applied for in Turku,
I would perhaps still be happily serving deaf people in that region

IF my friends had agreed to go to the country dancing place
to seek company for Whitsunday,
I would not have responded to the personal column advertisement
and met my husband

IF I had been little less choosy in my previous relationships,
I would not have had a grandchild without having my own children first

IF my husband had not become seriously ill and died,
I would have continued on the treadmill
serving the deaf people of the world till my retirement

IF I had not decided to let go of my important work
and started to enjoy life after all the hardships,
I would not be here writing these ifs and buts to you

Ferry and mitten

Säynätsalo municipality on Lake Päijänne consists of three islands: Säynätsalo, Lehtisaari and Muuratsalo. The municipality grew around the factories founded by John Parviainen. The Parviainen family did not only own the plywood factory and sawmill, but funded the building of the church, schools, rental houses and apartment blocks, as well as the general sauna for the workers from the factory. It was traditional in Säynätsalo that children followed their parents' footsteps as workers in the factory. Big families earned their daily living from the factory and planned their shifts to function as well as possible to suit the rest of the family. If someone decided to continue to secondary school, which meant taking a bus to Jyväskylä, it was the exception.

There was a ferry running between the first two islands and serving the transportation needs of workers from the two other islands to Säynätsalo, where the factory was. Later on in the 60's, after we had moved away from Muuratsalo island, the ferry was replaced by a suspension bridge. In between Lehtisaari and Muuratsalo there was an old wooden bridge which made a funny noise when the bus went over it.

During the first few years of my life, our family lived in a rented one-room flat with a stove in the Määttänen family house on Muuratsalo island. My father had got a job in the factory as a carpenter soon after he married and moved from the farm in Patana. Mother always stayed at home with we children.

My father used to bike to work no matter what the weather was like. When we had some errands to run either in Lehtisaari, where the closest store was, or in Säynätsalo where all the municipal offices were, we used to bike there. When we had to go to town, we took the bus. It always was an adventure to us children to take the ferry across the strait. Everybody had to get off from the bus before the driver drove it on the ferry. Adults were still talking about that one time, when the ferry had too many cars on it and had capsized, pitching a number of workers on their way home into the water where one six year old boy drowned. Our parents remembered to remind us how dangerous the ferry-ride could actually be.

One time our family was on its way to Säynätsalo to visit another deaf family. I always liked to stand by the side of the ferry and follow with my eyes how the metal rope hurtled between the big rolling wheels before making its way to the end of the ferry and disappearing in the dark deepness of the lake.

– DO NOT TOUCH! my mother often warned us.

But the rope was so tempting, moving so close by my hands. The rolling movement enchanted me. The rope darted before my eyes, when I tried to follow where it was going. By accident, my hands lifted higher up on the side of the ferry. I only intended to brush the metal rope running past my eyes. Only a light touch with my mittened-hand. Unfortunately, the part where my hand touched happened to have a broken strand. The strand caught in my mitten and off it flew. My mitten was jumping up and down, seemed as if it was teasing me as it moved farther away, disappearing finally in the water and never coming back.

I got so scared that I could not help but cry out. When my parents noticed what had happened to me, they first let my eyes see what they thought of my action and disobedience. The eyes of my mother and father were burning angry, faces were grim and serious, hands moving up and down in the air with fast movements and anger. When they finally got over their fright, they consoled me with their safe and caring hands.

Only a few years had gone by since the ferry disaster. The mental pictures of the boy who had drowned in that accident were still alive in people's memory. My parents must have first of all imagined what could have happened to me, if the metal rope had caught in any other part of my clothing. Even something more valuable could have been lost besides my knitted mitten.

Little brother

I was almost five. I had exciting times ahead of me – my mother had promised to bring me a little brother or sister. Now even I would get a chance to be the big sister. Thus far I had always been the little sister.

Suddenly, one day, my mother left without warning. She was gone for some time. My relatives took care of me and my brother when my father was at work.

Then my mother came back, as unexpectedly as she had left. But she came home alone. She did not have a little brother or sister with her as she had promised. I had been betrayed. I was very angry at my mother for breaking her promise. I was loudly crying out my disappointment. My mother tried to tell me that my little brother had come into the world too early and had lived only for two days. Explanations were no good for me, I was angry and disappointed.

I can still remember my little brother's funeral in the Säynätsalo church as if it were yesterday. It was wintertime, and at that time there were not too many flowers available. It was mainly cyclamens that were laid on little-Juhani's coffin. I, the disappointed five-year old, was screaming and crying out loud, enough to disturb the service. I had lost my chance of being the big sister, to have a little sister or brother to take care of. Even the pastor tried to calm me down, but my disappointment was too great for me to be able to quieten myself.

Only later, when I was older, did I get to know and understood that my mother's life had been in danger in giving birth to the premature baby. I did not receive a little brother, but my mother stayed alive.

The roots of this disappointment and sorrow have taken a long time to heal – cyclamens have always been funeral flowers for me, to me they have always represented death. I have never been able to buy cyclamens for home. It was only Christmas 2000 that I made myself buy a mini-cyclamen to give to a friend as a Christmas flower.

Going to school

My big brother is three years older than me. He had already started second grade in the elementary school in Muuratsalo. I was five and happy in the kindergarten, until one day in early September my brother brought a message to my parents from school: I should have started first grade that year.

I was big for my age and also very knowledgeable. I must have seemed older than my age because I was used to interpreting discussions between my deaf parents and the neighbours and hearing relatives. They had started to think at school that maybe my deaf parents did not know when I should start my schooling.

Next morning my brother took me along to school. He left me to the first grade teacher. The other first graders had already been at school for a few days, so my late arrival caused some interest and suspicion. The teacher started to inquire about my age and other skills. She was surprised to hear that I had turned five only in May, and would still be only six the following year. I was given drawing tasks, while the others continued with their school assignments. In the afternoon I was sent back home.

If only at that time there had been psychology tests for school entrants, maybe I could have started school at that age. Later on when I did start school at the age of seven in Kinkomaa, my teacher was sorry that she could not move me directly to the second grade because all my skills were not at that level.

Gone with the wave

Even as children living in Säynätsalo we were made aware of the famous Finnish architect Alvar Aalto and what he had created. (Aalto means a wave in English!) On the other side of the road from our house there was a boat-building yard owned by Mr Kosola. Even we children had heard rumours that Mr Kosola was building a boat for Alvar Aalto. I cannot quite remember how I was able to picture architect Aalto at that time when I was under school age, but I remember like it was yesterday when we children were told that we were invited to join the test ride on the Aalto's' boat on Lake Päijänne.

We little ones certainly were amazed at the luxury of the boat and its speed on the water, but the biggest wonder for me was the inside toilet on the boat. At that time, in the middle of the 50's, no apartments had inside toilets, we had to use the outhouse no matter what the weather was like.

Not too long ago I happened to notice a small advertisement for a forthcoming television programme in the Swedish-speaking evening news on our main channel, where a five minute programme on the Aalto boat was to be featured. I could not miss that, I had to refresh my childhood memories of that boat. They said in the programme that Aalto had designed the boat himself. Because he had never done anything like that before, his boat was called "Nobody is a prophet on his own land" in Latin; for short, the boat is called *Nemo*. The programme mentioned the old boat builder who had told Aalto about the particular difficulties in building that boat. The boat had too long a front and its balance point was wrongly calculated. That was why even the small waves on Lake Päijänne wet the front part, which was covered by a carpet.

The boat was kept on the Säynätsalo shore where the Aaltos picked it up on their way to their summer cottage. After Aalto's death the family moved it to the archipelago in Turku. Because the boat was not suitable for use in the sea, the Aalto Museum had taken it back and was looking for a good place to store it. Säynätsalo township, which over the years had become part of Jyväskylä city, agreed to find a place for it. Aalto's wife Elissa, an architect herself, designed a cover for the boat and for a while it was kept on an island in Säynätsalo where also tourists were able to see it. In 1998, when the 100th anniversary of Aalto's birth was celebrated, the boat received a more suitable home in the yard of Aalto's experimental house. It is now stands in a rack-type storage house designed by Danish architects.

But in the five minutes the programme lasted they had included a lot of interesting graphics and information about that boat which, all of a sudden had become very important to me again. For some reason not a word was mentioned of that important memory I had of it: as far as I can remember, the boat also had a toilet inside.

Alvar Aalto is famous for his works around Säynätsalo and Jyväskylä, places where we grew up. Later on when I visited Muuratsalo again I became familiar with the experimental house Aalto had built for his family. This strange and tempting building was far in the forest, unreachable by roads, on a forest path, which I walked once or twice when going to the cabin of a classmate's family. Aalto's cottage was reachable mainly by boat, via waterways. There never happened to be anyone at the cottage at those times when I walked past it, but still we hesitated to go too near this famous building. It was surrounded by a high wooden fence, painted in white, which formed an inner yard for the cottage. The cottage itself was typical Aalto-design with square forms and corners and windows, which were all of different shapes and sizes.

The Säynätsalo Town Hall was a familiar place for we children, which was also one of Aalto's most famous designs, which people came from far away to see. For our family, this famous building included the services of the town doctor and a sports store on the first floor, where my brother worked at one time, and the town library on the second floor which you could climb up to by steps sown with grass. Once in a while the local Deaf Club organised its annual meeting in the meeting room of this town hall. Then we children had the opportunity to wonder at the strange shaped lamps of Aalto design which gave hardly any light, his famous chairs with only three legs, sitting on which was difficult without tipping over, and vertical wooden shades on the windows, which made a nice clattering noise when we ran through the corridors and ran a stick over the shades. Sometimes I have wondered if this early influence of Aalto's famous designs has had influenced my brother's interest in art and design.

Later on when we lived closer to Jyväskylä, where we also received to our secondary education, we became familiar with Aalto's other famous designs: the main building of the Jyväskylä University and the Aalto Museum. When my mother moved to live in Jyväskylä after the death of my father, we often walked past one of Aalto's youth works on the top of the hill. Of course, I had to buy an Aalto-vase as soon as I got some extra money from my summer earnings. A bouquet of tulips cannot look as gorgeous as it does without this simple wave design by Aalto.

But it was not until my brother and I picked up a Japanese hitchhiker, who was an architect and was very keen on Aalto's work, from the roadside on our way back home, that we became Aalto tour guides. We wanted to show him some Finnish hospitality, so we did not only show him all the famous Aalto buildings nearby. He had asked us to take him to the Säynätsalo Town Hall. We invited him to stay overnight and introduced him to other Finnish secrets and traditions, such as sauna and what Finnish nature provides. We hope that this visit to the birthplaces of Aalto design has been an inspiration in the work of this young Japanese architect.

Rotten tooth

I might have been in the first or second grade in the elementary school in Kinkomaa, when a rotten tooth was found at the back of my mouth during the annual examination. So far I had visited the dentist only to have bad teeth taken out. It was always only when the pain was unbearable that I finally went to the dentist. My family did not have very much extra money to pay expensive private dentist's fees. My father was the only one who worked in the family, and the annual interest and instalment payments on our bank mortgage for the house were huge, even in the eyes of we children. We understood that we could not afford any extra expenses.

The school dentist only needed to look into my mouth to see how my tooth-ache could be cured: my back tooth – out it came! But the tooth, although it was rotten and aching, had strong and healthy roots. The older lady who was the school dentist had to work really hard to get it out. The tooth refused to come out in one piece. The dentist muttered after she had got most of the tooth out:

– I guess a small piece was left in there, but it will come out on its own.

I had already completely forgotten that tiny chip. But after some time my ear started aching badly. Regular pain medicine did not seem to give any relief. I had to go to see the GP in Säynätsalo. We had heard stories of his strange behaviour, but now I had a chance to see his eccentric ways with my own child's eyes.

The fat male doctor kept smoking a cigar even whilst attending to patients. The examination went alright, but when he sat down at his desk and started writing the prescription for me, all of a sudden the cigar dropped from his hand onto the desk and he fell asleep with his head leaning on the piles of paper. He woke up as instantly as he had fallen asleep and continued from where he had left off as if nothing had happened in between. He prescribed a pink, liquid antibiotic for ear infection for me. That should have relieved the pain.

But no – beside the painful ear-ache, my right chin started to swell up. It could have been mumps, but when my whole cheek and chin were rock-hard, it had to be something else. When the swelling disappeared, two swollen round rotten boils were left on my chin. One burst by itself before I had time to go to the doctor. He lanced the other one, cleaned it, and sewed the wound together. It was difficult to repair the damage, which had already occurred with the bursting of the first boil.

The chip or two which the school dentist had left behind had come out for sure. Not from the inside of my mouth through the hole where the tooth had been, but next to my jawbone, causing the rotten boils. For years afterwards I was stigmatised with the sign of the carelessness and indifference of the school dentist. Although the rotten boils and scar from the operation grew smaller and became paler in time, every time I met a new person there would be at some point in our discussion a question about my scar and where I had got it. I would have forgotten my scar if only someone else did not always bring up the subject.

Many times afterwards I have wondered whether a bigger fuss should have been made about what had happened, if my parents had not been deaf and could have fought against the results of the negligence and indifference their daughter had suffered. As a hearing child of deaf parents

I did not have enough information or skills to start claiming compensation for a permanent scar I had received. Sometimes, when I read stories in the newspaper on American court cases, which are fought for any little reason, I start thinking how much compensation would have been enough for my permanent cosmetic disadvantage. Even the thought of how much I could demand makes me happy.

Wild strawberries

We were visiting another deaf family in Säynätsalo. They lived in a factory housing complex quite near the church. As the deaf parents had their own issues to discuss, we hearing children tried to fill up our time by doing something. Margit was a few years younger than me, but at that age it did not matter.

Margit told me that she had found a wonderful strawberry field nearby, which was red with wild strawberries. There were plenty more than just for eating, enough to fill a bowl. Mrs Hantunen gave us a kettle and we took off for the strawberry fields.

Margit led me to the cemetery next to the church and to its furthest corner. The area was inside the fence, but still untouched moorland. It was filled with ripe, red wild strawberries. I had been taught to respect the peace of graveyards and the dead, but for Margit and her local friends, the cemetery was an exciting and challenging playground, with no adults around. I did ask if it was proper to pick and eat those strawberries. I could imagine the decayed bodies and worms crawling in the ground. I forgot my fear because Margit was so enthusiastic, and soon we had the two litre kettle filled with wild strawberries.

We were proud of our harvest, when we gave the kettle filled with berries to Margit's mother. She did not stop praising us. She must have seen strawberry jam jars in front of her eyes, when she poured a bagful of sugar on top of the strawberries to make strawberry jam after we had left.

I am not sure how she ended up asking us where the wild strawberries came from, where did we ever find so many wild strawberries?

– FROM THE GRAVEYARD! Margit signed, all excited.

Her mother's eyes widened to saucers, her face lost its entire colour. She was not happy about that piece of news. She grabbed the handles of the kettle and poured all of our wild strawberries into a waste bin. She was particularly mourning the sugar that had been wasted.

I have never seen such a wonderful wild strawberry patch in my life since that incident.

An egg as payment

There was a big farm near my childhood home. When I was in elementary school, there was a poultry farm there. One of my friends was Leena, who lived in the side house of the farm with her mother and sister. I cannot quite remember how they were related to the farm owners, but I remember that they did not own that farm themselves.

At the end of the 1950's, children did not get a weekly allowance from their parents, especially not in my family. Since my father had built us a house of our own, for which a big mortgage loan was needed, the repayments a couple of times a year meant that money was quite tight in our household. I had learned to understand that money does not grow on trees.

Seldom was there an opportunity to do little bit of work and get paid for it. In the poultry farm there was a busy day once a week, when they had to clean and polish the eggs that would be taken to a store the following day. One day after school I was at Leena's playing, when we were asked if we wanted to earn money and join the egg-cleaning task. It might have taken an hour or two, when I realised that it was already dark outside and I should be heading home. I was on my skis and home was more than a kilometre away.

As payment I could either have a couple of Finnish marks in coins or one egg! I was a sharp economist already at that time and could figure out that the egg was worth much more than the two coins. I asked to have the egg.

It was dark outside and freezing cold. I had difficulty in getting the skis on with the egg in my hand, but finally succeeded. I started off on my skis along the ski-trail by the road towards home. I had difficulties skiing because I was getting tired, but also because I had to secure the egg in my mitten. It was the uphill that finally did it. The skis slipped and I had to grab my ski-poles more tightly to keep my balance. The egg was squashed in my mitten.

I was tired, disappointed and crying, when I finally got home. I had been so proud beforehand to be able to show my mother what I had earned from my work. Now I only had the dirty, frozen mitten and a mind sore with disappointment. I guess I should have taken the couple of marks instead.

Wrong R

I do not know, which came first – the first names of my brother and me, both of which started with an R, Risto and Raili, or my quite bad, but in a way endearing and soft R-defect. Every time there was a Finnish word with an R in it, my tongue became stiff and in the completely wrong place, far back in my mouth, producing a soft burr, when it was supposed to rattle vigorously in the stream of air and produce a proper R.

This minor speech problem did not disturb me much. I did not know of anything else, until the bad boys got a hint of it and asked me to repeat my name over and over again as if they had not heard it the first time. They would have teased me more about it, if I had not always been big for my age and good at giving the same back. I could take care of myself. Adults would smile to themselves when listening to my speech, but they did not consider my speech defect to be so severe and worrying that they needed to interfere. My deaf parents were completely unaware of this speech defect of mine.

I went through kindergarten, four grades in elementary school and quite a few grades of secondary school before someone took more careful notice of this R-defect, which had become such a natural part of my life and personality that I did not even notice it any more. I cannot remember who this well-meaning adult was, who finally decided to change the stream of my life, and made me go to see a speech therapist to get my speech defect corrected. I must have been around 15 or 16 when I visited the speech therapist. For 45 minutes this older lady made me repeat drills and sentences, which did not have an R in them at all. I also had to do the drills at home for homework. With the help of the drills my tongue was led to a completely new place in my mouth, into a state of relaxation. After that practice, almost as a surprise, the stream of air all of a sudden got the tongue to tremble. I must have gone to see the speech therapist only three or four times, when it finally happened by accident: a trembling R!

After this practice there was no fear that my R would not tremble, sometimes a bit too much even. I kept trembling my R's to catch the lost time in years gone by. Sometimes I rolled my R's even in the wrong place and with force. It was time for me to show what I had learned: it was for the first time at the age of 16, when I finally knew how to say my own name right – R-R-R-Raili!

The following year I went to the States for a year as an exchange student. It was time for me to start speaking that foreign language, which I had studied for four years in school. In the beginning my replies were quite short and laconic, when I wanted to show that I had understood the question asked. It always took me too long to formulate the sentence correctly in my head to take part in the ongoing discussion. But I could show that I was following by saying: R-R-R-Really! I would not have noticed this new speech defect of mine, if my little brother Keith had not asked me to repeat what I said again and again. Back to square one: what was good, needed and right in the Finnish rolling R was too trembling and strong in the English language. My rolling R became the label by which I was remembered during that year.

When I returned to my old girls' school in Jyväskylä after my exchange year to finish the three last years of school in order to graduate, I also had a new language to start with: French. I was a smart and diligent student at that time, I could learn every other detail and rule in this new language, but I never learned to pronounce the soft, cotton wool-like R in the French language, it was supposed to be produced somewhere deep in your mouth by the uvula without any trembles. It was completely impossible for me to produce. It would have been like returning to the old way, which was no longer possible – unfortunately!

My parents' story

My mother, Toini Terttu, was born during the early February frost in 1919 in Ylä-Kintaus village in Petäjävesi, as the second child of Lyydia and Valde Lehtola. I wonder, if the small farmer parents at that point realised that their son, Leevi, born a couple of years earlier, was deaf? Working long hours in those days, I doubt they had time to follow or watch the possible reactions of the small child to sounds, or how his speech production was progressing. In the next 12 years in that family, six more children were born, so out of eight children four at some point proved to be deaf. My Uncle Antero always said, when someone asked him the cause of his deafness, that he had fallen down from the top of the baking oven and lost his hearing that way. However, it was more probable that my grandparents were carrying a strong deafness gene without knowing about it. The genetic strain was seen in the flock of children.

By contrast, my father, Eero Edvard, was born hearing as the fifth and second-to-last child in Edla and Jaakko Ojala's family in Patana village in Veteli, in central Pohjanmaa, in the first days of January in 1918. He had meningitis when he was only a few months old, due to which he lost his hearing. The inflammation damaged the hearing nerves, which also affected his sense of balance.

I wonder what kind of punishment from God my maternal grandparents felt they had received, when they had four deaf-mute children in the early 20th century? In those days, there was no guidance or information for the parents, no rehabilitation or therapy for the whole family, not to mention no sign language training as the language of deaf people. It must have been difficult to bring up a deaf child, to get them to understand matters and for the family to understand them. All family members learned to speak with exaggerated mouth movements, to gesture and to guide the deaf family member in the everyday tasks on the farm. The small farm had plenty of work for everyone. Each one of them had their own skills and area of responsibility in the hay field, or when the grain was threshed or potatoes collected in the autumn: everyone was at work.

Although the plentiful deaf flock must have been a burden for the parents or maybe even a reason for shame, the example and skills in guiding by the older deaf siblings were a blessing and lucky for the younger ones. Wherever two deaf people meet, there always is some kind of a visual and mutual manual language born. My mother must have learned a lot and received information from her older deaf brother Leevi, especially after Leevi started attending the Oulu School for Deaf-mutes. Unfortunately in those days, these schools were boarding schools, where they only had holidays for Christmas, Easter and during the summer. I am sure my mother Terttu received a whole package of information at once, when Leevi came home for holidays. Then my mother also learned sign language, although discussions with her hearing siblings and her parents were still carried out by exaggerated mouth movements without sound and by gesticulating. The younger deaf siblings, Antero who was born in

1925 and Lahja in 1927, were more easily led into the deaf world and information through sign language.

In those days the Oulu School for Deaf-mutes took a new class every other year. In the autumn of 1928 my mother already knew through her older brother Leevi, where she was going and why. At the Petäjävesi station the children got in the train going to Haapamäki, where they changed trains for Oulu. The school had organised escorts for the children from different parts of the country, who safely escorted the children to the school and, when the holidays started, back to their family members waiting at the nearest train station.

Unfortunately, I never discussed with my father in detail what his experiences in the hearing family in Pohjanmaa had been. Starting school probably followed a similar track as that I have heard from many older deaf people in the past in my work. I wonder, if the father of the small farm had time to see his son, ten year-old Eero all the way to Oulu, because of his work in the fields. Nor might the mother have had time from her work in the cow shed, kitchen and looking after the youngest, who was six at that time, to see her son to the nearest station in Kokkola. Nor did the parents have the skills to explain to the little boy where he was going and why. If they tried to explain, I doubt if little Eero would have had the concepts to understand what they were trying to tell him. He learned all that later in school. The happy days of childhood in the countryside were over. After this he would meet his parents, other siblings and village people, who had become important in his life, only during school holidays. Nobody could tell him either, when it was time to say goodbye again to them.

In autumn 1928, my mother and father started their eight year education in the Oulu School for Deaf-mutes in Lossikuja 6, in Tuira, Oulu. The class was led by a teacher called Saimi Tolvanen. The same teacher took the class right through to their graduation, when the students received their certificate of graduation from the school and also were confirmed. The pastor for the deaf, Otto Myyryläinen from Mikkeli district, came to school to teach their confirmation class.

My mother often told us children about her school times. Sign language was in those days completely forbidden in teaching. 10 students in the class sat in a semi-circle in order for them also to see the other students' responses from their mouths as well as the teacher's lips. My mother told us that teacher Saimi was very strict, but a good teacher. Although signing was used during the free time outdoors and in the dormitories with older students and her brother Leevi, the use of it was strictly forbidden during the lessons. If you were caught using sign language, you were hit with a ruler on your hands and told to stand in the corner.

My mother was probably a noticeably gifted and diligent student and that was why she was often favoured by the teacher. Mother even told us that she did some errands in the teacher's house, when the teacher had broken her arm and could not perform household duties. Because of her background, my mother already had concepts and information on different matters, so that when she arrived at school, she managed well there. She had very lovely handwriting and she liked writing very much. In handwork she was a master. During school she crocheted bedcovers, curtains, embroidered table cloths and other handwork. Later on she regretted that she had had to give them away for free because the materials were provided by the school.

My father Eero's background was different. In eight years he had to learn the language of the environment, to learn to articulate words that even strangers could understand and to receive information on everything. Although the curriculum used in the school in those days was demanding and generally with more lessons than in the hearing schools, most of the teaching time was spent on breathing and articulation exercises, teaching speech, and on the correction of pronunciation mistakes at the cost of the cognitive content of the lessons. There were only a few pupils in the class in order that the teacher could give individual teaching and guidance. The cleverer pupils had to wait for the slower ones to learn as their speech was corrected again and again until the teacher felt that it sounded close to being right. Although the teachers and other staff members in the school did understand my father's speech, it was never clear enough for a stranger to understand, at least not the first time. My father's strong and very monotonous voice often made people afraid at the first encounter.

My father and many other deaf pupils in the Oulu school were lucky to have Samuli Paulaharju as their teacher in handwriting, drawing, and boys' woodwork. He had entered the school as an apprentice teacher and worked in the school as a teacher for 30 years. My uncle Leevi, who died in 1941 in his early twenties, had painted some lovely watercolours and made drawings which were found in my grandmother's attic later on. Teacher Paulaharju had been able to pass his interest in the folklore-collecting tradition to his students. Leevi in his works had painted, for instance, a birch bark container and the traditional way in which a fence was tied.

My brother Risto writes in the Oulu 100th anniversary history book as follows: *The standards the students reached in handwork were much higher even than the comprehensive or vocational school of today. The furniture the boys made in woodwork was at a very high level compared to the work students are required to make today at the same class level in basic education. The difference can be explained by the fact that the students in the deaf school were a couple of years older in those days and the weekly hours in lessons were greater. Anyhow, teaching in handcrafts was equal to the level in vocational schools these days. The objective in deaf schools was clearly to give the deaf students preparation to manage in society as good citizens and also to give them preparation for work life.*

And my brother continues: *Teacher Paulaharju demanded good results from the students. And he got his boys to be interested because he understood his deaf-mute students, and the students understood him. And that aside, it was interesting to see that mutual understanding and friendly relationships prevailed between teacher Paulaharju and his pupils. The work of Paulaharju was not only limited to teaching drawing and woodwork. He was interested in the teaching of the deaf in general. He made educational posters, which were in use in the first grade. And he also made the drawings in the elementary school reading book by Naema Helsingius, which was used in general schools. Mr Samuli was a good friend of all deaf-mute people. He followed with interest how the students, especially the boys, progressed in school. And he followed their lives even after they finished their education. Nothing made Mr Samuli happier than to hear that his former students had succeeded in life.*

Grandmother Lyydia had her own plans for her deaf children, when two of her hearing children and the eldest deaf child died before their time: Rauni died of diphtheria, when she was under 20, Vilho was lost in the war at the age of 21, and the deaf son Leevi died of osteomyelitis at the age of 24, when his broken femur was not treated properly. It was expected that the hearing children would get married and live their own lives, but grandma Lyydia wanted to keep the deaf children at home working on the farm. But for deaf family members, life at the farm without contacts with other deaf people was even more boring than for the hearing children. My mother often told a story about how she had walked ten kilometres to the nearest railway station to go to an event at the Deaf Club in Jyväskylä. Once she had to tell a lie to her mother, when leaving home to stay with her deaf friends in town, although she already knew when she left that besides participating in the deaf church, her friend also had organised for her to visit the Schuman factory office for a job interview. Deaf people had a reputation as good and diligent workers, so my mother got a job right away. For the weekend she only had festive clothes with her, she had to borrow work clothes from the friend who had offered her accommodation. Grandmother must have wondered why mother stayed in town so long. She only came home the following Saturday after work. Mother had come home to the farm only to pack her things and clothes to move to town for her own independent life. Grandmother was angry of course, but could not do anything about her determined daughter who had a mind of her own.

Although my parents were classmates in school, the connection between them was born much later. My mother was dating a young deaf artist who had curly hair and made skillful wooden reliefs. Unfortunately, or should I say on my own behalf luckily, the deaf artist died of tuberculosis at some point. My mother met my father again at some national event for deaf people. Their wedding was celebrated twice because my father's family could not make it to the wedding organised in Ylä-Kintaus in my mother's home. A.V.Lehtola married them again on 16.6.1945 in Veteli. My parents lived for a while in Patana. But my mother, who was used to an independent life and income, soon got tired of the bossing of her mother-in-law and the two spinster sisters of my father, and wanted to move back to Jyväskylä. Another reason for this moving was that there were work opportunities for both of them in Jyväskylä as well as an active Deaf Club. My brother was born in the spring of 1947 and I three years after that on Mother's Day. And that is when my own story begins.

My father Eero

The main element in my father's history was that he was from Pohjanmaa, the north western part of Finland, and his home district was high in his list of values. When we were children, we could imagine the fierce men from Pohjanmaa raving with their sheath knives. When father Eero got angry, the sharp lightning of anger flared up in his eyes. When father got mad, there was no playfulness involved, and there was a long way to forgiveness.

One of the six children of the Ojala family, my father learned about farm work by imitating the others. How much my father understood of other people's work and how the family members talked to him before he went to school, to the boarding school in Oulu, can only be guessed. Sign language was not officially used, at least not in teaching, but when playing and discussing with other deaf children sign language was passed on from the older children to the young ones. The children went home for holidays only at Christmas, Easter and in the summer, so it was not very often that he was able to show his family members skills he had learned in school, new words that he had learned to pronounce. Discussion was not very deep with only individual words being used – PUU (tree), PATA (kettle), KUU (moon) – especially when no one else in the family knew sign language.

In spite of the teaching, which mainly concentrated on speech training at the Oulu School for Deaf-mutes, only a few hearing people among those who did not know him, could figure out what he actually was saying, no matter how many times father repeated himself. As mentioned earlier my father had a very strong, monotonous, gruff voice, the strength of which he could not control himself. Hardly ever could he figure out from the fast moving lips of strangers what they were saying. However, father never had any kind of communication problems with hearing people. He never was ashamed of his own deafness. If the hearing person could not figure out what he was saying, father used acting, drawing or guiding by hand as his tool to understanding. Father Eero was a born actor. When he wanted to describe what someone's appearance looked like by pantomime, it was clear from the start who that person was, if you knew them. He puffed his cheeks, twisted his eyebrows, pursed up his mouth, smacked or mimicked the person's way of signing or speaking or changed his own posture or way of walking to imitate that person. It is a pity that these performances never got recorded on videotape.

If my father had had difficulties in school in acquiring knowledge and language, he got to fulfil his potential in sports. Sports were not only part of lessons at the Oulu school, but were an integral part of the free time activities of the boarding school and in creating school spirit. Regularly there were competitions in school. The winners received sports gear and clothes as prizes which were donated for those children from poor families who did well in sports. My parents were good both in track and field and in cross-country skiing. Sports meant the world to my father. As a young boy in Pohjanmaa he had participated in competitions with hearing people, too, but his actual sports career he made in deaf sports. His main sport was javelin, but he was also good at discus and shot put, first in the national games of the deaf, later on in the Deaf Olympics in 1948 as a medallist and holder of the world record in javelin for the deaf. His world record was unbeaten for a long time from the end of the 1940's until the early 1950's. Beside different kinds of trophies, silver spoons and medals, his prize cupboard also included one gold medal from the Deaf Olympics, a couple of silver medals and a few bronze medals. When he got to tell the highlights of his career, he always mentioned a javelin competition with the hearing where he had competed with Tapio Rautavaara, who later became a famous singer in Finland.

To have been born in Pohjanmaa combined with sports in a way that can be almost be called an obsession. Father read the sports results in *Keskisuomalainen* morning paper very carefully. When in the late 60's our family finally bought a TV, father kept his eyes glued on the screen following the competitions and their results. There was not that much visual information for deaf people on TV in those days, not to mention starting and final lists of results, which nowadays are available through computer technology. The information was given in the background commentaries. I guess I could have interpreted even more of these sports programmes for my father, but I was young then and felt that I had more important things to do at home. My father had a surprising amount of information on the people who were shown on TV, about their backgrounds, results and what they were doing. He combined the moving pictures on TV with all the photos and information he had seen and read in the morning paper. The Finnish skills of my father were much poorer than my mother's, but he kept reading news in the paper and made some sense out of it all. The whole house had to sit and concentrate on watching TV, when my father's cousin, skier Hannu Taipale, was participating. He was the neighbour boy from Veteli!

In Pohjanmaa, my father's siblings and neighbours always came up with stories about how the harsh voice of my father made the gypsies stay away from the Ojala house, at least when father was at home. My father's hatred of gypsies originated from far back in his youth. He must have seen how distressed the family members were when they saw a gypsy group stopping by the yard. Someone went and collected all the washing off the lines just in case. The gypsies did not understand my father's speech nor followed his command when he told them to leave. He got a grip of one of the group's pants and leather coat and threw him out of the house. The gypsies were afraid of everything that was not normal. They never again stopped by the Ojala house to sell crocheted table cloths or to foretell the future. They increased their speed and went by the house quickly, never knowing if the strong madman, that mute boy, might be at home. He did not even hear if you shouted at him.

Our father was a carpenter to his very core. When we went on car trips in the 1970's, father always had to have his tool kit with him in the boot of the car. The spirit level was the most important tool in his profession. Father never did anything by cutting corners, he always had the dimensional drawings ready before he got his hands on anything and with the spirit level he made sure that everything was in line. So you never needed to regret anything or to repair it afterwards. This is what Uncle Olavi experienced, when our family arrived when they were still working on a new log sauna. He and the neighbours had thought that they would get the sauna building up in a couple of days and that it would be ready for them to use on Saturday evening. When my father joined the building crew with his spirit level that was the end of progress in building the sauna. Whatever had been built thus far was not good enough for my father. His spirit level showed that the foundation was not straight and he as a carpenter could not put another log on top before this mistake had been corrected. Getting the sauna building ready was delayed by a couple of days. But for once the sauna was so well built that I guess it still stands there and is in use. Uncle Olavi complained of his bad luck for a long time. It was a pity that the sauna had not been built before Eero's summer holidays had started.

Father had to get to Pohjanmaa during every holiday. When he bought the car, father would have driven the little under two hundred kilometres even more often, but mother was not that enthusiastic about visiting his family. He managed discussions with his siblings somehow; the most important news got exchanged with exaggerated mouth movements. For we children these visits to Pohjanmaa were a pain in the neck, especially when we stayed there longer. Father wanted to tour around half of the parish visiting every possible kind of relative. Those discussions with them were a handful to interpret. What made it especially difficult were all the names of relatives when only father knew who they were. We children could not picture all the first or nicknames as the speech sped past our ears.

We never knew how much fun our visits brought to the children of Uncle Olavi. It was only years after those visits, when my cousin Raija dared to tell me what happened after we had left. Somebody else might have taken it as rude and mocking of the disabled, poor deaf people, but I found the game the cousins came up with a great idea. Because of my father's strong and monotonous voice, strong expressions and signs in his huge angular hands, the girl cousins were playing the "Eero and Terttu" -game after our departure! They uttered strange sounds and were gibbering words out of their mouths, twisting their faces and furiously slashing their hands around.

The sound of my father's voice was sometimes piercing. Sometimes he just forgot he was making sounds even when talking to us children, although he could have just signed to us without using his voice. In these kinds of situations, especially when I did not want the people around us to pay too much attention to our discussion, I made a quick, closing sign on my mouth quietly, which to my father meant "turn the sound off!"

Another typical sound of my father was his whistling, which could be heard far and wide. Father cupped his huge hands over his mouth and pushed the air out of his mouth, and from somewhere there the sound was born. The whistle was different and easily recognisable. Nobody else had such a whistle. When my brother and I were playing Finnish baseball at the crossroads of Olympia village or were in the nearby forest playing, when it was time to come home for dinner, father only needed to whistle a couple of times through his hands and we were already running toward home. We were in a hurry for father not to blow his whistle again, as he kept whistling until he caught sight of us.

Wherever a workman was needed, father was always ready to help. Father was involved in building a home for many deaf families in our community. Our family house and the small outdoor sauna had been built with his own hands. My father was also busily involved when my brother built his home. In the cellar of our Kinkomaa house he had his own workshop, where all his tools were in good order and organised on the shelves. There he built a table and benches for my home, bookshelves, and many kinds of flowerpot stands for me. Father created a modern rocking horse with which he won first prize in the Deaf Cultural Festivals. In my first independent years living in my own home I never needed to buy any furniture. I just let father know what I needed and he produced it in the Ojala workshop. For a long time I slept on the floor in my first home as a protest against my mother who was too eager to clean and who was shocked when she saw my mattress on the floor. I found a photo of a low, wooden princess bed in a women's magazine. It even had night tables on both sides of the head board. I gave father the picture and guidelines about what I wanted, with the wish that whenever he had time, he might make me that kind of a bed. When I went home for my first free weekend from my new job in Turku, father guided me secretively into the cellar. There it was: an improved version of the princess bed! Father had come up with an idea of how to build it so that it could be broken up into three pieces to move it more easily. It was 120 centimetres wide. Father signed to me with a twinkle in his eye:

– A SINGLE BED WHERE EVEN TWO PEOPLE CAN SLEEP!

My princess bed served me well over twenty years until it was time to buy a real double bed with my husband.

I never could have guessed what a behavioural mistake I made and how much I hurt my father's professional pride, when after a short course in making knotted lace, I bought the necessary stand I needed for 15 FMK. I did realise that my father could have made it quite easily, but as I was so excited to continue making the lace right after the course, I did not have the patience to wait until he had time to make the stand. When I showed him the simple structure, I could see how hurt he was by my purchase. I explained that it would have been too complicated to explain the structure to him and the parts which were put together with wooden wedges. My father took offence at my having ignored him in this matter. He thought that the price I had paid for the four pieces of wood with the wedges was too expensive.

For a long time, father was a soft man who preferred to spend his time at the women's table whenever we had deaf families visiting or when we were visiting other deaf families. Deaf women gathered around the kitchen table to discuss. Men got together in the living room to exchange thoughts about cars or other technical issues. We hearing children had another corner in the household to play in. A car of one's own was a very important status symbol for deaf people. Deaf people got a tax refund from the purchase of a new car if you could justify that the car was needed for your work or because of bad public transport connections to your work place. That was the reason why deaf people got a new car every three years. Our family got a car only after my father had turned 50 and had his wild years. Before that father was never interested in cars or driving matters. All of a sudden the whole man changed. He had to go to the driving school. He had to buy a new car. Passing the written test at the driving school was difficult for him. My brother Risto took driving lessons at the same time and tried to explain the answers of the complicated questions in Finnish to him. Because my father's Finnish vocabulary was limited and the words when inflected did not look at all the same and familiar, he just tried to guess the right answer. He had hardly passed the written and driving test, and it was time to go to the car dealer's to buy the car. He found a brand new blue Mazda, which became the apple of my father's eye.

Father never was a good driver as he had got his license when he was over 50. With the car, the social circles of my father and mother were radically enlarged. Now it was easier to go to different deaf events in different parts of Finland and also to make family visits or meet schoolmates. I always was afraid when sitting in the car when father was driving. His driving and attentiveness behind the wheel was jumpy, unpredictable and uncertain. It was a wonder he never had an accident during those 15 years of driving. My brother crashed father's new Mazda in a multiple car accident on our way to Helsinki, and that father remembered for a long time.

Father's daughter – daughter's father

As I referred to earlier my father, Eero Ojala, was somewhat famous in his time in the deaf world. In the 40's he had achieved the world record of the deaf in javelin. He also had received gold, silver and bronze medals in the Deaf Olympic Games. He also threw discus and shot put; he was famous enough for his javelin-throwing that he got his sign name from that: JAVELIN THROWER. Deaf people usually give sign names to each other, which relate to a physical feature (hair, glasses, way of walking, dimples, thinness, largeness) or to some other typical feature in that person or his/her way of doing things (runny nose, sailor dress). The sign name can also come from the family name and what that means in Finnish. Usually these sign names stick to the person for the rest of their life.

When I started my career in the Finnish Deaf Association as an information officer in 1976 and visited local Deaf Clubs in different parts of Finland, my background was a big asset for me. When I introduced myself, I spelled out my name and told people my sign name, which is FLOWERS ON THE BREAST. This new sign name was given to me during the first sign language teachers' training course in 1973, when the students there decided that my old name BRAIDS was no longer good for me and did not describe my personality at all. During that summer I used to have many embroidered flowery blouses, which gave them the idea for my new sign name. Of course, that was not the only explanation of my sign name; some people who thought that they knew me better, came up with another explanation, which meant "always in love" or "many objects with which in love". The sign for flower in Finnish, signed on the left breast, also means "to fall in love". Well, at that time of my life, when I was free and wild, and constantly on the go in my work it might have been true, too.

Usually just telling the audience my name did not wake them up, did not create a bond between us, although I could sign myself. But when I added to the above that I am the JAVELIN THROWER'S daughter, connection was established. Someone had gone to the same school in Oulu with my mother and father. In the deaf world the term CLASSMATE has a very special binding meaning, but even a SCHOOLMATE was an important person with whom one had gone to school. It did not matter if the one person had been a first grader, when the other already had been in the graduating class. They had gone to the same deaf school at the same time, had been taught by the same teachers, and connected through what had been experienced together and through many memories from those school days. Another participant in the audience had been a sports mate of my father, with whom he had travelled abroad. Usually there were people in the audience who had attended some courses together with my parents or perhaps travelled together in trips for the deaf. It was my background that made me one of the group and I was totally accepted.

For many years in the deaf world I got to be my father's daughter, which made my road smoother and opened up doors for me, even in a group which I did not know before. Of course these connections of mine also brought happiness to my parents, when they heard from me about whom I had met during my travels. For deaf people it is very important to send regards to someone, but it is as important to remember to pass

70

them to that person, and not to forget. From my trips my parents received cards or letters where I tried to remember the names of everyone who had sent them their regards.

After some years I started to be a bit famous myself in deaf circles, I had been interpreting on TV, and also in the deaf video, or writing articles in the deaf magazines or my photos from different kinds of events had been published there. People had learned to know me as myself. There was a new generation of deaf people becoming active who did not know the old faces any more. It happened during the Cultural Festivals of the Deaf in Helsinki at the end of the 1980's. In the lobby I saw my father discussing vividly with some young deaf people:

– I am JAVELIN THROWER Ojala, I am the father of FLOWERS ON THE BREAST Raili Ojala!

Yes, the circle had been closed; a new generation had come into the picture!

Shopping with Father

When my brother and I were small, my father was the only one in my family who worked. We did not have very much money to spend. Whatever was bought had to last for a few years to come. Going shopping was a family affair in my family, to my big disappointment. I could not wait till I was old enough to be able to go shopping on my own, without the company of my father.

Our arrival in the shop could not pass unnoticed. We were always stared at. Our language was so visual and loud. We could sit in the bus and walk along the streets without talking to each other, but in the shop decisions had to be made and the purchase had to be discussed. That never went unnoticed.

The language of hands and facial expressions, of strong emotions, the language of my deaf parents, sign language, was a forbidden language in those days. Deaf people did not sign in public unless they had to. Also my parents had learned in school that sign language was the language of the apes, ugly and inferior to the spoken word, and should therefore be avoided. People thought then that sign language would prevent deaf children learning speech because it was so easy for them to produce. They would go over the fence where it was the lowest.

My father's idea of a good purchase was something that was well-made, big, strong, thick, stiff and cheap. Qualities, which were quite the opposite from my ideal purchase. Of course I was always allowed to try on anything I wanted, but before the final decision was made the piece had to get a closer check-up from my father. Poor mother was in a difficult position, somewhere in the middle, she understood my wishes and wanted to please us children. But in the end, it was my father who always had the last word.

Buying clothes or other practical school gear was not so bad. Father never could do much harm with his inspection of those pieces. Buying shoes was my nightmare. It was not only that I never got the shoes I wanted. They always were impractical, too small, of too thin a material and usually too expensive. Of course my favourites were red, shiny and light to wear.

Well, if I insisted on getting the pair I liked, it was time for my father's check-up. I would have given anything to avoid his quality control, but without it nothing was bought or paid for, it was inevitable. There was a lively discussion between our family members, which was followed by all other people in the store with curiosity. The movements of our hands were abrupt and strong in pleading and intransigence, the facial expressions changed from devoted pleas to sharp denial. This all was accompanied by the utterances of strange sounds, puffs, snorts and whooshes, followed by slapping of hands on different parts of the body, which made no sense to hearing people. For us it was just our normal conversation in sign language, when opinions were worlds apart.

My father always won at the end. He took a firm grip of the new shiny shoe. He turned it around, inspected it inside and out, checking its flexibility, to find faults or weaknesses in its production. If the shoes passed this initial phase, there was more to come. He started bending the shoe. First one way, then the other. In his opinion shoes had to be flexible and the leather should be strong. In his opinion there should always be room for growth and in the winter, room for many socks. Sometimes I was sorry that there were no more children after me in the family who could have used the well-worn shoes, which were already too small for me after a couple of years.

Always after his handling, my new shoes did not look new any longer. Not to mention all those pairs which did not pass my father's quality test and were lying on the floor of the shop. From the store I had got new, durable shoes which would last a long time, but no one could tell that they were new to me. I often wondered afterwards if it was because of that, because of our behaviour or different communication, or because of the mountain of shoes on the floor I had tried on, that we got angry looks when we left the store.

Deep coma

It was a hot August day in 1983. The Indian summer had already been around a couple of weeks. It was time for the First World Games to be held in Helsinki. Something my father was really looking forward to watching on TV. But first he had to finish what he was doing, digging a ditch around our house to get the insulation installed for the approaching winter. He was a hard worker: whatever he did, he did it thoroughly and well. It might have been that even a shallower ditch would have been sufficient for the insulation, but my father was digging a ditch a couple of meters deep and approximately one meter wide around the house. We do not know if he had a certain task he wanted to accomplish that day, but one thing was for sure: he had planned to sit by the TV, when the World Games started.

Mother had looked out of the living room window once or twice to see how father was doing, and was now waiting for him to come to have lunch. But there was no sign of him. She could not see the movement of his shovel either. When he did not arrive after a while, mother went out to see what was taking him so long. She was shocked to find father lying on his stomach at the bottom of the ditch. My mother could not climb down so deep, she did not know how he was doing, when she started running for help.

We did have a text-telephone at that time, which could have been used to call for help. But getting through to the emergency number via the text-telephone was not very easy. Calling via the text-telephone relay-service was so painstakingly slow: first you had to introduce yourself, then ask for the number you wanted to call and after that you could say what you wanted to say. At that moment it was too complicated for my mother. I am sure that she did not even consider using the text-telephone herself, she was so shocked. She had learned to use the text-telephone in her old age, she was one of the first to have a text-telephone in

Finland, but it was mainly intended for keeping up with the children and close deaf friends. This auxiliary device was of no help at that time!

Our closest neighbours were at work during the day, so my mother ran as fast as she could to the next closest neighbour some couple of hundred metres away. The wife was a bit simple, she did not know how to call the ambulance either. At least now my mother had two extra pairs of legs and hearing ears to run for help, they both ran in the other direction over the road and they were banging the neighbour's door. Unfortunately that neighbour had a big watchdog outside, which did not like two women dashing into their yard and bit the neighbour on the leg. At last they got the ambulance called, but it took some time before it arrived from over 10 kilometres away.

When my father finally was taken to the hospital, he was considered almost a hopeless case. It was said that he was in such a deep coma that he did not react to sounds. He was not resuscitated fully, only his basic functions were kept up. When he was taken to the hospital, my mother had told the ambulance men that my father was DEAF. Somehow that piece of important information had disappeared somewhere along the way.

When I was first contacted by the hospital that same afternoon, the nurse told me laconically that my father's situation was critical. When I was uncertain what to do in that confusing situation, if I should leave Helsinki to see my father, the nurse told me coldly:

– Your father might already be dead, when you finally arrive here!

The five hour bus trip from Helsinki to Jyväskylä felt like eternity and hopeless with that thought for company.

When I finally arrived at the bus stop closest to my childhood home, where my mother and brother were waiting for me, more comforting news was waiting for me: my father had started to react to the surroundings, that was why they had decided to operate on the haemorrhage in his brain the following day after he had been moved to Kuopio University Hospital. Would his prognosis have been better, if the operation had been carried out when he was first admitted to hospital? The doctor who operated him was one of the top experts in Finland. My father got the best possible treatment, but unfortunately in spite of all those efforts he died three days later of pneumonia. He had swallowed his own vomit while lying at the bottom of the ditch and that had caused the pneumonia.

When we visited him in the intensive care unit of the university hospital, we could see from the monitors how he was reacting to our touch, no matter how deep in his coma he was. He could not hear, his sight, which had been so important for him, did not function either, but at least he had his touch left. How could this piece of information be passed on to medical experts so that they would not treat every person as a mass and draw their own conclusions based on wrong assumptions?

What was most comforting for us in this tragic situation was the encounter with the top surgeon. He was very open and honest about the situation. The operation had been successful. The big aneurysm in one of his veins had probably been there for a long time and perhaps had been oozing and even causing distress for some time already. It had been fixed during the operation, but because it had been so massive, the tube might possibly have moved or not hit the right spot. The brain operation could be said to be successful, but unfortunately my father did not have the strength to fight the pneumonia. The surgeon's humility made a big impression on us. At the end, everything possible had been done for my father, although he did not get all the help he needed in the beginning. Who can be there to talk for a deaf person, when he cannot do it himself?

At the funeral parlour

My father had died less than a week previously. Grief at his sudden and unexpected death ate all my energy, but I had to have strength enough to take care of all the practical matters connected with his death and to arrange the funeral. Luckily there were three of us. Besides my mother there was my brother with whom I could go over the first big loss in my life. I guess one is never well enough prepared for the departure of one's parent, but my father's death came too soon, he had just retired and started enjoying everything that the freedom of retirement could bring along. My mother had been close to death so many times before that we did not even think that it would be my father, the athlete, and the healthy man, who would go first.

My brother and I took care of most of the arrangements because it was so much easier for us than for our deaf mother. There were also situations where one of us had to interpret for our mother. So it was when we started off to a funeral parlour in Jyväskylä to agree on the funeral arrangements. I had never before visited or even thought that there was a funeral parlour connected with the old, popular flower shop called Somman Kukka in Jyväskylä. I often had bought flowers from there.

We entered the shop in a threesome. We were served right away in the flower shop, but when we told them that we actually had come to buy a coffin, we were asked to enter further back in the shop where the funeral parlour was. I had not even noticed before that there was a door to this backroom. It was filled with different kinds of coffins along the walls. We turned and looked around a while, there seemed to be no-one in there to serve us. Like magic, an old woman appeared from behind black curtains. She looked like a witch with hair hanging dishevelled over her face. She looked as if she had been imprisoned there in the midst of all the coffins and that she had not seen fresh air for a long time.

When that woman opened her mouth, the spell broke as syrupy sweet words started to flood out of her mouth:

– Well, how are you doing, my dears? She asked, fawning upon us like she had read American guidebooks for good salesmen.

– Which would you prefer? she continued leaving me completely dumbfounded.

I was the interpreter for my mother in that situation. I could not believe my ears. All strength escaped from my muscles, all I wanted to do was to escape from this horrendous situation, but at the same time I kept interpreting her 'sweet' questions for my mother. How dare she act like that, when our father had just died? Why did people come to the funeral parlour in the first place? My brother hardly even noticed the grotesqueness of the situation and did not react to the situation as emotionally as I did, continuing the matter of the purchase.

The effective sales-cannon did not give up.

– Of course your father has to get the best possible coffin, which even has nice lining in it because it will be his last resting place! You could not place your father in a simple wooden coffin, could you?

If only I had had any strength left to fight against that magic and had not been the interpreter for my mother in that situation, I would have walked straight out of that shop and that situation as a demonstration against that bad, cheap and vulgar service. But I submitted to my faith, adjusted to the situation, did not want to hurt my mother more than she had already experienced, so I went on interpreting the syrupy-sweet questions and comments as matter-of-factly as I could.

My father received his coffin, his last dignified resting place, a wooden coffin well suited for a carpenter without any extra ornaments. In spite of that American-style top salesperson! After that I have made sure that I always go straight past the old, honourable Somman Kukka-shop in order to avoid falling into the spell of that old witch again.

A fall

My mother was often ill in her life. Everything started in the year 1968, when she caught an after-illness of the Asian flu, a strange bacterium which started to destroy the blood-cells in her spinal cord which make the blood thicken. Cortisone repaired the situation for a while, but her doctors wanted to decrease the dose little by little because of the bad side-effects the cortisone had. At some point, as the dose was too small, my mother started getting bruises all over her body just from a touch, and soon it was time to call the ambulance and speed to the hospital to get her a blood transfusion. We family members were kept on our toes trying to watch for an increase in symptoms in order to get her to the hospital before blood started flowing from her nose, when there was no stopping it. A spleen operation helped her for a while, but soon she was back to cortisone again.

Whether it was due to the cortisone or not, the bones in my mother's hips had been deteriorating badly so that at the age of 70 she needed an artificial hip operation in both of her hips. She had already been imprisoned in her own home for two years because two people were needed to carry the wheelchair down the five stairs from the elevator to the front door to the street. It was time for the first hip-operation. Of course, my mother was afraid of the big operation, but on the other hand she was willing to undergo anything to get rid of the constant pain. Unfortunately my mother had caught something just the day before the operation, a high fever a few hours after she was taken into the surgical ward for the operation next day. It was unbelievable that it can take hours before a patient in a hospital can get help and a diagnosis. It was a Sunday night and all the doctors on call were tied up in operations and emergencies. We had taken her in at noon and we arrived to visit her again at 6, but it was after midnight when she finally got her diagnosis and medicine: a urinary infection!

No operation this time. My mother was waiting to be moved to another ward from the surgical one. She waited in her bed in the hallway for the doctor to come and finish the papers for the move. I, her daughter sitting by her bed, tried to get the attention of the busy nurses to fulfil my mother's small wishes. She was feverish and under thick blankets. The antibiotics had not started to take effect yet. She was thirsty and often asked for something to drink. Finally one nurse stopped by and paid a bit more attention to my mother's condition. I do not know what made her think of taking my mother's blood pressure in the middle of her busy schedule? Her blood pressure was very low. There was no time to wait for the doctor to arrive, my mother was taken to the intensive care unit with speed. They hardly had time to take her papers along. This time: blood poisoning!

I do not know how many times it had happened before that I, without any medical training, understood the seriousness of her condition before anyone else did. Before her blood was too thin. Before some busy nurse or doctor would have time to stop by and give an expert glance over my mother. Why is it always so difficult to beg for attention for someone else who cannot do it herself? When would it be proper to lose my temper and start demanding attention? Would that have helped?

My mother recovered in the good care of the intensive care unit in a few days and was ready to be moved to the intended ward. I felt so safe, when spending time at her flat, to know that my mother was getting the best possible care and the attention of the nursing staff and the monitors, which controlled all her systems. I could not help smiling every time I visited my mother in the hospital because everyone was complimenting my mother's communicative skills: what a good lip-reader she was! Well yes, she could read lips better than an average deaf person, but a lot of it was merely guessing or luck because people talked too fast, with small lip movements, or were using language too difficult for my mother to understand. We had given our contact numbers and also the contact information of the deaconess for the deaf in case interpreting was needed. I also tried to explain to the nurses that I was in town just to take care of my mother, I could be called to interpret at any hour. But that call never came.

One afternoon I arrived in the ward to visit my mother. When my mother lifted up her head from the pillow, I was shocked, her eyes had black circles around them. I asked my mother what had happened. She did not know. I took a mirror from my purse and showed the eyes to her. She looked surprised. She had not known that she had black eyes. She started telling me that in the morning during the doctor's round there had been many doctors around her bed and after that she had been taken to be X-rayed. That's when I really got worried. I rushed to the nurses' office to ask what had happened. The nurse in charge told me that my mother had told them that she had fallen and that was the reason why her head had been X-rayed, but nothing had been found.

Back to my mother again to find out what really had happened.

– They told me that you had said that you had fallen?

My mother signed:

– The doctor asked me this morning, if I had fallen. I did not understand why he asked me that, but I remembered that I had fallen. You do remember, when I fell on the rocky shore nearby Aunt Lahja's house? After that my hips have always hurt me.

So much for easy communication between hearing and deaf people. And my mother's excellent lipreading skills.

Little-Risto

Little-Risto was just plain Risto before he came to live with my family. Because the first name of my big brother was also Risto, there had to be a way to distinguish these two boys from one another. Because Risto Toivonen was both younger and smaller than my brother at that time, he became Little-Risto after he came to live with us. We two were less than two months apart in age, but otherwise our lives had been worlds apart. It was only at the age of 11 that Little-Risto, who was deafblind, started getting education and going to school. That same autumn I had started first grade in the secondary girls' school in Jyväskylä. Little-Risto did not know many words or signs when he came to live with us. Most discussion with him had taken place by pointing at objects or with a few home signs the Toivonen family had invented.

Measles had been the reason for his loss of hearing, along with almost all his sight and his sense of balance, and had caused minor mental retardation for Little-Risto. He was the first deafblind child to get regular education in a deaf school in Finland. After him, compulsory education was extended to other deafblind children who started to be taught in the

Jyväskylä School for the Deaf. In that respect Little-Risto was a pioneer in the field of deafblind education in Finland.

When his parents started to organise his regular education in Jyväskylä, a private teacher was found. Mrs Elsa Närhi, who had a deaf background, deaf parents, and who had been quite active in the deaf community in Jyväskylä, had shown an interest in starting this new experiment in teaching a deafblind child. She did not have official qualifications as a teacher, but it was thought that her sign language skills and knowledge of deafness would be the best way of getting started. Mrs Närhi knew all the deaf families in the Jyväskylä district and she was the one who suggested my mother as Little-Risto's carer. It was impossible even to think of leaving him to live in the understaffed school dormitory with other children. Little-Risto needed more personal, individual care and attention, which the dormitory could not provide him at that time. The only big problem in placing him in our home seemed to be the daily transportation to the school and back. We lived in Kinkomaa, 10 kilometres away from the school in Jyväskylä. It was not a problem for the government, who provided the children in the boarding school full board and a few trips home every year, also covering my mother's bus fares.

The complication arose from the fact that my mother had literally to take Little-Risto by the hand to school in the morning, take the bus back home, and return to school in the afternoon to fetch him home again. She had only a few hours in between at home, but it was considered part of her work as the carer. What made these trips by bus so demanding for my mother was that the buses she took in the morning and in the afternoon were the ones the school children usually used and were packed. Little-Risto's balance was really bad and he was very clumsy walking, which made the long walk to the bus stop demanding for my mother. At that time there were no separate paths for pedestrians on our road. Both the school and Little-Risto's parents contacted every possible official body to get the bus stop moved a bit closer to our home. That did not seem to be possible. The road officials referred to the hill we lived close to, which made visibility bad if the stop was moved closer. Another excuse was that in the countryside there had to be a certain distance in between the bus stops. Our neighbours who lived by the road and closer to the bus stop did not help at all. They did not want to give up their short walking distance. What was not possible officially was made possible unofficially. The bus drivers and conductors felt sorry for my mother and Little-Risto, so it became customary that the conductor gave a signal to the driver after the official bus stop to let him know that he should stop by the hill. Usually this system worked well when familiar people were involved, but once in a while my mother could see the bus flying by our house over and down the hill to the next bus stop. It was quite a climb for my mother, trying to keep Little-Risto on the side of the busy road by holding his hand. If my mother's toes had not been squashed already in the crowded bus where Little-Risto could not keep his balance when standing up, he also stepped on my mother's toes at least once or twice when climbing up the hill. Till very old age my mother remembered to show me the nail of her little toe, which never grew normally again after being stepped on so many times, and another toe, which always kept hurting.

Little-Risto was our new family member for almost eight years. Whatever he had learned in school, new words, signs or information and naming the objects in the world around him, he kept practising with us at home in the evenings. Gradually his world started to take shape and order. People and things got names and relationships, there was past and future in time beside the present, there were signs, which described feelings and thoughts. The family members in his own family had names and name signs as well as the teachers, pupils and carers in the school. Little-Risto's world grew to include new people, when he visited other deaf families and deaf community events with my family. Whatever Little-Risto learned he usually remembered for a long time. When we met him afterwards, somewhere else, he always remembered to ask how our relatives or certain deaf friends of his were doing. Communication with him happened in short, simple sentences and expressions, with a few signs or written words. I can never forget the happy expression on his face, when he had understood something, answered correctly, when we had been talking about the same thing or when he had received an answer to his question.

I do not think I have ever met another person who was happier and more positive than this young deafblind man who lived with us. Little-Risto did not feel sorry for himself or for his own destiny, what he had lost. He was happy for what he had. He was always very helpful, ready to serve. If my mother was not too fussy about the result, she let him help her do the dishes. He was there outside helping my father to shovel the snow. Fetching the morning paper was one of his duties at home. Cleaning the blackboard was his favourite task in school. Because he could see signing and people only up close, there was many a time during the evening, when he rumbled and clattered to check what we others were doing in the other rooms of our house. After a few words he continued back to the kitchen table where he was doing his homework with my mother or father or doing craftwork or putting a puzzle together.

When he returned to our house after spending the weekend at his parents' near Helsinki, where he flew almost every weekend, he always had something he wanted to share with us. If he happened to stay with us a couple of weeks in a row and received a package from home, he made sure that everyone got their share of the goodies. The contents of the package was divided evenly between our family members, his teacher Elssa and her daughter Päivi, and his schoolmates Tapani and Outi, who were the next deafblind children the school accepted a few years after him.

Little-Risto could see a little, he was not completely blind. He could make sense of signing, if it occurred close to his face in his sight circle. He did not need hands-on signing. Reading and writing was successful, when the text was big and clear enough. It was our task to draw darker lines five centimetres apart from each other in notebooks or paper for Little-Risto to do his writing. These kinds of papers were filled with Little-Risto's news to his parents and sisters during the school year and to us from his home or his parents' cottage during holidays. We received little gifts he had made himself for our birthdays, namedays or Christmas. He never forgot his friends' name days or birthdays because they were clearly marked in his calendar at school, which helped him to make sense of the passing time. I still hold dear a little purse which Little-Risto made for me sometime in the 1970's. During my travels I keep my passport and vaccination card in it.

Our roads parted when the Jyväskylä deaf school got new premises further away from the city centre, in the forest behind the Laajavuori skiing resort. In the 1970's it was the tradition to put all disabled people out of sight, as if disability was a contagious illness. The old school was right in the centre of Jyväskylä, the town people had got used to seeing deaf pupils on the streets. It had been easy for my mother to take just one bus from our home to the school. My mother did try to take the two busses together with Little-Risto to the new school, but when it took her almost an hour one way to get to the school, it became too hard for her to continue taking care of Little-Risto. He was moved to live in the school dormitory. Of course our family still kept in touch with him. Soon we noticed how his communication and other skills were drastically deteriorating, when there was no one who looked after him in the dormitory in the evenings. All he did all evening long was to wander around the corridors of the dormitory alone. He would have needed a personal carer in the dormitory who could have looked after his homework, made him do something in the evenings, and discussed with him the things he had learned in his private teaching during the day. Little-Risto did not get by in a big group because he could not make sense of the signing, if it was too fast, too far away or too complicated. Little-Risto began to be beyond the age for compulsory schooling. He received permission to stay a couple of extra years in the school because he had started only when he was 11, but at the age of twenty his schooling was over.

When Little-Risto lived with us, we got to know his family, the Toivonen's, pretty well and this friendship stayed alive even when he moved out of our house. For some reason Mrs Närhi became some kind of a hearing authority in our family who thought that because she knew better than my parents how to raise children, she could tell them, especially my mother, what she should do with us. In her opinion we children were too radical, rebellious and liberal. But she did not succeed too well. My brother and I had been left to grow freely and to believe in our own sense of what is right. Whatever she tried to tell our mother about how we dressed, behaved or the about my brother's long hair, only caused heartache to mother. Usually mother did not even bother to tell us Mrs Närhi's comments, but believed in our decisions and trusted us.

There are a few funny incidents I remember about spending time with the Toivonen's. The first time, when we were invited to their summer cottage and had a fancy lunch with their relatives I could not enjoy it at all because it was the first time I saw people using knife and fork at the table. In our house we got by with shovelling food in the mouth either with a fork or a spoon. It must have been at that time when I decided that one of these days I would be a lady and know how to eat properly like other people.

Another incident took place when Little-Risto's father took us children to the zoo in Helsinki. After walking around the island for some time and taking a break in a café he said that he would go to the WC. I had never heard the word before and because I thought that it was something exciting, I told him that I wanted to go there with him. He told me that a toilet is a place where even the royals go alone. That was how I learned what Water Closet meant.

After finishing school, Little-Risto spent a few years in the vocational school for the blind in Espoo. He also lived at home with his parents for a few years till a home was opened for young deafblind people in Hyvinkää. There Little-Risto found his own home with a room of his own where he could keep his own things and furniture, but where he got all the services and care he needed, when he needed them. His moving about had deteriorated quite a lot over time and as he had become heavier and clumsier, he got around best sitting in a wheelchair. His parents had built rails in both their home and summer cottage for Risto to get around in the house and there were rails also on the walls in the Marjaana-home where he lived, but the safest way for him to get around was the wheelchair. When my mother was still alive we did go and see him there. He still remembered and enquired after his friends and our relatives in Jyväskylä.

When I look back on the history of my age-mate Little-Risto and myself, I have to admit that his starting point for life, learning and human relationships were much weaker than mine from the beginning, but that he actually might have lived a much happier life being satisfied and joyful for the things he had received or what other people had given him. Little-Risto never learned to miss what he did not have. That was for us others to grieve about. Little-Risto has been an important part of the lives of the Ojala family members, especially me. He keeps reminding me that the most important things in one's life are health and friends!

Deaf nanny

Salmi Anne Mikkonen appeared in the life of the Ojala family in the autumn of 1970, when a Saab station wagon drove into our driveway in Kinkomaa. Three months old Salmi was sleeping innocently and happily in her baby-basket in the back of the Saab. She was completely unaware of the important decisions which were to be made in the house about her future. It was after this visit that Salmi got a deaf nanny. It was quite a brave decision for her parents in the atmosphere of that time which was not too positive towards deaf people and sign language. One big reason for making this kind of a decision was that Salmi's parents were already somehow connected with deafness: her father being the head of the hard of hearing dormitory in the School for the Deaf and her mother being an audiologist in the Kinkomaa hospital. That way it was easy for her to drop her daughter at the nanny's on her way to work and to collect her again on the way back home. It was just a minor detour off the route to Säynätsalo to our Ojala Lane and back again.

My mother did not have any work at that time after giving up looking after Little-Risto a couple of years earlier. It was from deaf school circles that the Mikkonens had heard about my mother and the possibility that she perhaps might take a new day-care child. Of course my mother was a bit hesitant about taking a hearing baby to look after from a family she did not know, because she had not taken care of little babies since I grew out of my nappies some twenty years earlier. However, the Mikkonens trusted my mother's capability completely and were quite desperate in their situation, where Anna-Liisa wanted to return to work and nannies were difficult to find.

It was very interesting for me at the age of 20 to see how my deaf mother was looking after a little hearing baby, responding to her sometimes very loud demands. My mother was very good in organising her household work so that she always could keep her eye on the baby's needs. When Salmi took her nap in the carriage outside, my mother had to take a few extra steps to the window throughout the day to check that the baby was all right because she could not hear her crying. If I remember it correctly, at that time Salmi did not have a special baby-alarm to attract my mother's attention visually.

Salmi grew up and was a happy, satisfied little girl both with her nanny and at home with her parents. It was so heart-warming to watch the daily reading and playing sessions she had with both of my parents. My father also took his share of the moments after he got back from work around three in the afternoon. That was a special hour always dedicated to Salmi. My parents, although they were deaf, used their voice and spoke to the hearing child, as they must have done when my brother and I were small, but they also used signs and sign language with her. It was not a big surprise to notice that Salmi's first language was sign language. In those days we used to have a female cat called Tutu in our house that Salmi just loved. No wonder her first sign was CAT, which she made with a long stroke from her elbow down to her wrist instead of stroking the head of the cat on the top of the hand upwards from your fingers. It was exactly how Salmi was petting the cat: from the tail towards the head, stroking the cat the wrong way. BREAD was Salmi's second sign, also quite early at the age of eight months. I guess the need to get more bread had had some influence on the development of this sign. Salmi had learned that sign when making bread rolls with Aunt Ojala. It was also an easy sign to learn because her nanny often made bread rolls that way, tapping her hands against each other. Salmi proved right the results some sign language researchers have found: pointing in little children changes into sign language which children incorporate into their own language.

It was interesting to notice when it was exactly that Salmi realised that her nanny could not hear anything. I was at home sometimes during the day and could hear how Salmi tried to get my mother's attention by shouting:

– Ojalan tätiiii! Täätiiii! (Aunt Ojala!) from the bedroom or from outside, if she had lost my mother from her sight.

The voice grew louder and stronger. No results. From the corner of my eye I could see her disappointed little face, shrug of the shoulders, deep sighing, when she finally started taking small steps toward where her nanny was. A quick pull of my mother's skirt, if she had not noticed the approach of Salmi, there was an eye contact again and her needs could be responded to.

Salmi started producing her first signs at the age of eight months and was speaking words and two word sentences well before the age of one. When we discussed this with Salmi's parents, we found a simple explanation for it: my mother did not speak understandable amounts of language to the child, but used a very clear and simple, well-articulated words with her when discussing or reading books with her. Of course my father also had his important part in introducing the world of politics to Salmi by reading the daily newspaper from the table aloud to her when having his afternoon coffee after work. Salmi's favourite food was the sweet rolls dipped in the coffee of Uncle Ojala.

Salmi was one year old and it was time for her first annual check-up with the paediatrician. When he heard that Salmi had a deaf nanny, he was utterly shocked at the thoughtlessness of the parents and told them how this arrangement could slow down Salmi's speech and other development. Otherwise everything else seemed to be in order; the child was balanced and well developed to her age. Salmi took everyone by surprise by saying good byes in many words to the tight-lipped doctor on the way out.

Somehow I had thought that my mother, who was very fussy about the cleanliness of the house, would have been very strict about how the child ate her meals. But surprise, surprise, meal times were made into a nice game. My well over fifty year old mother was very modern in her upbringing of the child: it was not important how the child ate, but it was important to her to get Salmi to eat her meals. At the Ojala house, eating sessions were like a game. It was not the point to use a spoon and fork and eat from the plate, but sometimes the pieces of pasta were lined up like soldiers on Salmi's tray, another time pieces of sausage and potatoes were counted individually before they disappeared in the hungry little mouth. Food disappeared from the tray, the child ate and was happy with her nanny.

Once in a while I myself had some free time to take Salmi for a ride in her pram to go the local store. There were interesting nests of trolls in the old birch trees, which we never could pass by without Salmi pointing at them and asking for more troll stories from me.

Salmi was a lovely-looking little girl with dark brown eyes and well-tanned brown skin, which attracted the attention of many passers-by in the Kinkomaa village. When Salmi was a bit older and could answer questions directly herself, her first name seemed to be a big puzzle to many adults. When Salmi was asked what her name was, she responded eagerly:

– Salmi!

– Yes, yes, but what is your first name? stupid adults kept on asking because in Finland Salmi usually is a last name and Salme a girl's name.

It was a bit complicated to get a two year old little girl to explain the history of her first name, which had originated from the village named Salmi in Karelia and the priest who had married her parents had the last name of Salmi.

I had difficulties keeping a straight face when somebody started telling Salmi what beautiful, dark hair she had. In our family we used to tell her that the back of her hair looked like the butt of a chicken, when it was all tangled up when she woke up from her nap.

– Not beautiful, chicken butt! she might respond to a person talking about her beautiful hair. It was difficult to try to change her opinion afterwards.

About a year later after Salmi's arrival her little brother Mikko Mikkonen also came to my mother to be looked after. Mikko never was the same kind of a special treasure as Salmi was, but that often happens to the second child, and the same applies to the nanny. Everything becomes a normal routine. Also the children's clinic had eventually accepted the fact that the children had a deaf nanny and there was no sign of linguistic underdevelopment in these children at all. The children of the family friends of the Mikkonens did have some difficulties understanding, when the children spoke of their three grandmothers. They asked Salmi to name them, to find out the truth. Salmi started counting: mother's mother, Mikkonen's grandmother and Aunt Ojala. All the children could do was to accept the fact that, given her age, my mother seemed like a grandmother to them.

Dimness

How do you know, when it has become dim, if you have never been able to see like other people do, if the world from your perspective looks different from other people's, if the arrival of twilight happens slowly, gradually and takes years? How can you prepare yourself for complete darkness, if you cannot even see when it is dim? How can anybody ever understand what losing your sight means to a deaf person whose whole connection to the outside world, communication with other people and perception of your own language, is based on your sight?

The wife of my deaf uncle, the world champion skier, was for my family and other deaf people just one member in our small Deaf Club and our deaf community. The only way that she was different from the others was that she had good Finnish language skills, because she read a lot and spoke well. That might have been proof that at some point she might have heard better and learned the language of the environment through her hearing. No greater attention was given to that fact, either in the deaf school during her time there or later on in deaf circles. In those days there were no screening tests available to find out about sight problems among deaf school-age children.

When my cousins were in their adolescence, Aunt Anja little by little started to withdraw from the activities of our deaf community. She did not seem to be interested any more in coming to the Deaf Club. She did not attend the deaf church or any other events organised in our home town. People were discussing her absence, but they thought that Anja was too clever to enjoy being among regular deaf people and that she was not interested in the simple things discussed at the Deaf Club. She was able to read books and gather information from different sources, which were too difficult for other deaf people to understand. Of course, there were some deaf people who considered her to be too proud. As long as Uncle Antero came to the Deaf Club, to the events, it was enough for the others.

Slowly rumours started spreading, which later became the subject of common discussion, that Anja had problems with her sight. At some point it became public knowledge that Anja had tunnel vision, which belongs to the so-called Usher Syndrome. The typical features of this syndrome are that the person usually has hearing loss from birth and later on their vision gets narrower because the retina in the eye starts deteriorating and slowly leads to probable blindness. Anja had given up coming to the Deaf Club because she could no longer follow discussions in sign language. The movements of the hands were too big and often went beyond her vision and she could not make any sense of the signs. The moving hands constantly jumped out of her sight and her narrow tunnel vision. When she could not follow what was happening around her, when she did not have any idea how other people saw or heard, she decided to stay at home, and became isolated and depressed.

Luckily we had a sharp-eyed deaconess for the deaf in our home town who really cared about her clients and who after a while noticed Anja's constant absence and got her an appointment with an eye specialist. A difficult process started: to prepare herself for the expected total loss of sight and to start learning to use the technical equipment available for blind people. I am sure that the difficult adolescence period of my cousins was not made any easier by the painful process their mother was going through. Facing the facts and finding the answers to the problems she had encountered released considerable resourcefulness in her and her whole person changed. The problems she had had participating in discussions with other people, in accessing information and being uncertain about the whole situation were now in the past. Aunt Anja devoted her time to learning Braille, to using her new technical equipment and to finding new hobbies, but now as a deafblind person. After she mastered Braille, books in Braille kept coming to her regularly from the Library of the Blind. She learned to knit with a knitting machine and started producing jumpers, caps and other knitted things to be sold in the blind shop. But that was not all: she met other deafblind people in the rehabilitation courses and got interested in the organised activities of the deafblind organisation and even got elected to the board. One of the most touching sights for me, which I will never forget, were when Anja performed signed poems she had translated herself from Finnish at the Cultural Festivals for the Deaf.

But if Aunt Anja had the guts and courage to overcome the paralysing effect which her new disability brought with it, making her circles so much smaller, she could not have accomplished it alone. My Uncle Antero was there by her side, as her support, as her guide and interpreter, as her safe-guard, always smiling, positive, and as her spouse, with a good sense of humour. Uncle Antero never got tired of interpreting for his wife in every place where there was no other official deafblind interpreter available. When the paid interpreters could interpret from hand to hand for little over an hour at a time, he interpreted as long as there was something to interpret, as long as someone was saying something in sign language. Maybe it was also little easier for Anja to face the hard reality and to see the possibilities her rehabilitation and her own attitude brought to a manageable life, when her husband had such a positive attitude and a never-ending sense of humour. The Lehtola couple never stayed at home inside their four walls after the diagnosis was made, but were instead always present when something was happening among deaf or deafblind people, no matter if it were in their home town, in Helsinki, or even in the northern part of Finland.

Fortunately deaf children are screened nowadays and many times during their school years to find out if they have this hereditary gene. This way they have the possibility of starting their rehabilitation and learning to use the technical equipment as soon as their diagnosis is made, so that no one will have to move from dimness into complete darkness without any warning or preparation.

It's never too late

I AM SORRY I HAVE NOT RESPONDED TO YOU FOR A LONG TIME. OLD COMPUTER BROKE. IT TOOK LONG TIME BEFORE I GOT NEW ONE. FIRST I HAD TO GO TO COURSE TO LEARN NEW SOFTWARE. I AM OLD, NEED MUCH PRACTICE BEFORE I LEARN.

I had made an appointment with the social worker at Sampola Service Home to visit deafblind Anja, the wife of my late Uncle Antero. I had had no replies from her to my email messages for a long time. My reception at the door was hearty and warm as soon as I had signed "Flowers on the breast", my namesign, into Anja's hands. When she finally realised who I was, her laughter came from deep within her breast, just as she had always laughed.

– I PUT COFFEE SERVING ON TABLE. THAT WAY WE DO NOT WASTE TIME. NICER TO TALK FREELY AFTER COFFEE. WE MEET SELDOM.

First I was led by my hand to their bedroom. On the side table there was a brand new computer. Communication-discussion equipment was installed in it, which changes the written text into Braille for Anja to read. She had finished her course in the Deafblind Service Centre in Tampere and now it was time for her to keep practising her use of the software.

– AT COURSE THEY TAUGHT ME FIRST LATEST VERSION OF WINDOWS. I HAVE USED IT MANY YEARS TO READ MY EMAILS AND DAILY NEWS. SOMEONE CAME UP WITH NEW IDEA THAT WINDOWS IS OLD AND OBSOLETE SOFTWARE. BETTER FOR ME TO LEARN LINUX. THAT WAS ALL NEW TO ME. I DO NOT KNOW IT WELL YET, BUT YOU KNOW ME, I WILL LEARN FOR SURE WHEN I PRACTISE.

My almost 80 year old deafblind aunt was guiding me into the secrets of her new computer. She showed me how the addresses of important people and services in her email programme functioned and how every day she reads the newsletters, magazines of her own organisation, the Finnish Deafblind Organisation, and newspapers in Braille. I had known Anja almost all my life and been following her progress since she lost her sight in the 1970's, however her ability to learn something new and the fact she could still, in her old age, keep up-to-date felt unbelievable. Linux had until then been for me a programme used by young nerds. Now Anja was hands-on teaching me how it also served deafblind people in practice.

Anja had been using a knitting machine for a long time. She had knitted jumpers, scarves, socks and mittens, even selling them. At some point Anja wanted to learn how to knit gloves. The teacher had told her right away that it was just too difficult for a deafblind person to knit them. Anja started doing her own research by touching gloves someone else had knitted to find out how the fingers had been made. By trial and error she finally figured out how to do it. My visit happened to be at the very time when she had finished her first pair and I was given a pair of gloves knitted by a deafblind person herself.

In the Jyväskylä service centre for physically disabled people, Anja had for many years taken care of her totally paralysed husband, my Uncle Antero. When I visited her there after Antero had passed away, Anja was complaining how lonely she was and that her deaf friends did not visit her very often to share their news with her. The services of the centre were there for her to use, but Anja insisted on making coffee for her guests herself. As a hearing and sighted person I felt strange being served, but everything functioned so well for Anja in her own home. She kept her finger on the side of a coffee cup to feel how full she should pour it for it not to overflow. The furniture and things in cupboards were in the order she had put them in so that everything could be found, and walking around without sight was easy for her. But loneliness was another matter. Some caregivers there in the centre had learned the manual alphabet, but it was too slow and complicated to have a longer, deeper conversation with them.

At a deafblind event, Anja had met deafblind Samuli, the same age as she was, who had just lost his deaf wife. They got to know each other, fell in love, and it did not take too long before I heard that Anja had moved from Jyväskylä to Hämeenlinna to the Service Centre for the Deafblind. Love does not care about age. Both of them were well over seventy years old then.

When I visited Anja and Samuli in Hämeenlinna I was moved by the joy and happiness they spread around. Now Anja was no longer lonely. A couple of hours flew by fast because there was so much to talk about and questions to ask talking hands on hand. I was always so sorry that I just could not talk to both of them at the same time. You need both of your hands when talking to a deafblind person. When I was driving back home I felt joyful and refreshed. I had spent time with two people who were happy and satisfied with their lives, who did not complain about their fate because now they had each other.

The Säynätsalo ferry.

The funeral of my little brother Juhani.

At the kindergarten in Muuratsalo in 1954, second from left wearing a cap.

Family photos through the years.

Family photo in Kinkomaa.

Mother and father in Kinkomaa.

Women in festive clothes, mother making a face.

Mother's parents Lyydia and Valde Lehtola.

Grandfather Jaakko Ojala.

Grandmother Edla Ojala.

The Lehtola family in Ylä-Kintaus in Petäjävesi.

The Ojala family in Patana in Veteli in 1947.

Class photo from mother and father's class in the Oulu School for Deaf-mutes, mother standing beside the teacher, father on the left.

Confirmation photo of mother and father in 1936, mother at front right, father third from the right in the back row.

Graduation photo from the Oulu School for Deaf-mutes; Samuli Paulaharju, the dark haired man on the left in the middle row.

The first wedding at my mother's home.

The second wedding at my father's home.

At my grandmother's farm with deaf people.

Father throwing the javelin.

Father by Lake Patana.

Father throwing the discus.

Father with his caricature drawing of Lasse Viren.

Father with a mirror cabinet he made.

Father at the Parviainen factory in Säynätsalo.

Father on his 60th birthday.

Mother with her siblings Rauni and Leevi.

Mother's confirmation photo.

Mother in her spring outfit.

Mother crocheting.

Mother in her official photo. Engagement photo of
mother and father.

The Lehtola siblings with their spouses in Lehtola.

The Lehtola siblings and Anja Lehtola.

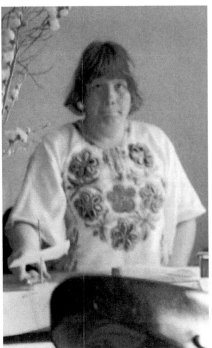

Ojala the javelin thrower.   "Flowers on the breast" blouse.

The President of the Finnish Deaf Association, Runo Savisaari, and me.

Risto Toivonen with Aunt Ojala in 1961.   Little-Risto at my graduation party in 1972.

Little-Risto with Aunt and Uncle Ojala in 1967.

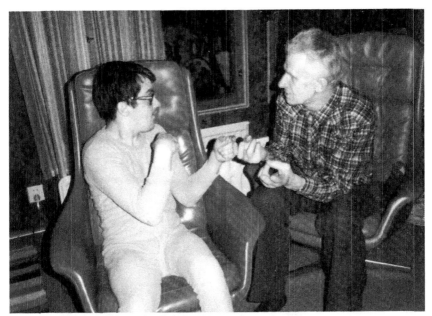

Little-Risto signing with Uncle Ojala in 1983.

Little-Risto at the Säynätsalo Deaf Club, upper right.

Salmi Anne Mikkonen signing.

Salmi and Mikko Mikkonen by the sauna stairs with Aunt and Uncle Ojala.

Salmi

III

Bridge between two worlds

Sign language – mother tongue

light movement of hands in space
touching the breast or the head
reaching out to the other hand
my mother tongue is also my father's

full of emotion rising directly from my heart
gestures facial expressions all simultaneously

eyes receive it
heart feels it
share history and experiences
of deaf people

not possible to write or to record
the inheritance of a small minority

sign language - forbidden language
survived as everyday hand-talk
lived and flourished as needed
did not die, hearing got interested

international? by no means
based on culture and customs
grows from experiences
lives as used by deaf people

Finnish – language of environment

words one after another
sentence by sentence
my ears received
this second language of mine

from relatives neighbours
playmates I learned it
final touch at school
in a well of information and books

with this language reached the hearing world
stories fairy tales
its unwritten rules
language, key to power

Names of my life

My deaf parents certainly did not realise what kind of a mistake they made when they chose names for their children. First there was Risto, the oldest child. I was born three years later. On 11.6.1950 the neighbours in the Määttänen lodging house wrote in my parents' guest book, received as a wedding gift in 1945: *Little Raili Marjatta has received her name today and we who have been celebrating the occasion have drunk many cups of delicious coffee and eaten home-made pastries. Good luck to the tiny sweetie starting her journey of life as well as her happy owners!*

As I referred to earlier, my first language was sign language, our home language. I learned to speak Finnish when I was little over two years old, although I did have many good models besides my big brother, including hearing neighbours and relatives, the kindergarten carers and all my friends there. Surprisingly, my parents were wise enough to put me into a kindergarten, although my mother was not working, but was at home. In those days, the authorities looking after the welfare of children did not pay much attention to those who might not have 'normal' language development or enough input from the hearing environment.

Neither the trained kindergarten teachers or my elementary school teachers paid any attention to the fact that I was not rolling my R's correctly. The fact that the names of all our family members had strong R's in them made the situation even worse. I always had to produce these names in all kinds of introductions or when going to different municipal offices with my parents or when official forms had to be filled in. When they asked for our names I produced a soft R in Ee**R**o, Te**R**ttu, **R**isto and **R**aili. My little brother Juhani, who was born prematurely and received his name in an emergency baptism in the hospital, did not belong in this group. He died after two days, when I was five years old.

My soft rolling R was my trademark till my late teens. Once in a while some nasty person made me repeat either my name or whatever I just had said, as if he did not quite get the sense of it the first time. I swallowed the bait and repeated what I had said. It was the same kind of abuse we heard from stupid people who called us "children of the mutes", and our language "the ape language" and mocked our deaf parents, even when they were present, not taking into consideration that we children heard and understood what they were saying.

I do not have any recollection who the person was who, in the girls' school, finally paid attention to my speech defect when I was already in my teens. I was told that speech therapy could help in correcting the minor speech problem. I only went to see the older female speech therapist with her hair in a bun when my R started to find its right place and started to roll. First, different kinds of exercises and drills were used to relax the tongue. The right place for the R was found by practising the closely related letters. When my R started to form and roll the right way, it felt unbelievable that this speech defect of mine had not been corrected earlier. When my name was **R**aili Ma**R**jatta and I learned to pronounce it correctly, I uttered it a couple of extra times because producing it right was such a joy. The only trouble with this huge achievement of mine was that I never learned to pronounce the French R right nor produce the soft English R at the beginning of words. Now I had to repeat the wrong pronunciation to please my American family and especially my little brother there: **R**eally!

I do not have a clear memory whether I had a name sign when I was a child, before I started to be BRAIDS, when I started secondary school. I was known by that name among my relatives and in the local deaf community in Jyväskylä. Especially for the deafblind Little-Risto who lived with us as a family member, this name sign of mine remained. I think that even today this name sign would always bring a smile of familiarity to Risto's face, when I signed BRAIDS in his hand.

My long braids were cut during the spring of my graduation. Taking care of my long hair, which reached to the middle of my back, started to be too laborious. Among deaf people, the name sign you get usually stays throughout your life. During the summer of 1973, when I was participating in a course for sign language teachers, I complained to my course mates that BRAIDS did not feel like it was me or mine. They did not need to look at me long to come up with a new name sign, FLOWERS ON THE BREAST, as I have mentioned earlier. During that summer my wardrobe consisted of different kinds of shirts with huge colourful flowers, tunics with flowers stitched on the breast, which my mother had brought to me from Israel, and a couple of jackets my mother had decorated by hand and sewn together from small pieces of fabric available during the war before I was born: these also had flowers on the breast. The new name sign described my lifestyle in those days well, because FLOWER signed on the breast in Finnish Sign Language also means "to fall in love". The man of my life was still missing when I was in my twenties and thirties. There was often a burning feeling in my breast, but the object kept changing. I wonder if that is why there are so many variations of my sign name among deaf people.

When I toured around the Deaf Clubs in Finland as the information officer of the Deaf Association, it was easiest for me to introduce myself as the daughter of Ojala, the JAVELIN THROWER. As my father was known till the late 1970's as the holder of the world record in javelin and the medallist from the Deaf Olympics, my father's name sign was like a business card for me in the new deaf community where I was always received with warmth and acceptance. Many people I met had gone to the same deaf school as my parents. Others had been my father's sports mates or had otherwise spent time with my father or my parents on joint trips or courses. But a new generation also came into the picture in the deaf circles of the 1980's. Young people did not know my father in the same way. At the Deaf Cultural Festivals I once saw my father introducing himself to a younger deaf person as the father of Raili, with FLOWERS IN THE BREAST.

A loved child has many names, it is said. This is also my experience when it comes to nicknames. For my secondary school classmates I always was *Rallu*. That name was also adopted by my brother and later on his fiancée, Anita, who later became his wife. When this nickname of mine was used in my brother's family, his children also inherited the use of it, although they were born at the end of the 1970's and early 1980's. I feel a warm sensation from the past in my breast, when I hear this name *Rallu* still used by my nieces and nephews today. I have only kept in touch with one of my classmates from that time, but when the Jyväskylä girls' school was celebrating its 140th anniversary and both of my classes had a reunion there, this nickname of mine had a renaissance for a moment.

After I spent a year as an exchange student in the States I came back and was put in a new class one grade lower. For three years my nickname was *Rällä*, which I guess was invented by Lissu with a raffish mouth. In the beginning I did not like that name, it sounded so rough, but gradually I guess I just had to get used to it as a part of myself, to describe my constant talking and very often too loud a personality of mine. Nobody told me to be quieter and not to laugh so loudly, so I never learned to be ashamed of my loudness. Contacts with my graduation class survived until late in my university years, but I guess it is only the family of my godson Nuutti who still uses this *Rällä* nickname.

My name has had longstanding influence in my brother's family so that even one dessert has got my name. For the three children the huckleberry whipped dessert was called Raili-porridge. This porridge gets its light purple colour from being whipped and looks so much like the colours of my clothes, according to the children.

In 1973 when I started my working life, the big dream of getting a redheaded little son was my obsession. First I had to look for a father who carried the right genes for this little boy. Ireland and Scotland certainly are the best places to look for these genes as there are plentiful redheaded, freckle-faced people there. This task became a bit more difficult, when I decided that I also wanted to find a man with the last name of O'Riley or a similar version in English of my first name Raili. It was my obsession to get O'Riley as my married name in order to become *Raili O'Riley*. I used this name as a pseudonym for a while, when I wanted to write some lighter articles in the *Deaf Magazine* from my travels and other observations than what was expected of me as the information officer.

The first person that filled the requirements was an American interpreter called Chip Reilly. I met this pleasant young man for the first time during my trip around the world in Bangkok. He was working in a project in the local Deaf Association there. Unfortunately he was already taken by a young Thai deaf woman. Next summer at the WFD Congress in Finland, I met a deaf British man with a curly hair by the name of Terry Riley. Once again my dreams hit the shore and cracked, although he told me that one of his five children did have red hair and freckles. However our friendship and collegiality has lasted all these years. Maybe some dreams are just not meant to be fulfilled?

Once again I was in the process of choosing names, when I decided to get married to my long-time partner Pärre. There was a choice of becoming Mrs Karjalainen. Pärre had been planning to take back his the name of his real father, who had died in the war, instead of the name he had received from his adoptive father. I really did not feel like becoming Mrs Karjalainen II. As long as his adoptive father had been alive, Pärre chose not to hurt his feelings by changing names. After he died, Pärre wanted to wait till he retired, because all his working life he had been known as Petteri Karjalainen. In 1998, soon after he retired, he was ready to take the big step and become Per-Olof Signell again, the name he had last had when he was five. There was a lot of paperwork with the Hyvinkää magistrate before the new names were official. The funniest part of this

117

process was that for one whole day in my life I was Raili Signell before my double name Ojala-Signell took effect.

After the change of names got legal approval, I sent out a release about this new name of mine via the Deaf Association intranet, by email and with change of address cards to my friends and colleagues. I also had to get new official documents with my new name, including my social security card, my ID-card, my driver's license and my passport. Hardly had I sent out these messages of my new double name for the world to know, when I met an old CODA-interpreter colleague, a good old friend in the Light House cafeteria. When you have sign language as your mother tongue, you also see the world around you visually, through sign language.

– Oh, you have taken a new name in order for you to become SIGN-L? asked Tuija, with a big smile on her face.

Once again I had been blessed with a new name sign.

Music and me

My deaf family has not given me any models in the world of music. I have had to create my own relationship to it. My parents did not give us examples of singing or playing any instruments, nor did they encourage us as children to study any particular kind of music as a hobby, but they did not forbid us to listen to anything we wanted. We got a radio in our household quite late, when my brother and I were already in our teens. In the fifties people in day-care or elementary school were not so enlightened that they would have encouraged our deaf parents to take the hearing needs of their hearing children into consideration.

However, my brother and I did not live in a musical vacuum either. The influence my mother's mother had in listening to classical music was discouraging to say the least. When the Tuesday concert by the Radio Symphony Orchestra started playing, Grandma Lyydia turned immediately towards the Helvar-radio and turned it off, saying:

– They started the squeaking of the violin again!

In our Pohjanmaa grandmother's house, they played the tango constantly, always and everywhere. The radio was usually turned off when other kinds of songs or bands were playing, especially when songs were in some other language than Finnish. The tango was played in the living room, in the attic rooms, in the cowshed, and also in the yard, when my cousin played tango-melodies on his accordion.

A few years after we had got the radio, my brother bought a tape recorder with his summer earnings. It was the early phases of the Beatles and Rolling Stones. My brother was keeping up with the latest from very early on; if I remember it correctly he was one of the first in our home town, Jyväskylä, who had long angel curls and colourful hippie-clothes. In our attic rooms, music was playing constantly and loud. Our friends from that time have later commented that it was always nice to visit our house because our parents always greeted them with a friendly smile and never came to tell us to turn down the loud music. At some point my brother and three of his friends formed a band, which practised in our cellar. We were fond of the melodies of the Beatles, Donovan and Dylan, but actually the way the Rolling Stones broke all the boundaries and their jagged sound were more our kind of music. Of course the Stones also had beautiful, melodic pieces, of which *Lady Jane*, *As Tears go by* and *Paint it Black* were our favourites.

From the music lessons in school only a few names of composers have stayed in my mind, but hardly any of the pieces they composed. The deaconess for the deaf in our home town Jyväskylä, sister Aune, was like a hearing mother to we hearing children of deaf parents there. She was a hearing adult who firstly understood our parents and could communicate with them in sign language, but who secondly always had time also for us hearing children, listening to our small problems and answering our endless questions. She also was the first person who tried to introduce classical music to us, guiding us to listen to her favourite kind of music. Long and deep discussions were conducted over this theme, but it was not that easy to get us young people convinced and to change our taste in music. For us it had to be rock & roll and rhythm & blues.

It was almost pure accident that I was finally led into the world of classical music when, during my exchange student year in the United States, my host family and I were given free tickets once a month to the Washington Symphony Orchestra concerts. This extraordinary possibility was offered to us by Mrs Merriweather Post, at that time one of the richest ladies in the world. It is not until much later that I realised what a golden introduction I got to the world of classical music because during that year, for instance, David Oistrakh and van Cliburn played as soloists with the orchestra. Because I was a philistine as a listener to classical music, the only concert I actually remember was held on the 6th of December in 1967, when the Washington Symphony Orchestra played *Finlandia* by Jean Sibelius as their extra number. The whole concert audience stood up then to honour the 50th Anniversary of Finland. I still get chills when I think about that concert: it was then that I really felt that I was a Finn and was proud of it.

But my actual entrance to the world of classical music happened by pure chance. I never knew, when I went to see the movie called *A Clockwork Orange*, either how violent the movie was, or that that *Beethoven's 9th Symphony* was the movie's soundtrack. There were scenes in that movie which I could not watch at all, but the music fascinated me from the very beginning. I guess it was because of the music that I went to see the movie again a couple of times, sitting through it mostly with my eyes closed. It was like a door had been opened for me into an enchanting, fascinating and inviting world, which inspired me, gave me something new to think about and supported my creativity. First, I bought all the nine symphonies by Beethoven. Next, all the violin concertos. Although I have heard and listened to a lot of beautiful classical music, which I like very much, there has not been anyone like Beethoven for me. I guess it is because we also have much in common: deafness!

Dangerous telephone

When I was a child, we did not have a telephone in our deaf family. It was not the way of taking care of business at that time. When we needed to get an appointment for the doctor or someone else, we went to see the deaconess for the deaf, who made that reservation for us. At the same time the interpreter for that situation was booked, according to which times or dates suited her. Visits to our deaf friends were agreed upon at the Deaf Club or when visiting other family members. In those days it was usual to just drop by to see if someone was at home during our evening or Sunday walks without making any agreement beforehand. Our family lived quite far away in Kinkomaa village, 10 kilometres from the town of Jyväskylä and three kilometres from the Säynätsalo village centre where the factory was. That was why we continued our way to another address, if the first family was not at home. In the 1950–60's telephone were not part of deaf households and their everyday life.

Once in a while there might be an exceptional situation, when a call needed to be made to a hearing relative whom we met quite rarely, for example. In those cases I wrote down on a piece of paper what my mother or father wanted to tell them or ask them, added their telephone number to that piece of paper and walked along the road some way to the nearest house, where they had a telephone. At that time I was not allowed to speak on the phone, but I stood nearby, while a family member made that call. If something needed to be added, answered or clarified during the call, I was nearby to answer it. This was another way in which things were agreed upon in our family.

I was sixteen when I got a summer job in the nearby store. Besides me, there was the couple who owned the store and one assistant. When engaged, I did not dare tell them that in my whole life I had never used a telephone myself. The office of the store was a dreadful place for me, especially when the telephone was ringing. A few days went by when, although I might have been closest to the telephone and free to answer it, someone else always got it first. The longer it went on, the more often I happened to be the only one free to answer the call. Then I made myself out of sight. I always made sure that when that happened, I was either in the toilet or in the cellar fetching potatoes. The mere thought that I should have answered the call and discussed matters on the line which I did not know the answer to right away, terrified me. I might not have understood what was being said. I had heard how the others spoke on the phone, but even the thought that I might be in the same situation made my mouth dry. I would have needed to ask the others for the answers anyhow. I felt so stupid and hopeless in that situation.

It might have been the lady of the store who finally noticed that I was never around to answer to the call. She took the subject up with me and finally I could confess to her. After that I was given clear instructions about what kinds of calls were expected in the store and when and how they should be answered. Only at the age of 16 did I get guidance on how to use a telephone properly. It was comforting that they promised that every time I did not know the answer, I could always ask somebody for help, no matter if they were serving a customer at that time or not.

The fear of telephones has followed me through my life. It has always been difficult for me to take care of matters by telephone. Especially difficult it has been to interpret over a phone because people tend to speak on top of another and especially because hearing people who are not familiar with deaf people do not seem to understand that the interpreter always is a bit behind and needs time to finish what the deaf person wants to say. The deaf person might be in the middle of what he is saying, when a hearing person starts speaking and giving his answer while interrupting the interpreting completely. The interpreter sees the signing and hears the speech, but it is impossible to produce both at the same time.

I have felt so sorry for those hearing children of deaf parents for whom the parents have got a telephone in the house, where the children have to call this and that place on behalf of their parents. Text-telephones arrived in Finland only during the International Year for Disabled People in 1981. My parents got a text-telephone then for the first time, after which they also could contact we children by telephone.

Sack race champion

Competitions and games at the Deaf Club, courses for deaf people, and summer camps organised by deaf people have been familiar to me since I was a kid at the Säynätsalo Deaf Club. Usually there were always enough volunteers to participate in these games and competitions, nobody was forced to join in. These funny games were usually quite physical and demanded good fitness and precision in doing them. Trying out hard on the stage or in the field brought team mates together to strive to do their best and to try and win. The audience was not left out either, but joined in by cheering the participants and trying to goad their favourites into even better results with their facial expressions and gesturing. I still can remember a few games, which were quite X-rated, where the audience was dying of laughter, when the touching got closer and closer to forbidden parts of the body. But for deaf people touching is a natural part of communication and allowed even in games.

I had been out of town for a couple of years studying at the University of Tampere and had been away from my familiar deaf circles for a while. I had settled down in Tampere quite well, but I never actually felt at home in the Tampere Deaf Club. It was not a second home to me. I was used to my little, safe Deaf Club of 20–30 deaf people in my hometown, which took care of its members with warmth. The big membership body and many different activities for different ages of deaf people at Tampere did not offer me what I needed from a club of that type. That was why it felt so good to return home during the summer and to meet old friends at the sports and sauna evenings the Deaf Club used to have in the Muurame church's summer place.

One weekend there was the summer weekend of the Jyväskylä Deaf Youth Club not too far from where we lived. Many of my good old friends from our bus tour of Central Europe, where I had been the tour leader and interpreter a few summers earlier, were there. I had really got to know them better during the tour and we had so much catching up to do.

Different kinds of competitions and games were also included in the programme of this summer event besides giving people an opportunity to see each other again. Members of the youth club had asked different stores in Jyväskylä for the prizes which were to be given out. I had heard that the sack race (which we call sack-running in Finland) had been a popular type of game in many places, but I had never actually seen it in practice. I had no idea about the different techniques this game demanded. But as my father's daughter, I was very competitive, I put my name down as a participant in the sack-running competition.

I must have been in the third pair to start, and did not have very much time to look around to see how other people were doing it, what the technique was, before I had to try to get myself into the sack and move to the starting line on time. I took a good grip of the opening of the sack on both sides and moved clumsily to the starting line. When we got the start mark, my feet found their way into the two corners of the sack by accident. I had not had time to practise or think about the possible techniques needed for this special race, but when my feet were comfortably in the corners and I could move them in turn one after another the length of the bottom of the sack, I started feeling like the stitch made by a sewing machine, with a limited length. By accident I found the rhythm, after that all I needed to do was to get some more speed into my movements. I have always been a bit plump and with short legs, but because of my guts and endurance I have always been good in different kinds of competitions. My partner was far behind me, when I came to the turning point with a good rhythm. As the technique was so good and functioned well given the circumstances, all it needed was more speed in this machine.

By running in the sack I beat all the other competitors very clearly. That was where my difficulties started. The judges had a meeting and decided to disqualify my performance because it did not follow the rules. I would not give up that easily. I complained about my disqualification:

I informed the judges that, if the game is called the sack race, or, as we know it in Finland sack running, running in the sack could not be forbidden! If other people had chosen to jump with their sack it was not my fault, because I had never seen this game being played before and I could not know beforehand that running in the sack was forbidden and that the whole stretch should have been covered by jumping with the sack. The judges met once again, but this time they had a more serious problem in front of them: it was not only that I had disobeyed the rules, but also that it was a hearing person who had won the sack race at the deaf youth summer games.

At the end, I was given the first prize, but not with completely happy faces. The prize was a charcoal grill. This grill served us well for almost ten years at the cabin before the bottom of it burned through. I do not think we grilled anything at the cabin without me thinking of the circumstances in which I had received the grill: when it had been a lovely summer day in the Central part of Finland and I had been crowned as the winner in the sack race of the deaf.

Sleep talker

The Course Centre of the Finnish Association of the Deaf is in Heinola, little over two hours' drive from the capital. One weekend years ago it was filled with course participants. The workers for the deaf, pastors for the deaf, deaconesses, social workers and directors of the institutions for the deaf had gathered there for their annual get-together and study weekend. Even we, school counsellors from the boarding schools for the deaf, had been accepted as participants as we were seen as important bridge builders between the deaf children in school and the adult deaf world.

A good friend of mine, who also had deaf parents and who had grown up in the deaf world and become bilingual in a deaf family, as I had, had his summer job in Malminharju Course Centre that summer. He was lucky to have received one of my favourite rooms there as his base for the summer. He lived in one half of a cabin, which lay on the shore of the lake. Although the cabins did not have any conveniences, the outhouse was in the nearby woods where you had to go even in the dark and cold. It was so nice and easy to leave for your morning jog from the cabin and plunge into the refreshing lake after jogging. Because this course was fully booked, over the weekend he had had to share his half of the cabin with one of the other participants.

On Saturday evening in the programme after the course day there was a sauna and after that a course party. Although these weekends for the workers for the deaf had originally been organised only for church workers, after the network of social workers for the deaf under the Deaf Association had spread all over the country, to all districts, lay-people started to form the majority in the worker group. At some point in the evening, some of these participants' worldly habits included getting drunk and partnering up.

It started to be time bedtime. My friend disappeared, but came back pretty soon scowling timidly. Only a friend could notice that. When I asked him what had happened, he said that there was no going to his cabin for him tonight because the cabin was already occupied, but not for sleeping. Well, a friend in need is a friend indeed, I figured, and invited him to spend the night at our cabin. He needed to get some sleep because he had a work day tomorrow. We had only two beds in our cabin-half, but my roommate had nothing against sharing our bed with this man. We pushed the two beds together so he could sleep in the middle. She was hard of hearing, so her only complaint was that now she had to keep her hearing aid on the whole night to know what was happening in the cabin, and that would make her ears ache tomorrow.

We wished each other good night and lay down next to each other with a smile on each of our faces. The situation was quite tempting for sure! During the night I woke up when I heard him laughing aloud. I thought that he was awake and was laughing at the situation. When I propped myself up on my elbows, I could see that he was still sound asleep. He was smacking his mouth and signing and speaking at the same time:

– Good food!

At the breakfast table I kept teasing my friend about what a typical Finnish man he was: sleeping between two women but just thinking of food! I was disappointed to find out that he did not believe me at all, but thought that I had made up the whole story. I should have woken him up in the middle of the night and told him then what he had just said. I wonder, if he would have believed then that he speaks in his sleep – even in two languages simultaneously!

One in a million

There will be only one man in a million who will not take you away from the deaf world, but who is willing to accept how important a part deaf issues play in your life. This man will be ready to join you in deaf events, even to study sign language.

Once in a while this prediction of a deaf colleague in 1974 has come back to my mind. My circumstances have changed many times since those days. At that time I was married to my work. When I was in my thirties, I worked hard to find a suitable companion for my life. My men hunting was such a known issue in my circles that it was almost a joke. In deaf circles it is normal to date, get married and have children. I felt pressure to settle down, but how could I combine my private life in the hearing world with my work, which filled my whole life? So I had to find the one man in a million!

It was also possible to marry a man from my own culture, that is, a deaf man. During my childhood in the Säynätsalo deaf community I knew mixed couples, where the wife was hearing. That was never very common or popular among deaf people in Finland. Deaf people tended to marry another deaf person. And although these mixed couples were involved in deaf events, contacts with them were not as close as with the others. Hearing wives never made it to the inner circles of the deaf community. They did come to deaf events, visits and communicated signing fluently, but from the deaf viewpoint, they always remained hearing.

It would have been different in my case as sign language is my mother tongue and I had grown into the deaf culture and its values. In those days the barrier in my case would have been, and I am not sure if it still is, whether I would have had the willingness and energy to always be the hearing person who knows, interprets, and helps within my own closest relationship. In those days there were no highly educated deaf people in Finland. A relationship with a regular deaf person could never have been completely equal. I already became tired and irritated with all the hearing-based information which I had to convey to my parents, so how could I function as an interpreter and intermediary to my own spouse? This society of ours still functions so much on hearing people's needs and is based on both hearing and on the Finnish language.

Sometime in the 1980's a slight passing hope occurred in my life for the possibility of finding a deaf spouse at my own level. A lovely, young

deaf man, one of the first ones in Finland to study at university, was list-
ing his requirements for a suitable companion in his life: fair haired, clever, with a sense of humour, well educated... I was smiling to myself, when
listening to him. He is clearly speaking of me. Until he dropped a bomb,
which again showed where I stood: DEAF! The Deaf Awareness movement had arrived in Finland via Sweden as one version of the American
Black Power movement. As a child and in my youth, my hearing was one
of my biggest assets in the deaf world; now it was a big minus.

Sign language started to be accepted as a language among other
languages and has been approved as one of the domestic languages in
the Constitution of Finland. More hearing people were coming to work
among deaf people. Sign language was studied at evening and intensive
courses like any other language. But after all, there is always that big
BUT, which makes it difficult to learn and internalise the language and
culture of sign language users. You do not fully learn a language on a
course, but there is no Deafland available where you can travel to practise what you have learned on the courses, in real life with deaf people
in everyday situations, to acquire customs and values closely connected
with the language.

In my working place at the Deaf Association there were only a few
hearing people who really had a free choice, when it came to choosing
company during lunch or coffee breaks, to sit either at the hearing or the
deaf table. All hearing workers had the opportunity to study sign language, more or less depending on their position. In practical situations,
all hearing employees could take care of the issues connected with their
own work with their work colleagues, in sign language. At meetings and
more complicated situations there were FAD interpreters to help out so
that everyone had the right to use that language which was most comfortable for them. It is not solely a question of the language and the command of it. It is a question of common experience, the capability to understand the content of issues not only at a language level, but through
values and the history connected with the experience. One has to have
the sensibility to understand and to interpret the richness of the sign
language user, but also to be interested in deaf people as people.

The issue can also be looked at from another point of view, the deaf
viewpoint. When your daily life is full of communication and other problems connected with information accessibility, you do not have the extra
energy during your breaks, your own time, to try to understand a hear-

ing person who is signing only a little and awkwardly, or to change your own way of signing, making the discussion with your own deaf friends or colleagues simpler so that even the hearing person who signs a little bit can understand the discussion. Usually students at sign language courses are told to go to the local Deaf Club to get practice in sign language and get some practical knowledge about deaf people. Some braver teachers even tell their students to find a deaf friend with whom an especial understanding of sign language can be developed. A deaf friend or girl/boyfriend could also make it smoother to enter the deaf world.

Finally I did find myself a husband in my later years, to the big surprise of my friends and family, and even got married to him. But it might never have happened, if I had not divorced myself partly from my work in the Deaf Association and the deaf community, which had always been my first priority in life and which filled my mind and heart with only one thing: advocating the rights of deaf people was the most important thing in my life. My husband never learned to sign. He did start a sign language course, but unfortunately the teacher started with teaching the manual alphabet. My husband went there a few times, but because his fingers refused to bend in the necessary positions even to spell his own name, he quit it. I could never be his sign language teacher. But he was accepted in my deaf family and circle of friends just as he was. He communicated with his openness, smile, eyes, facial expressions, and he had a good mouth for clear articulation. Without any worries I could leave him with my deaf mother for a day when I went to work. The only quarrel they had was about the TV channels they wanted to watch.

Now that I am alone again the prediction my colleague made years ago has come to haunt me. At Midsummer time I met a deaf friend and her hearing companion on the street. This already older retired man seemed to enjoy himself at the deaf table, kept talking and joking with the deaf guests in sign language, which he had only recently learnt. Together we laughed about how difficult it is to get deaf people to leave a place where there are other deaf people. In addition to learning a new language, this man seemed to have quickly learned the values and customs of the deaf world. So these kinds of men do exist! One in a million, but this time not for me!

Good mouth

When you are born as a hearing child of deaf parents, in your mother's milk you receive, as well as sign language skills, a good mouth. It might be difficult for a hearing person to understand the significance of this important feature. Among deaf people I have even received glowing praise for my good mouth.

In my childhood and early youth, when sign language was still a forbidden language and even deaf people were ashamed of using it in public places, I kept explaining matters to my parents with a big and clear mouth. This all happened without any sound. That is why outsiders did not pay much attention to our discussions. With my mother this always functioned better. She had better Finnish skills and a bigger vocabulary. She could better control the use of her own voice. Her voice was more pleasant to listen to, even to a stranger's ears. My father, coming from the north-western part of Finland, did not care what other people thought of him. He did not hide his signing, nor did he save his voice. To the point that when everyone around us turned to look at our discussion, we children were signing to our father that he should lower the volume of his voice or turn it off completely.

When I started working as the personal sign language interpreter for the executive director of the Finnish Association of the Deaf, I started receiving attention and praise for my good and clear mouth. In the beginning we had a shared office. Our desks were opposite each other. As the interpreter of the deaf director, I received the calls she was getting. We had a cane back-rubber hand as our technical aid. Her attention could be attracted with it, if the call was for her. As a deaf person, she was able to concentrate on whatever she was doing no matter what kind of noise or bustle there was around her. Not even flashing the light of the table lamp could attract her attention, so I had to use the extended hand. Only when I had her attention could I start interpreting the call for her. When I was taking my own personal calls my clear mouth caused some problems. My boss could read from my lips whatever I was saying. When I noticed her attentive look, I had to cover my mouth with my hand in order not to reveal all my personal secrets to her.

I had the gift of a natural born speech therapist, a speech trainer. Whilst at that time the teachers in deaf schools spent most of their lesson time in different subjects trying to teach speech and words, for me it came quickly and easily. I did not need mirrors, or to hold a hand on my throat or cheek to feel the air stream. I opened my mouth and produced a word or a sentence, articulating clearly, and it was easy for a deaf person to understand. My deaf discussion partner could almost see into my pharynx how the muscles in my mouth were moving and where and how the tongue in the mouth was put.

I have spent many an uproarious moments with my deaf friends, when I have been trying to get them to correctly pronounce foreign words, which are not pronounced as in Finnish words. It took a while to get my boss to remember that the abbreviation WFD (World Federation of the Deaf) is not pronounced like in Finnish "vee-äf-dee", but that the W is in English called "double-u". So the abbreviation in English is pronounced "doubleyuu-ef-dee".

But how to teach English to a Japanese deaf person? I learned that through trial and error also. I had noticed during a few meeting trips that when a Japanese deaf person uses English words, it is difficult for him to stop at a consonant. In Japanese all words end in vowels. A hearing discussion partner usually heard these English words to support the international signing: IMPORTANTO, TOILETO. During our trip to China I brought this subject up, when I heard this Japanese person to ask for a TOILETO from the Chinese hosts. Green tea served at the places we visited had done its trick to us others too, but the bladder of the small Japanese person must have been even smaller than ours. I told the gentleman that the English word for the place he needed ended with a T consonant. I articulated the word to him with clear lip movements so that my tongue stayed behind my upper teeth slightly, to be seen between my lips.

My teaching was received with Japanese gratitude and bows. This matter seemed to be important for him. When we were sitting on the first seat row of our minibus with my interpreter colleague, we could hear the Japanese person practising aloud what he had been taught: TOILET-O, TOILET-O. My teaching had not quite made the point. I had to find out a different approach to prevent the vowel after the consonant coming out. I was fighting against centuries-old Japanese language rules, but finally I did succeed. I moved to the back seat of the minibus to continue my speech practice lessons. I gave positive feedback to my diligent pupil, to whom I explained that in his speech production there was a minor detail to be corrected. I opened my mouth wide open and produced the word TOILET, clearly and slowly articulating it. This time I used my right hand on my mouth to stop the natural air stream right after the T consonant. That trick seemed to function well.

The Japanese man started practising the word. To my big surprise the vowel O did not slip out behind the mouth covering hand. The rest of the trip we could hear the words TOILET and IMPORTANT many times with a slap on the mouth and with a Japanese giggle. I had succeeded in my task. What a wonderful speech teacher the world had lost in me!

Passenger in fear

Richard, beware of the cyclist! You are driving far too fast in the neighbour-hood. Beware of the lorry! You were driving too fast for you to see it! Hyacinth Bucket is giving instructions to her husband Richard in an English TV-comedy series *Keeping up Appearances*. For me and my husband this series was one of our favourite TV programmes. I could find so much of myself in Hyacinth and in my own attitudes concerning my husband's driving. I was observant, sharp, well in advance, I anticipated the forth-coming situations in traffic, gave my comments and constantly reminded him of the traffic rules.

In my childhood home we always travelled longer distances by public transport. Shorter ones, under an hour, we walked or went by bike. Using a car became customary in my family only at the end of 1960's when my father got car fever in his crazy 50's. He had insurmountable problems in passing the written exams in the driving test. He had many attempts, and finally made it. A brand new blue Mazda appeared in front of our house. He could afford it, even with his factory worker's salary, because he was eligible for a tax refund because his deafness. Father's chatting at the women's table was over. Now he moved among the deaf men to discuss cars.

My father was a hopeless driver. My fear in the passenger's seat is due to his bad driving. If there was a way to avoid getting a lift from him without hurting his feelings, I usually used other means of transport. If to get a lift from him was the only way of getting somewhere, I refused to sit in the front seat. In the back seat I tried to concentrate on the scenery going by the windows in order not to have to follow my father's clumsy driving.

When my father got the car, he became an active visitor and tourist.

Finally it was possible to visit all those deaf friends and relatives who had been difficult to reach by public transport. Later on my poor mother reported on close accident situations they had encountered.

It did not ease my situation much, when I myself got a driver's license at the beginning of the 1970's. During the first year I did not have a car to use, so the theory in driving did not move into practice and I never learned to trust in my own driving. Or possibly I did not trust the other drivers on the roads. I had had a driver's license for three years and I had driven very little, when my driving completely stopped for over twenty years, when I moved to Helsinki. My driver's license was used only as an ID with a photo.

My fears in traffic were not diminished, when I was sitting in the passenger seat, when my deaf colleagues were driving on working trips to different parts of Finland. One needs hands and eyes for driving the car, but they are also needed in sign language discussions. It was alright for me, if the driver was using one hand in communicating and just glanced the sign language reply in. One deaf colleague of mine often forgot that he was driving the car. He carried on a lively discussion signing with two hands, as well as following the answers of the discussion partner on the passenger seat. I got stomach ache, when I was watching those discussions through the mirror as I sat in the back seat.

One does not need hearing for driving. Deaf people communicate through their eyes. Most of them have a wider peripheral vision than hearing people do. They notice and even see things which hearing people miss. There are no separate statistics available on accidents occurring to deaf people. Usually it is noted that there are no more than is normal. Getting a driver's license is not self-evident in all parts of the world. In many countries, such as Japan and Colombia, deaf people were not allowed to drive a car. In my work at the WFD Secretariat I kept writing statements and recommendations based on the information we had, when the deaf organisations of various countries asked them to advocate for the rights of deaf people to drive a car. But usually this was in vain. In Finland the only limitation was in obtaining a professional driver's license to drive a lorry. However, we do have a couple of deaf people who even do that, too.

On a working trip to Bogota, Colombia, there was a deaf young man at the airport to meet us with his VW Kleinbus. Right away he told us that deaf people were not allowed to drive there and that he did not have a driver's license either. He had avoided police raids by good luck only. With my colleague we had decided to stay a few extra days in the country after the regional seminar and WFD Board meeting. We had got that far, so we thought to make the most of it. The deaf hosts were happy with our decision. Volunteer guides were available to show us around the vicinity of Bogota and its surroundings. Also the deaf driver without a driver's license and with his minibus was ready to serve us. Our alternatives were limited: either to sightsee on our own by public transport in this dangerous country with its bad reputation for drug crimes, with our limited Spanish skills and limited time available, or to accept the offer from our deaf hosts in spite of my fears. To be shot, robbed or to die in a traffic accident?

I thought that I was being clever, when I asked my travelling companion, who knew only a little sign language, to sit by the driver in the front seat. Maybe the young man would concentrate on driving better, following the dangerous traffic and keeping on the road on the dangerous winding mountain roads. I settled in the back seat with three lovely Colombian young deaf women. When my colleague could not communicate with the driver, he started to carry on a conversation with us who were sitting on the back seat. I glued my gaze on the scenery flying by the window. I kept asking my colleague what the driving speed was as the speed seemed to be constantly rising. My fear did not decrease at the sight of all the crushed cars on the roadside. A skeleton of a totally burned-out bus made me think that there might not be a safe way of travelling in that country.

During a filming trip with the Deaf Association video team, I understood that my fears as a passenger were not necessarily always connected with having a deaf driver. On our onward journey from Lusaka to Livingstone and Victoria Falls, the other car twice had a flat tyre. We made it to the destination with the spare tyre, but we did not dare to drive back on the bad asphalt road without getting the tyre fixed. The road was full of craterlike holes. We were behind schedule and darkness was falling. It was not safe to drive in the dark not only because of the road, but also because of bandits. The price of a human life was not very much over there. In addition, we had expensive video cameras and recording equipment with us. A few of us had to get the equipment safely back to Lusaka during daylight. The four wheel Jeep was left behind with the other interpreter to look for a place to get the tyre fixed.

At a road block the leader of the group explained our situation to a driver behind us going in the same direction. He was asked if he could take three of us with the video equipment to Lusaka. An elegant young man was on the road all alone with his fast sports car. He agreed to take us and I got the seat of the socialiser in the front seat. The deaf colleagues sat in the back with the equipment. The accelerator pedal was pushed hard to the floor as we set off in the direction of Lusaka to reach it before darkness fell.

The young man proved to be the son of a British Ambassador. Discussion with him could have been pleasant, if I had not been so afraid in the car. The car did not have seatbelts. When we got on the road, we found out that the driver seemed to love the top speed he could reach in his car. To save myself from more fear I stopped staring at the speedometer. If I had been driving, I would not have dared to drive that fast even on a many lane highway. We were speeding among other traffic on a two lane road, where the driver constantly had to circumvent the hard-edged holes via the opposite lane not much caring about the oncoming traffic. We passengers were stiff with fear. I remembered all those guardian angels my friend Aune had always sent along to protect me on my travels. Hopefully they had been keeping up with us at that speed! We reached Lusaka in record time before the darkness fell. With shaky legs we stepped out of the sports car at the gate of our hostel and thanked the young man for his help.

The only positive side of my husband's falling ill in 1999 was that I had to take three driving lessons in a driving school to retrieve my driving skills. I became the permanent driver on our trips to the cabin during the summer. When my husband became paralysed, I also had to learn winter driving, otherwise I would not have made it to visit him at the local ward daily. I remember how surprised my deaf colleagues were on my husband's funeral day, when they saw me behind the wheel, when I told them to follow my car to the memorial service place.

– WHAT, RAILI IS BEHIND THE WHEEL AND DRIVING THE CAR? My work colleagues expressed with surprise.

I have moved from the passenger seat to behind the wheel. The best feedback was that I received from my friend Ritva last summer, when we were driving back home from the cabin:

– Remember, when you once said that there are only three drivers whose driving you have never been scared of? I think they were besides me, your brother Risto and your husband. The same can be said about your driving now! She commented from the seat of the passenger-in-fear.

Deaf salad

I was once again on a working trip in Geneva. The other international interpreter was my colleague, and good friend Liz from Scotland. Liz's parents had also been deaf. If the life of deaf people and their common background and experiences make them world citizens, the same seems to apply to the hearing children of deaf parents, too. Wherever I have run into hearing children, whatever their mother tongue, culture or political system in their home country, our common background, similar experiences and common deaf language have immediately built a bond between us. It has always been so easy to talk to this kind of a person, no matter if the only common language has been the international gesture language. There has always been enough that has joined us in communication, although we might not always have had spoken words to share.

These common experiences, background and culture have made the hearing children of deaf parents form their own organisations and organise get-togethers both nationally and internationally. Of course the Americans were always the first ones to start with a national and partly international CODA -organisation (Children of Deaf Adults). These kinds of organisations exist these days even in Australia, U.K., Denmark and Finland. A big international meeting is always organised in connection with the World Congress of the Deaf. At the meeting in Australia the theme was *Passport without a Country*.

But back to Geneva. It was there that Liz and I first realised that there were some international rules in our behaviour, which we were following. When either of us needed to go to the toilet, she informed the other one about that. We started pondering if hearing people do that in general, to inform their companions about every little move they plan to take. I remembered staying at my mother's where every time I needed to leave the sitting-room and go either to the kitchen, bedroom or toilet for something, I had to inform my mother about it. Of course, there is this explanation to it that hearing people can always hear where the other person is moving about and what he is doing. A deaf person does not know that, that is why he has to be told about it, preferably beforehand. This is why in a deaf family every toilet visit is reported.

In Geneva at the local Deaf Club we foreign visitors were served ra-
clette together with baked potatoes and gherkins. For dessert canned
fruit in sugar syrup was brought to the tables in small bowls. Liz kept
shaking her head.

– It cannot be true! They also know deaf salad even here!

We others did not understand what she meant without her explanation. We were told that ever since she was small, she was used to getting
this kind of canned fruit-salad for dessert wherever they went to visit another deaf family. When deaf people were visiting each other, the
deaf hostess always prepared for the guests a cold meat dish as the main
course and canned fruit salad for dessert. This was how also the hostess
could fully participate in the ongoing discussions, meeting with one another and exchanging of news in her own language. The situation where
one participant was needed in the kitchen for too long away from the
group tried to be avoided. It is almost impossible for deaf people, or at
least difficult, to do something else with their hands and eyes and keep
on participating in a conversation. Eyes and hands are generally actively
needed in deaf company.

In those days I do not remember that canned food was as much used
as that here in Finland, but I do remember having them as a reserve in
the cupboard for unexpected guests. For us it was common for our mother to make a big kettle full of rice-porridge and mixed-fruit soup, which
was there on the table ready for whenever someone got hungry, while
guests were visiting us. That way we children did not disturb the adults'
conversations with our needs.

Why always me?

Once again we are planning to have a get-together of the Foundation for
Overexhausted Workers in the field of Sensory Impairments in Lahti
after a long while. This unofficial foundation that was founded over 40
years ago to celebrate the 50th birthday of Aune, the pioneer in deaf work,
gets activated every time someone in our close to ten-person membership reaches a significant birthday, is defending her dissertation or is
otherwise in need of attention. A couple of times we have organised other kinds of recreational weekends during the summer. Once in a while

I have complained, if not aloud then at least in my heart, why it always has to be me who gets the ideas, tries to motivate the others, collects the birthday gift money, buys the present and puts together the scrapbook pages, and tries to keep the spirit of over-exhaustion going and the membership entertained? No matter how often I tried to hint that my over 40 years of being a secretary in the foundation was getting close to its end and that it was time for the younger ones to put their hands on the wheel, it was always me who put together the agenda and background materials for the annual meeting. The foundation revitalises its membership itself with new suitable overexhausted members in order to get younger and more enthusiastic blood in its activities. However, the most active participants and supporters have been the four founding members of the foundation, the reason being that they have the right kind of spirit of exhaustion, which can only be reached by serving and organising fun events for the others.

Of course, I well understand the situation, when I am enjoying the wonderful time of being free from work duties, that every morning when I wake up I can think about what fun I would like to do or organise today. My other overexhausted friends, in spite of Aune, who is the oldest of all of us, are still doing long days serving deaf or other disabled people. It was not that long ago, when I was still in that same wheel working fulltime. Yet I did not lack time to take care of matters which I felt to be important. If I have inherited my connection with the deaf world from my parents, I guess I have received my organisational abilities from my mother's milk. My mother used to be the secretary of the Deaf Club in Säynätsalo for almost as long as I lived at home. The Deaf Club was the other home, the living room also for we hearing children of deaf parents. After I finished my studies and returned to my home district I worked as the secretary for that Deaf Club myself.

Deaf people in Finland and overall in the world share sign language and being deaf in the hearing world. In 1976 at the annual meeting of the Finnish Deaf Association in Kuopio, a couple of we hearing children of deaf parents who were working fulltime in the field of deafness realised that there were many things that were also common to hearing children. That is how we got the idea to start gathering hearing children together. The first conference was organised in the FAD Course Centre Malminharju in November 1976. I had access to the "free" postage and calls of the Deaf Association. That is why I worked as the convenor for the conference, although I could not participate in that meeting myself because of a work trip abroad. From that very first meeting we started talking about setting up an organisation of our own. The organisation was not seen as the most important point in the 1970's and 1980's. The regular meetings started to fade because I got tired of organising them due to my amount of work, travels and other activities. The Association of the Hearing Children of Deaf Parents was founded on 8.9.1996, when 20 years had passed since the first meeting. I worked as the secretary for that organisation for many years. A new impetus to organise these meetings after a long silence started from the changes in the Finnish Constitution where the rights of sign language users were secured by law. This also applied to hearing children of deaf parents who had learned sign language as their first language.

A slowdown in the activities of the hearing children of deaf parents might also have been caused by the fact that at the end of the 1970's and early 1980's I had work up to my ears in setting up sign language interpreting services and interpreter training courses in Finland. The hearing children of deaf parents who earlier had functioned as sign language interpreters in their home towns were the group who were trained and got certified to work as paid sign language interpreters. During the first years of sign language interpreting services, the Deaf Association also functioned as an advocate for the interpreters concerning their fees and other rights in relation to the government. It was in 1982 that sign language interpreters were ready to set up their own advocacy organisation, The Finnish Sign Language Interpreters' Association SVT. For the first couple of years I functioned as the secretary for this new organisation, although I felt that there was a conflict between my work at the Deaf Association. Because I had the best contacts with the sign language interpreters in the field and had the communication means at use, I felt that my involvement was important at this starting phase of this organisation.

I had already started my career as an international sign language interpreter in 1975 before I started working at the Deaf Association. At different conferences, seminars and meetings I met sign language interpreters from other countries, many of whom were also from deaf homes. The initial idea of an international organisation of sign language interpreters was brought up by the working interpreters at the WFD Congress held in Washington DC in 1975. At the First International Conference of Sign Language Interpreters in 1981 in Bristol, a working group was elected to prepare statutes for this organisation. However, these free-lance interpreters did not have a deaf organisation behind them to help in the work, so this first attempt died out.

At the WFD Congress in Finland in 1987 where I functioned as the interpreter co-ordinator, the idea arose amongst European interpreters of the possibility of securing funding to establish co-operation amongst EU-countries. In 1988 I participated as an observer in a seminar in Scotland and in 1993 in a meeting in Brussels. The representatives of the EU-countries were ready at first to accept only the original EU countries as members, but together with the Swedish representative we raised the issue of whether they really could afford to lose the knowhow and experiences we had in the two Nordic countries, where long traditions in sign language interpreting services and training already existed. That is how our countries were accepted as ordinary members. Once again I had the pleasure of being active in setting up a new organisation. For a couple of years I functioned as the Vice-President for the European Forum of Sign Language Interpreters EFSLI and after that as a Board member.

The international experience and my contacts in the world were partly the reason I was asked to be a member of a working group, which after the 1995 WFD Congress started to prepare for the establishment of an international organisation for sign language interpreters. Because of my husband's illness I had to cancel my planned working trip to the WFD Congress in Brisbane and the sign language interpreters' meeting there, where the draft statutes for the new organisation were to be discussed. A new working group was elected to develop the structure of this new organisation, where I was still included. I could not participate in the next meetings for interpreters in 2002 and 2003 either. The founding meeting for the World Association of Sign Language Interpreters WASLI was held in Montreal, Canada, and the first Board for the organisation was elected in South Africa in 2005. My spirit was present at that meeting, because my Russian colleague Anna gave our joint presentation there and my name was even printed in the conference programme and proceedings without my being present in person.

The invitation for the annual meeting for our housing co-operative Väli-Pirkka has just arrived. I think I will give that meeting a miss because every time I have been present, someone has suggested me for some task. Nowadays it is so difficult to get people to become active in running joint issues, to work on behalf of the others. I feel that I have done my share. Now I only live for myself. My mission is to continue bringing joy and happiness to other people and my friends. I never want to be a secretary again.

New role

It is pitch dark all around me. Completely black wherever I look. I try to turn my head around and to see at least a little ray of light. When I have been staring at the darkness long enough lights like shooting fireworks start to flicker in my sight. I guess I just have to believe that there is no light here. My dinner will be eaten with the help of the sense of touch only and I need to get oriented to the environment only through my hearing.

I try to perceive the room of the restaurant relying on my hearing only. It is almost impossible to believe that there are close to 60 people in the room having dinner with us. The room feels small, although once in a while I can hear the cackle of laughter from the other side of the big room. I can pick out vaguely a discussion going on in Swiss German. I make an effort to hear, if there really are no other tourists beside us. The restaurant is unique, one out of the two or three in the whole world. Hearty laughter right behind us, from the side and from the other side of the room disturbs my perceiving task. The customers seem to be having a good time: they are enjoying this new kind of an experience in their own company – having a dinner in the dark.

My blind friend wanted to treat me to a dinner in a different kind of place for my birthday. He took me to the Blind Cow (*Blindekuh*) restaurant in Zurich during my holiday trip there. In the restaurant all the workers, including the waiters and waitresses, are blind or partially sighted. We were given the number of our table at reception. The menu was scribbled on the blackboard, in German only. After asking we received a version of it in Braille, but after reading a bit my friend found out that that was also in German, it did not help him much as an English speaker. The receptionist did not know enough English to give us help in translating the menu, we had to be satisfied with the combination of languages we knew and our previous experiences of menus and what it all could be. Luckily there were not too many alternatives for making a wrong choice.

We were asked to leave all our extra things in a locker in order that no-one trip over anything lying on the floor. The bill would be paid only after coming out. I left my whole rucksack with all my travelling belongings and my mobile in the locker. We were asked also to leave anything that might have light on it, like watches. It took my friend a while to decide to leave his white cane in the locker, he decided to trust on my guiding skills and the fact that it would be safe even for him to move in the dark.

It was time to ask our waitress to come and guide us in the restaurant. Rita who was blind appeared from behind a black curtain. Already after exchanging a few words we could see that she did not know very much English, but her happiness and positive attitude, together with her laughter would help us out even in a difficult situation. Were we ready? She asked my friend to put his hand on her shoulder and I joined in the queue. We stepped to the other side of the black curtain. It was dim, to get the eyes of a sighted person used to less light. A handrail followed the hallway, which one could use to move to the next curtain independently. When that curtain was opened, we were surrounded by pitch darkness.

We had been given information at the counter that people would be sitting on tables of six. We wanted to sit side by side. It felt safer for me and was easier for discussion. Rita showed us our places by placing a hand at the back of a chair. She showed us by guiding the hand where everything was on the table. There were people already sitting at our table, but it took me a while to distinguish that there was another couple and they were sitting left of us, but whether side by side or opposite each other, that took longer to find out.

Rita's attention was gained by calling her name. Communication with her was some pig Latin, English and German words added with a big laugh of success, when she understood, or her disappearing somewhere further to ask someone else what a word in English meant or what a German word would be in English. My hands were quite unaccustomed to trusting movements in the dark. By touching and trying to feel how things were placed in relation to each other on the table I finally dared to put down my aperitif glass on the table, even to be recover it again and not knock it over with my hasty movements. When Rita brought the red wine bottle, I was more certain of myself as I knew how the glass stood next to the cutlery.

During our first course, carpaccio salad, I was trying to use the knife and fork together as one should in a fine restaurant. I found it hard to find the pieces of food on the plate, get them on the fork with the knife and after that get the fork in the right position into my mouth without dropping too much on the table or floor. It certainly would be interesting to see how messy everything looked after the dinner in daylight. Soon I decided that the knife was just a complication because I had something that was much handier – my forefinger! Nobody would notice anything! Over and over again with the feel of my fork on the plate I could be sure that the plate was empty. I had even managed to get the last big piece of lettuce and small piece of shrimp into my mouth.

The chef of the restaurant seems to serve almost everything sliced up in mouth-sized pieces. My friend enjoyed his duck with chutney sauce, although the rice brought some problems for him, too. But the use of fingers was not forbidden there. My red snapper was soft enough to get sufficient pieces with my fork. Little by little I learned to find the potatoes Parisienne from the plate, even to give a couple of them to my friend to taste.

My nervousness caused by this completely new and strange situation for me started to disappear slowly and I started to enjoy the darkness around me. I found out that by closing my eyes I could concentrate on listening to the sounds in the room better. We were in no hurry during this celebration dinner, we could hear others being guided out to the dim hallway behind the curtain. My friend exchanged a few words with our tablemates, but otherwise we were the only tourists and people who used English in the restaurant. While eating our delicious dessert of seasonal berries with vanilla flan we decided that this restaurant certainly could be recommended also to other tourists. Surprisingly enough there was not a word mentioned in the Zurich tourist guide about this rare and new kind of eating experience. The name of the restaurant could only be found in the Zurich restaurant list on the net.

The only accident during the dinner took place when my friend tried to help Rita a bit by lifting up his plate with the knife and fork on it. The fork fell tinkling on the floor. With Rita's experience, collecting the used dishes would have gone more smoothly directly from the table.

According to my friend: *this experience does not simulate how it is to live as a blind person because blind people do not live in the dark, but experience the life around them with their other senses. Rather this experience sensitises people to a loss of vision and how one after that can learn to live in the world of sighted people. Blind people are at home in the non-light.*

Rita guided us back to the light. My friend paid for this delicious dinner with his credit card. I had never thought before how the credit card can also be used as a sign of the line where the signature is wanted. We waited for the taxi for a while. My friend took hold of my arm, when I told him that the taxi had arrived at the gate.

– Taxi? I asked the driver, pointing my finger at both of us.

The driver lifted his forefinger for the sign of waiting, rushed past us and expressed himself in the international language:

– Woof-woof !

The receptionist must have ordered the taxi for a blind man with his guide, but the driver only knew guide dogs. I just burst out into a loud laughter, which I could not stop even when we were sitting on the back seat of that taxi. People certainly have taken me for many kinds of things and called me by different names, but never before have I been called a dog.

Performing with my brother at an event at the
Säynätsalo Deaf Club.

Angel choir at the Club's Christmas party, Ojala siblings on the right.

Hearing children of deaf parents in Säynätsalo.

My best childhood mates.

Masquerade at the Jyväskylä Deaf Club.

With Aune at the Malminharju Course Centre masquerade in 1977.

At my first sign language course at the Deaf Association Course Centre, Malminharju, in 1973.

One in a million was found, we got married in 1996.

Uncle Martti's car.

IFA-car of Hugo Mäkinen.

Father with his Saab.

A deaf driver in Columbia.

Interpreting at a sightseeing tour in Riga.

My interpreter colleagues, Anna and Liz, at an interpreters' meeting in Finland.

Atmosphere of a final banquet in Moscow.

The 25th Anniversary Conference of the World Federation of the Deaf in Rome in 1976.

The official Finnish representative in the back row.

The medal received from the Pope.

IV
As a sign language interpreter

First interpreting assignment

As the hearing child of a deaf family, interpreting had already become familiar to me from when I was a child at home. I got to practise interpreting in discussions between the neighbours and my parents. In between my childhood games I interpreted for my relatives who did not know how to speak with a big mouth or whose lip movements were difficult for my parents to understand. Although my parents tried to get on their own as long as they could, sometimes they wanted to make sure that they had understood everything correctly. Then we children were called to interpret to avoid misunderstandings. I do not remember any situations or matters which would have stayed in my child-mind as scary or troubling.

In return for this bigger responsibility than parents usually entrusted to their children, my brother and I received quite a lot of freedom to come and go as we pleased. We did not have any set times to come home, we were trusted. Usually we proved to be worthy of that trust. Freedom brought responsibility with it, why would we have been foolish. It was usually for us to bear the consequences, too. That is why I have been so sensible, thoughtful and conscientious since I was a little child.

From situations at home, our interpreting responsibilities slowly moved on to the occasions organised by the local Deaf Club, for instance, telephone calls connected with the arrangements of different events. The whole deaf community and its issues became familiar to us from the time we were small children.

The first interpreting situation, which I could consider work, was a weekend camp organised by the pastor for the deaf for those deaf people who lived in hearing families. It was organised in a beautiful campsite on a lake. This annual camp was almost the only opportunity for these deaf people to meet one other and other deaf people who used sign language. They returned home, after school or vocational school, back to their parents, where at that time sign language was not much used or known. They might have been an extra pair of hands, which were desperately needed in the farm work. Because sign language had been completely forbidden in rehabilitation and education for the deaf, their mental and linguistic connection with their folks at home was quite weak. Internal communication within the family with its deaf member was almost limited to pointing its instructions – eat, fetch logs, feed the cows, to the hay field. In those days there were not even TV's in Finnish households, the access to information for these deaf people was limited to glancing at photos in the newspapers and magazines. They could not understand the difficult Finnish language. They were often present in situations where matters that were discussed passed by their deaf ears.

For the participants, this camp was the highlight of the year. I had been asked to interpret there because the pastor for the deaf could not make it and because the deaconesses from the different congregations did not know how to sign. I was in my senior years in school. Sign language skills of the participants were quite rusty, basic and simple. In those days my signing skills were not that good, but I had got by quite well in my own deaf community. It was connection to other deaf people that these people needed badly in their lives. Communication functioned somehow, when you made everything simple enough and tried to explain only the main facts.

Before this camp finished there was Sunday service in church. It was held in a beautiful summer chapel on the lake, where the altarpiece was a glass window overlooking the lake scenery, with the blue of the lake and a couple of rocky islands in it. I had arrived in the chapel early enough. I knew that from the sign language interpreting point of view the situation would be not only difficult, but impossible: the sun was shining from behind the interpreter directly into the eyes of the deaf participants. I wanted to hear everything properly, so I placed myself near to the hearing pastor, who would carry out the service. I had time to find and mark the hymns in my hymn book, but I had no idea what the content of the sermon would be.

The pastor started reading the texts directly from his notes and the Bible. He read so fast that even if I had had more experience of interpreting, I would have suffered. I hardly grasped half of what he was saying. If the deaf audience had been a bit different, I could perhaps been able to transliterate some of the text for them in signs, and leave them to understand it themselves. My audience, straight from the woods, deaf people who had been "integrated" among hearing people all these years, who had possibly forgotten the biggest part of what they might have learned in school, would have needed the text well-processed, clearly thought-out, in order for the core of the message to be clear to them. Words flew by me. Hopelessly I continued my waving of the hands knowing that the sun was in the eyes of the deaf participants and that they possibly could not even see what I was trying to sign. I kept opening my mouth like a fish on the shore, my hands were beating the air forcibly. Luckily at some point the service ended, my misery was over.

I walked down the church aisle towards the door. The deaf participants were smiling in a friendly way at me from their pews. I felt like apologising for my failure to interpret. I felt that even a more experienced interpreter could not have done much more than I did in those circumstances. A deaf man was walking towards me. He grabbed my hand, lifted it up in the air towards the light and signed:

– BEAUTIFUL HANDS, LONG FINGERS!

I guess that was how my short, thick fingers had looked in the sun with the lake scenery behind them!

An official delegate

When I was cleaning out my drawers, I happened to find a small velvet envelope, which had a gold-plated medal in it. On one side there is a relief of a man with a beard with a scroll in his hands and on the other side there is a text *PAULUS VI PONT MAX* and his coat-of-arms. An old souvenir, but not until now it has started to mean something to me. It was time to clean dust from the medal and take it, if not into everyday use, at least to be part of my jewelry in use. I took the medal to a goldsmith and had a catch made in it in order to use it as a necklace in ceremonies. The souvenir was a memory of the time when I got to meet the Pope himself.

In October 1976 I was enjoying my holidays in between two jobs. I had promised to go and interpret at the 25th Anniversary Conference of the WFD in Rome. At least that was the original intention. The Board of the Finnish Association of the Deaf had at its meeting made a decision that the finances of the organisation could not bear the expenses of two people travelling to Rome. However, it was important to have a delegate at that conference as the Finnish Association had been one of the founding members of the WFD. It was impossible to send the deaf executive director there on her own as most of the presentations would have been in spoken English. I as a hearing person with English skills was available, so the Board made a historical decision to send a hearing interpreter as the official delegate to this WFD Conference. My task was to produce a written report for the Board about the conference and for Finnish deaf people to read.

Because the conference lasted a long weekend, the cheapest way to travel was to book a two week tourist trip to Rome. I had time both before and after the conference representation to familiarise myself with the Eternal City. Even arriving in the city from the airport, it felt as if my school history book had come alive before my eyes. On a sightseeing tour organised by the travel agent, I first got to know Ancient Rome and with the help of a guide the Vatican, its museums and St Peter's Basilica. It was an unbelievable experience for me to see with my own eyes the frescos of Michelangelo, my favourite artist, *The Creation of the World* in the Sistine Chapel and his altarpiece *Final Judgement*. I had read his biography, admired his works in many books, but now I could imagine him lying on his back high up on the ladders in the cold and damp church and painting the ceiling frescos. *What is the power in a human being that makes him create something so splendid and skillful, to leave everything else in life as unnecessary, to suffer from hunger, pressure and people's mockery?* I had written in my travel report in the *Deaf Magazine* after my trip.

Besides history and art I was thrilled to follow the traffic in Rome. For a long time I could stand in the crossings near my hotel to see how the Italian temperament affected their driving. I could not figure out any clear rules about how the cars, by honking, were able to squeeze from five lanes into two at speed, but compliantly. It seemed to function smartly and with cooperation. All of a sudden in the middle of the dense traffic a driver could decide to start backing up his car. He must have forgotten something? The others courteously made room for the reversing.

The best way to get to know an unfamiliar city is to walk along the unknown streets with a map in your hands. After two weeks I could say that I felt Rome in my bone and marrow because I kept walking on my days off from eight to ten hours a day along the streets of Rome. Once in a while I sat down in a street café to enjoy a cappuccino or a delicious Italian ice cream, and to watch Italian people going by and their way of life. Men in Rome were pretty as a picture and dressed elegantly like mannequins in a showcase. Roman women did not seem to have anything else to do but to keep themselves well taken care of, fashionably dressed and to tread in their high heels along the pavements, glancing at the windows in passing.

Of course, there were also others beside me who enjoyed the late autumn warmth and sun in Rome. Under the trees and bushes and ancient ruins cats were teeming. As a cat person I had difficulties not patting them. There was rabies in southern Europe, so my contact with these scabby fluffy-haired creatures had to be limited to patting them with my eyes.

In the evenings it was lovely to wander along pretty, shady small streets. Rome is full of small, atmospheric eating places, trattorias and pizzerias where you could get delicious Italian food cheaply and in big portions. Some adjustment was required to get used to their late eating hours. It took me a few days to learn that the eating places were not always open when I started to be hungry at Finnish eating times. Some of the waiters could not understand when I ordered and asked only for a portion of spaghetti, lasagne or ravioli. Besides the conference banquet, I just could not fit the whole Roman dinner into myself: starters, pasta, main course, dessert, cheese and coffee.

The opening of the conference took place on Friday in Campidoglio city hall. Amintore Fanfani, the President of Italy, was the patron of the conference. There were high level representatives of the Italian government, the city of Rome and the UN special agencies and of course, deaf people and experts in the field of deafness from all over the world. The official language of the conference was English, but everything was interpreted into Italian and American Sign Language. Deaf people from other countries were waiting to see international interpreting, but that had not been organised. This assured me that it was the right decision not to send a deaf person there as an official delegate without an interpreter.

Before the trip I had been afraid how I would manage with my language skills in this international conference of the deaf. It was not a question of the spoken or heard English or talking to hearing people, but whether my signing would suffice to talk to deaf people and, after all, how international sign language was. From the first day I met deaf people from different countries and was happy to find out that contact was possible and discussion was lively. The more I could give up my Finnish signs to express matters in pantomime using facial expressions, gestures and my whole body, the better the discussion flowed. It took a moment or two before I could figure out the numbers in other sign languages and the personal way in which each deaf person was signing. My true language bath was when I ended up by mistake in the bus reserved for the conference organisers on a planned visit to a deaf school. Instead of seeing the school I ended up having a huge magnificent lunch with the Italians and discussing deaf education, pregnancy prevention and many other matters with them.

Sunday was a day off at the conference. A fieldtrip was organised for the conference participants to an old Etruscan town called Tarquinia, approximately 70 kilometres outside Rome. There was an excellent chance to get to know the participants better during this trip and ask them about the situation of deaf people in their countries. The conference working days had been so full that it had not been possible for this kind of interaction before. After visiting the Etruscan museum and the underground catacombs, and after a plentiful lunch, there was a moment for taking a walk along the seashore. Only one person from the Soviet Union was brave enough to take a swim and was splashing in the waves of the sea. I was sorry that I had not thought to take my swimsuit on the trip.

Since its founding in 1956, the office of the WFD had been within the Italian Deaf Association offices on *Via Gregorio VII* next to the Vatican. The long-time WFD General Secretary, Dr Cesare Magarotto (who as a hearing person had followed in his deaf father's footsteps) had been able to organise an audience at the Vatican for the conference participants. One delegate from each country had received this invitation, in other words including me, as the official delegate from Finland. When we arrived at the Vatican, we first met the Swiss Guard in their orange, red and blue outfits. They still wear the uniforms designed for them by Michelangelo. The Vatican Palace is a museum in itself where all the walls and ceilings are full of wonderful paintings and art treasures. We heard that the Pope was often so interested in discussions with the invited guests that we had to wait for our turn for an hour and a half. Finally we were invited in, and after walking up numerous steps we were seated in a room with the throne of Pope Paul VI in front, and the statues of the apostles around the walls. When the Pope entered the room, we got up and applauded him. The Pope blessed us all in French. In his speech he noted that the WFD was doing great work to improve the situation of deaf people all over the world. Before he left the room the Roman Catholic representatives in our group went and kissed his ring and got a blessing from him. From our visit to the Vatican we all received the gold plated medal I mentioned in the beginning.

There was yet another official situation where I needed to represent the Finnish Association of the Deaf to give its congratulations and make a presentation to the WFD representatives at the banquet. It had been really complicated to get the FAD gift to me because the FAD pennant had had to be engraved with the name of the recipient and the occasion. The executive director had carried the pennant box on a working trip all the way to Iceland after which she was to hand it to me at the Helsinki airport, before I boarded the plane to Rome. That part was successful, but when I studied the box more closely in my hotel room, to my frustration I noticed that the screw, which should have been there to screw the pennant to the marble base, had been lost somewhere along the way. Instead of handing the pennant as it should have been handed, upwards without the box, I gave it to the hosts, along with my congratulatory words, lying flat in the box. Luckily nobody tried to put it together during the celebrations.

So even at the beginning of my career in the Finnish Association of the Deaf, I had managed to get to know the bigwigs and celebrities in the deaf world. It was these contacts, which later in my 30 year career in the Deaf Association and later in the WFD Secretariat in Finland, brought me joy and many opportunities.

The Vatican and the whole papal institution has been a big interest for me since this visit. Pope Paul VI, who also was known as the "pilgrim pope" because he was the most travelled Pope at that time, died a little over a year after our visit. His successor Pope John Paul I lived only 34 days as the Pope. Again people had to wait for the cardinals gathered in the Vatican to make a decision on the new Pope, and for the white smoke to rise from the chapel chimney, which had been installed on the roof for this purpose.

Me in many

I have always been easily distinguished from a crowd both because of the colours I wear and my own distinctive style. In the early 1970's when I started my sign language interpreting career, my deaf clients had to try to follow my signs in between my flying Indian cotton dress sleeves, bright colours and colourful figures on my tunics. As a pioneer in the field, I was one of the five sign language interpreters in the whole country who knew English, so deaf people did not have many to choose from. In those days deaf people were happy to receive interpreting services in general.

Because interpreting the morning and evening prayers and Vespers was part of my job description at the Turku Christian Community College, for the first time I had to think about what to wear. In everyday life there my colours and styles were not a problem, but for the inauguration of the new college building, I really had to think hard about what to wear because the Archbishop Simojoki was going to participate in the ceremonies. I did not have any of the religious people's favourite colour, black, in my wardrobe. I thought that I was well dressed when I put on my full-length Indian silk beige dress, but in the photo published in the college newsletter, the Archbishop had his eyes glued to me when he was watching my leading the sign language choir. I wonder if he was interested only in my signing.

In those days we sign language interpreters worked alone. Meetings, seminars, conferences and all kinds of study trips had to be managed all alone. For other participants the breaks in the programme were for recreation or talking to the others. For me as an interpreter, it was hard enough to have time to go to the loo or to have a cup of coffee to stimulate my tired brain and body. I had to agree the loo visits with my client. Many a time I had heard complaints that an important or interesting hearing person had made contact with her and had wanted to exchange a word or two in the loo queue, when I had been somewhere else. By the end of the meeting day I did not have any energy to sit straight and to sign erect. The long day of interpreting had its effects, as with tiredness in the brain, accuracy and fluency suffered, but in addition, my arms, neck and whole upper back got tired. Once in a while, I had to put the other hand on the armrest and continue with one handed signing. The dinners and get-togethers for the meeting participants were a nightmare for the interpreter. Everyone was talking at the same time and a lot. The evening turned slowly into night, others did not have worries about tomorrow, but I had to be sharp and spirited from early morning to start yet another day of interpreting.

Sweden recognised the professionalism of sign language interpreters a few years before us. The Swedish sign language interpreters criticised me for agreeing to take on long assignments on my own. In their opinion I should have declined to take on the task if I was not given an interpreting partner. My problem was that I worked for the Deaf Association, and I knew how tight their budget was. Often we were happy to get funding for one deaf participant and one interpreter. The Swedish interpreters also emphasised their professionalism by the interpreting uniforms they wore. The Americans had begun to disseminate the idea that all interpreters should dress in similar dark uniforms, which separated the interpreters from other participants. I immediately made the decision that my interpreting career would come to an end that day when we in Finland decided to move into wearing black or some other dark coloured interpreting outfits. I felt that these standard uniforms did not look good on anyone.

As a pioneer in the field and a trainer of interpreters, I slowly had to submit to the facts and give up my multi-coloured, huge-patterned and flowery tops in interpreting situations. No one paid any attention to multiple patterns in skirts and trousers if my outfit was otherwise suitable for the situation. I also felt that there were other colours, which were a good background for signing hands beside black, blue and brown. As an interpreter I dressed in different shades of green, purple and red, which offered a peaceful background for my hands, but nevertheless allowed me to be me.

Working as a fulltime interpreter in the Deaf Association for three years, experiencing long days of interpreting at meetings, powwows, negotiations and seminars and conferences, travelling around Finland, different parts of Europe and the world, were sufficient for me. Every morning before leaving for work I had to check the day's programme and think about what kind of outfit was needed during the day. In the corner of my work room there was a closet where I kept my clothes for emergency situations in case the empty-looking work day suddenly acquired an important interpreting task or visit. After this fulltime interpreter's career, it felt great to be able to put on any multi-coloured, patterned clothes in my own style or to dress in clothes which felt good and were me.

I have never received any remarks on my clothing, but I have received comments from clients on interpreters' clothing in general. Young interpreters especially do not seem to have an understanding of the dress code for the occasion. A miniskirt, t-shirt, or jeans are not really a suitable working outfit for every situation. Because deaf people have to take in the information visually through their eyes, even a small detail might grow to be a big problem for them. Once I received a complaint about a platform interpreter who worked at an important event for the organisation, who was wearing a festive outfit as expected, but who had everyday walking shoes on, which were even muddy. Dangling, shiny earrings, brooches and rings can turn into visual noise, when the deaf person has to look at them on an interpreter for hours.

One of the most important features in a sign language interpreter is flexibility. She has to have an eye both for the interpreting situation and the people with whom and for whom she is working. The interpreter has to move to be close to the source of information, in other words the presenter and what he is presenting on a screen. The interpreter cannot be confined to one place only. If needed, she has to be ready to move. If, for instance, the presenter moves from the podium to be close to the overhead projector. It is also important that the interpreter has enough light on her, but the light cannot come from behind her for it must not shine in the deaf person's eyes. Many a time, I have had to ask for more light, when the lecture room has been dimmed for a presentation on the screen. One of the most memorable ones was the greeting by the UN Secretary General on a video screen. We interpreters were sitting in the darkness when the video started. The greeting was given in spoken French, when the official language of the congress was English. When the lights came on, it was not only the deaf participants who shook their heads.

The work of a sign language interpreter is comprehensive and demands full concentration. We always hope that we will receive the background materials of the meeting beforehand for preparation. We cannot follow just from the paper what the presenter is saying or establish what we are hearing from a written text. Since 1975 I have worked as an interpreter in international settings. My English skills are based on my school English and the year I spent in the States as an exchange student. Basically my skills are in everyday English. The register of my English has not been sufficient for all situations. I have needed hands-on guidance to UN jargon and to interpreting the luncheon in which Princess Diana participated. When interpreting into a foreign language in a fast moving situation, I have not always been able to come up with exactly the right, politically correct expression. Sometimes it has been good enough, if I have been able to utter something. Afterwards the deaf client has sometimes had to explain that my choice of word in the interpreting situation was not her political statement, especially in light of how some Americans seem to take it nowadays.

Training of interpreters, the increase in the number of interpreters, and professionalism in the field has brought improvement in working conditions, one of which is working in pairs. In the 1980's the Deaf Association adopted the use of two interpreters in situations longer than two hours. When you are working in pairs, you do not need to work up to your last morsel of energy. You have extra ears and hands to help in problem situations. 20-30 minute active interpreting sessions are followed by support interpreting. You cannot leave the situation to have your well-earned break. You have to monitor your partner's work by her side and help her deal with any difficulty which might arise. Especially numbers, names and foreign words have to be picked up and kept in your active memory to be thrown to your colleague, when she reaches that point in her interpreting. We interpreters use the term "sitting on a hot bench". The pressure on the working interpreter is so intense in some situations that she would not hear if someone in the presentation mentioned her name. As a support interpreter I have given hints to my partner or whispered words or sentences in her ear for her to be able to produce the accurate concept to the microphone. I have had wonderful experiences from these kinds of joint working situations with many colleagues. When confidence between us has been strong, the support interpreter has bravely jumped in and continued interpreting if I have got stuck, if she has noticed that, for some reason, I am not functioning well enough during my session.

In 1976, when I started as the interpreter for the FAD executive director, I received a lot of positive feedback on how important it was that the sign language interpreter had a good enough general knowledge and a university background. Even that has not always been sufficient, when at the World Congresses we have had to interpret every possible different scientific fields and even from what is a foreign language for us. Even dictionaries have not been sufficient to translate the medical, psychological, linguistic and other special scientific terminology to be able find the exact equivalent and meaning. Nowadays, the Internet has brought solutions to this problem and is in constant use. Many times I have tried interpreting at linguistic seminars and conferences. No matter how many times I have looked up the meanings of the linguistic terms, the field has not opened up for me. That is why it has been a pleasure to leave this impossible field to younger ones with better background information and language skills to interpret.

As an older veteran, I have been trying to encourage younger interpreters to interrupt the speaker every time it is needed. When the presenter is reading directly from his papers and in addition, with a strong accent, it is impossible to process interpreting into sign language. Interpreting colleagues have always praised the brave one who has dared to interrupt the speaker. The deaf signers, who sign like lightning, have always been too risk-averse to interrupt. Many interpreters have lost their reputation doing that. But the fact is that even when signing at normal speed, it is difficult to produce good, rich and vivid spoken language if the deaf person does not take the interpreter into consideration at all. In sign language, information is produced simultaneously by hands, facial expressions, body, size of the signs and localisation. Reproducing all that in a functioning linear spoken language often is very difficult.

The strangest interpreting trip I have made must have been the one I took to Iran, where even the interpreter had to take into consideration the laws and cultural traditions of that country. When sitting in front of hundreds of Iranian conference participants, I had to make sure that my scarf stayed on without revealing my hair or ears, that my long cape and long sleeves kept my wrists covered and that my ankles were hidden under my long skirt and winter boots. All the other women were dressed in black. Luckily that was not demanded from me over there.

I have always been easily spotted among a crowd, seen from far away. Once I was waiting in the lobby for my boss before a seminar. She was standing nearby me and I expected her to notice me. But her gaze was wandering in the distance around the lobby and even swept by me. I went to her and touched her shoulder:

– Is it me you are looking and waiting for? I have been standing here next to you and waited for you to notice me.

– How is it that you are dressed in green? I have been searching for someone dressed in red. That is how I have always found you even in a big crowd of people.

...and the name was?

I had agreed to function as an interpreter at the baptism of my first niece during the Mothers' Day church service in Kuhmoinen church. At the end of March a little baby girl had been born with dark brown eyes, dark hair. The first grandchild in my family would get her name the following day, in the Finnish tradition.

The family was getting ready for the celebration where the little one would be the centre of attention. Kuhmoinen church was packed full for the Mothers' Day church service. My brother had reserved a couple of rows in the front for my parents, my aunt's family and for the deafened group, who were at the Course Centre where my brother was the director, taking a course. When the organist started playing, I found my place in the front near to where the minister would soon be, on that side where the people who would get the service with their eyes were sitting.

The sermon by the minister went somehow, although I could not provide the exact meaning for every little phrase and word because Bible studies was not my thing. Depth was therefore missing from my interpretation. I had received information about the hymns beforehand, I had glanced through those texts to get the meaning. My mother's hymn book with big font was in front of me, I did not need to rely solely on the singing of the congregation.

Towards the end of the church service was the moment our family had been looking forward to: the name giving to the little one. My brother and his wife had decided to hold her in their arms themselves with the godparents standing nearby. I moved closer to the minister and the group participating in the baptism. The look in the eyes of my parents got sharper: What would the little girl be called?

The minister followed the text for baptism and sank his palm in the water bowl to pour it on the head of the child. The mother, Anita, moved the child's head closer to the bowl.

– I baptise you So... ... in the name of the Father, Son and Holy Spirit...

I could not make any sense of the name. I had never heard such a name before. The minister's otherwise clear speech became a mumble in my ears and I just could not convey the name just given to my parents, relatives and the deafened group. My parents' eyes were full of questions:

– Yes, but named what?

In any other kind of circumstances I could have interrupted the minister and asked him to repeat himself, but not at the Mothers' Day church service packed with people, as I stood at the altar as an interpreter. My eyes were desperately trying to catch the eyes of my brother standing close by as my hands went on interpreting further. He was deeply involved in the baptism ritual, and as a proud father was looking at his wonderful daughter. He would be of no help to me.

I thought that I had another chance to correct my mistake and failure, when the minister repeated her name once more. But I still did not catch the name that time either. However, I signed:

– S – O and something else that I cannot figure out.

My long-term memory worked hard trying to go through the list of Finnish names for females starting with a letter S, but the name I had heard did not resemble any of the names I remembered. I was counting out the wrong one: Soile, Saila, Sorja…

Anger started bubbling inside me. Why did I not ask for the name beforehand? What a stupid custom this is here in Finland that the name of the baby is kept secret till the last moment before the baptism. My strength was draining from my system. Why did I agree to take this interpreting job in the first place? A professional interpreter would have managed the task much better than me.

The church service was over. The organ was playing to guide people from the church out to the lovely spring weather. My task was over. I could see the questioning eyes of my parents and the others who did not hear the name. The answer to their question had been given from the altar twice, but the name had flown rapidly by my hearing ears without the brains to be able to register it and my hands to interpret it into sign language. I had failed in my job. Only anger and frustration was left. I just shook my head to my parents' question:

– NAME WHAT, NAME?

I rushed after my brother to the front door of the church.

– Why did you not tell me what the name would be, as you chose such a name, which I have not even heard ever before? I burst out my disappointment and anger to my brother, maybe even too strongly.

– You go and tell mother and father what the name of the girl is! I expostulated.

– SOLJA KASTEHELMI! ("Melting morning dew") my brother spelled out to the deaf and deafened people, who had gathered around him.

He just could not understand why I was so angry.

After this unsuccessful interpreting task, I swore that I would never take this kind of an assignment again. Until, three years later, there was another baptism in my family. This time the celebration was at home. I was interpreting the minister's speech to my parents and telling them that the little girl would be called:

– HELJÄ SUVI-TUULI ("Soft summer wind")!

I had been able to blackmail that name from my brother beforehand. Otherwise I would have refused to interpret the baptism.

I

It is one of those days again, when I have to rush into an interpreting assignment which I am not well prepared for. I have never met the deaf patient before and I do not have time to discuss with her the forthcoming
interpreting situation at this doctor's appointment. I rush in just as her
name is called. I fingerspell out her name and a deaf woman gets up. She
might have seen me interpreting on another occasion? My profession
has not yet labelled me, I hope. My interpreter's name-tag is, of course,
pinned on my other outfit at home.

I enter the doctor's office following the patient. She introduces herself
and I start voicing it as soon as I am finally in the room. The doctor greets
me and starts talking to me. How could I make him understand that I am
just the interpreter in that situation and that he could talk to the deaf
person directly?

I cannot completely understand what the deaf woman is signing. She
has her own ways of expressing things. I cannot understand much at all,
when she starts explaining her symptoms to the doctor. I guess this is
not my day – I have to ask for clarification, repetition and the same thing
all over again. Also the doctor seems to have difficulties understanding
her. He is trying to ask clarifying questions, but of course he is using
medical terms, which in turn I do not understand. He still does not look
at the patient, but talks to me. How can I get out of this situation suc-
cessfully, and soon?

The doctor asks the patient to lie down on the examination bed and
starts examining her. I rush from my chair to beside her head in order
to interpret the doctor's wishes and orders to her. The doctor looks at
me with surprise. I was not needed there in his way, I could read his
thoughts. The deaf woman seems to have resigned herself to her fate,
she gives over her illness to the hands of the wise doctor. I still cannot
completely understand what it is all about – and I am supposed to be the
interpreter, to convey information between two languages and cultures.

The woman returns to her seat, which is situated badly in relation to
the doctor's position. Once again I should have taken more time when we
first came in and arranged the seats so that it would have made it possible to have direct communication between the doctor and the patient.

The doctor takes a thick book in his hands – Pharmacia Fennica – to
find the right medication and dose. I wish I could have that book for my

bedtime reading. Maybe after that I could be a bit wiser during these doctor's appointments. The deaf woman gets her prescription and orders for further treatment. I shake hands with the doctor and leave the room.

In the hallway the woman has lots of questions to ask me, but I have to hurry to my next assignment. I wish the bus would come quickly in order not to miss the next appointment. I did not feel too successful after this interpreting. I wonder how one could succeed for once? After all, how much did everything depend on me?

You

You sit insecurely in the waiting room for a doctor's appointment. You arrive well in advance because you would like to meet your interpreter beforehand and discuss it with her before going in to the doctor. The interpreter is late. You start to feel tense. Maybe someone else will be called in your place before the interpreter arrives. You have registered at the counter where they did not understand your speech. You had to write down on paper your name and date of birth. The woman showed you where to sit down and wait till you would be called in. You have risen a couple of times to walk around just to show them that you still are there, for your name to be called. Your papers have been clearly marked with a red pen DEAF!

Luckily the interpreter rushes into the waiting room at the same time as your name is being called. You have seen her somewhere before, you recognise her as she walks in the door. You relax right away, when you see the interpreter fingerspelling your name and you know that it is your turn to go in. You go first and shake hands with the doctor. You spell out your name for the doctor and introduce your interpreter. The doctor almost slammed the door on the face of the interpreter who barely made it in the room after you. You wonder if the interpreter even saw what you were signing to the doctor.

The whole time there, you cannot calm down. The doctor does not even look at you, when you tell him about your symptoms. The interpreter does not understand your signing, you have to repeat what you have signed over and over again. You think that maybe it is better to simplify for the interpreter what you want to say to make the process faster. The doctor appears to be nervous, when you look at him beyond the interpreter. The doctor's questions seem strange. You are wondering if the interpreter is even interpreting correctly what you are signing to her? Maybe it would have been better to ask your social worker to come with you to this appointment, but that would have meant postponing the appointment because this date did not suit her at all. You are starting to doubt whether you are getting help for this irritating illness at all from this doctor with the help of this interpreter.

The doctor points you to the examination bed. For a while you are unsure what you are supposed to do, what is it that he is going to examine. Luckily the interpreter jumps up from her seat and appears from behind the doctor to be beside your head and interprets the doctor's orders. The examination is over. The doctor seems even more hurried than before. He glances through a thick book. He writes a prescription for you, which he gives to the interpreter. He tells you to eat lightly, drink more water and come back to him if the symptoms do not disappear after taking the medication. The doctor says goodbye to the interpreter and hurriedly also to you. Maybe he is trying to catch up with the appointment times, which are running late.

Some issues are still unclear to you and you would like to discuss them with the interpreter in the hallway, since there was no time to go through them with the doctor. The interpreter is already half-way to the door, trying to excuse herself from the situation – her next appointment is on the other side of town in half an hour. The situation remains uncertain to you. You did get the prescription and a few instructions, but still you feel that you did not get that help you came for.

He

He has had a bad start to the day: first an argument with his wife and children at home before starting out for work. About money, as always. The family does not really understand that a doctor's salary is not what it used to be, they are not that rich. At reception, the schedule started slipping even during the first patient, which usually affects the rest of the day and brings a sense of pressure.

At 10 o'clock it was Mrs Tianen's appointment, a little bit later even than that. She had been at this medical centre before, but never as his patient. It took a little while before he understood that the patient was deaf and that she had an interpreter with her. He almost closed the door in front of the interpreter. He was wondering to himself why this deaf woman did not speak for herself, but started to sign to him. He did not understand sign language. Everything was taking too much time and his schedule started to slip again. He started to worry about the slowness of the situation. It was like watching a silent film without a plot. This patient did not know much of anything; she was very unclear and using very odd Finnish language. He almost had to guess what the illness was all about.

Although he was in a big hurry, he still had to examine the patient, to show willing. The interpreter was lovely and precise, but it was hard for the poor patient even to understand what was expected of her. The interpreter had to leave her seat and come to the side of the examination bed to tell her what she was supposed to do. There were some strange noises in her stomach, maybe something to calm down her digestion was needed. The next patient was already waiting, he did not have more time for Mrs Tiainen. Everything would go so much easier and faster if only the deaf people would learn to speak for themselves.

Coffee & cognac

It was in those days when we only dreamed about having a team-mate with whom you could have shared the long day of interpreting. At that time sign language interpreters were working alone. Well, in general it was enough then to have some situations interpreted for deaf people. At that time lectures were important. It was important that the interpreter interpreted everything, being truthful to the speaker's text. There were some breaks put in the programme – coffee break in the morning and afternoon and a bit longer for a lunch break. These were important to the deaf participants. Then they had a chance to meet and discuss with the speaker or the hearing participants at the seminar. It has been said that actually it is during the breaks that the most important issues are discussed, when it is important to try to influence, to inform about issues that are of importance, especially when it comes to the needs of deaf people.

I was younger then, more energetic and full of enthusiasm in my work. I did not have any difficulties waving my hands the full long day, all alone and without any proper breaks. I felt that interpreting during the breaks was especially important. They were the moments of success, when I made it possible for the hearing and deaf person to meet and exchange ideas. It was in my opinion really influential, although I only acted as a conveyor of messages in these important situations.

Once again, it was effectively a whole day seminar. My hands had been waving in the air smoothly and actively during the morning and my brain produced successful translations. After lunch the speed started to slow down a bit. I was getting tired. At the same time, the schedule for the seminar started to fall behind. The interventions were longer one after another and the afternoon coffee break, which I had dreamt of since lunch, started to be just a vanishing dream. I had thought that I would have time to walk around a bit to sharpen up and go to the toilet. Only a few minutes would have been needed. My neck started to ache, my arms were tired. At times, I was only signing with one hand, the other leaning on the armrest of the chair. Even that felt like a rest.

The seminar schedule was half an hour past the scheduled start of the coffee break when the chairman made a constructive proposal to the participants: Would it be all right to enjoy coffee while working in order for the seminar to finish on time? I could not believe my ears. How about me? Where is my well-deserved break? How can I drink coffee and interpret at the same time? I gave a desperate glance towards the deaf participants. They seem to be nodding at each other and supporting the chair's proposal. This way they would make it at home on time. I guess my glance, which I directed to the seminar chairperson, was full of suffering, because he beckoned the waiter, who was distributing coffees and pastries to the participants, to him.

Surprise, surprise – in a minute the waiter was bringing a small table to my chair and a cup of coffee and a glass of COGNAC! That was a friendly gesture from the chairperson to the tired sign language interpreter.

The seminar continued its work for a little over an hour. The coffee turned cold in my cup. I could smell the aroma of the cognac. Everyone wanted to get home on time, the seminar programme was even tighter than before. My hands were tied up with the non-stop speeches, I did not have a single opportunity even to grasp to my coffee cup, not to mention the cognac. I guess it would have not been proper either – to drink while working in the middle of the day.

Cello concert

When you discuss deafness and the seriousness of that disability with hearing people, they often feel sorry for deaf people because they cannot hear the birds singing or the voice of their dearest loved one. When hearing people think about losing their own hearing, their biggest loss would be the loss of music. Sounds and music form such a big part of the everyday life of we hearing people that the loss of hearing would feel much more serious than the loss of sight.

Deaf people in general have as good a sense of rhythm as any person, neither better nor worse. Deaf people can feel the rhythm of music with their hands, the bottom of their feet or with their whole body, if there is a vibrating surface somewhere nearby. A wooden floor is the best type as a dance floor for deaf people. They can also feel vibrations from the side of a purse or holding a balloon on their lap. Usually deaf people love dancing. Music for them should have low bass to have the right vibrations. Deaf people are also very sharp using their eyes, they can pick up the rhythm or steps from another dancing couple next to them.

Another type of music, which deaf people like very much are signed songs. There are some deaf people who are against them because they feel that only songs which are produced in sign language are part of true deaf culture, that signed songs are only translations of hearing people's music. At their best these kinds of songs can be visual art. Deaf people in the former communist countries especially practise and have signed songs as their hobby. The performances are fabulous with choreography and outfits.

How do you interpret music for deaf people? I have one experience of this, which I will never forget and after which I have never again tried to interpret music for deaf people in a visual form.

Some years ago there was an experimental cello concert in connection with a seminar for disabled people. The concert was publicised as a visual concert suitable for all disabled people. Beside the cello player on the stage there was an overhead projector, which was used to show the notes of the piece played on a screen. Beside that there was a poet reading a poem written to suit this cello piece.

The cello player started playing. Another person responsible for the overhead moved the transparency following the music. The poet was reading his poem here and there. Interpreting the poem was no problem

174

because I could also read the text on the overhead and the rhythm was nice. But how to interpret music visually? Especially cello playing? First I tried to draw slow movements in the air. I was not satisfied even myself. Next I tried to describe the sound which the cello produced. Oh boy! What to compare it with? Violin? The sound of a cello is low, stretching, peaceful and sad. The sound of a violin is high, jumping and happy.

– WHAT DOES LOW MEAN? the deaf person asked me.

I had a hard time trying to come up with similar visual images in my mind. What could I compare low with? All of a sudden I got the idea of a visual comparison. It is like throwing stones in the water. When you throw a small stone, there will be a small circle forming and the sound is a high "PLIMP!" On the other hand, when you throw a big rock in the lake, it will make a huge enlarging circle on the surface and produce a low sound, "PLUMP!"

When I looked at the deaf person, I felt happy and satisfied, like I had made a new invention.

– IT LOOKS THE SAME! he said.

After that I have not even tried to interpret music to deaf people.

It stretches, but does not break

What is a good sign language interpreter like? What kind of features are needed from an interpreter for her to manage well in an interpreting assignment between two languages and cultures? These issues have been discussed in working groups and seminars, whenever training for sign language interpreters has been planned in different countries. Language competence in both languages of course is the Alpha and Omega for an interpreter. Sufficient education, at the least graduation from secondary school, and wide general knowledge have been seen as necessary for an interpreter. As for personal and social features and skills, these have varied in the discussions depending on which experiences and needs deaf and hearing people have had in different interpreted situations. A sense of rhythm certainly does not seem to be one of the most needed qualities in the work of a sign language interpreter. However, its importance became self-evident for me in the summer of 1978 at the Deaf Nordic Cultural Festivals in Aalborg, Denmark.

Denmark had chosen a challenging theme for the festivals *The music of the Deaf.* Finns took on this new branching out eagerly as a subject to be worked on. What does music mean to a deaf person? How can deaf people sense music and enjoy it without acoustic sensations? What else is there in music beside sounds? The cultural group from the Deaf Association had fierce discussions on how to approach this theme, how music could be taken into the presentation so that even deaf people could feel part of it and experience musical sensation. Although deaf people cannot hear music even with a hearing aid, nevertheless, they can enjoy the rhythm of music, the vibration of low sounds and resonance from different surfaces. Deaf people have always enjoyed dancing. Folk dances have always been a part of Deaf Cultural Festivals and in social evenings at the local Deaf Clubs. Tambourines and wooden sticks have played their part in the music of the performances, to accompany the rhythm of dances and to make them visual.

Deaf people had seen a dance performance at the Helsinki City Theatre on Charlie Chaplin's life. The piece was no longer in the theatre's programme, and we were given permission to do further work on it to turn it into a performance in pantomime and dance by deaf people, called *Smiling Boy.* Excerpts from the movies of this popular silent film personality were included in the manuscript. When the main details for the less than half an hour performance were complete, the group was happy to get the choreographer of the city theatre to give some professional guidance in polishing the performance. During the practice sessions, suitable dances and their length had been agreed upon. Music for it would be agreed later on. Just before the trip I was asked to watch the dress rehearsals of the performance. A wish was expressed that I would find suitable music for this piece. The working group had decided that the deaf participants in the audience at the festival were to be given balloons before the performance so that they might feel a musical sensation from the vibration from the surface of the balloon.

I received a list of all the dances to be performed in this Chaplin dance performance from the deaf director. I was asked to find suitable music to be played in the background. The wish was a surprise because I had no previous experience or knowledge on this subject. I contacted the choreographer in the City Theatre to find out what might be needed. We only had a couple of weeks before leaving for Denmark. They trusted me as a hearing interpreter as a ram trusts his horns: of course I would find the right kind of music, I was hearing, was I not? I got a hint that there was a very good music store in Helsinki called Digelius Music where I probably could get expert help. The professional dance expert trusted that I could find suitable music from there.

I felt pretty stupid, when I walked into the music store. The wish felt just crazy and impossible. To try to find a record from among thousands of records, which could exactly describe and support this performance rhythmically along with every different spirit of its various scenes was a wish too far. My list included a waltz, a Charleston, several kinds of marches, Dixieland music, and music that would be played in the background to keep the right spirit going. I was a bit perplexed, when I phrased my question to the man behind the counter, probably the owner of the store. He did not consider my wish stupid or impossible, but had a few questions to fine tune the content and spirit of each scene. First he found an LP that contained Charlie Chaplin's film music. According to him that could be played both as background music and in different scenes to give rhythm to the dances. From a waltz record he recommended three different Finnish waltzes. *The Best of Dixieland* -record had the needed Charleston, a march, and a piece that suited Chaplin's daydreaming scene.

We did not have time to have rehearsals together with the music before the trip. The Danish organisers had promised to give us enough practice time at the festival place with the help of an expert technician. Both the performers and their support group filled the bus and headed for Denmark. I had four precious LPs in my bag, which would play an important part in the performance of the Finnish group. At home I had listened to the records very carefully many times over and over again and made a manuscript of the music for the performance for the person responsible for the technology. The biggest challenge was that the performance was already together, the music had to be adjusted to it, not vice versa. The technician would need to have fast fingers and sharp senses because the pieces were not in the right order on the records. The LPs had to be changed at speed and the needle of the record player inserted on to the right track. The deaf performers handled the performance as a routine, but I had the big responsibility of providing the musical sensation to the audience as well as showing the rhythm of the music to the deaf actors, and keeping an eye on the technician to ensure he changed the record track when the scene and rhythm changed.

As soon as we arrived in Aalborg, we went to the festival venue to start our rehearsal of *The Smiling Boy* for the first time with music in the background. Luckily the technician who was employed to work for the festival was flexible, with a good sense of humour and he was willing to give his all to the success of this work. I explained the structure of the performance and the objective to him. We went through my music manuscript. I gave him the four LPs where I had clearly marked the A and B sides, and to be sure had even circled the numbers of the pieces that would be played. I hid between the stage curtains during the practice, so as not to be seen by the audience. However, the deaf performers had to see from my hands the rhythm of the music played. With my other hand I was showing the technician what would next be needed. A piece that lasted for only two minutes needed the music to be replayed from the beginning as long as the scene continued on the stage. Sometimes only a part of the piece was needed. I had agreed with the technician different signs for continuation, interruption and changing of the record. Besides that, he had to follow my manuscript with his other eye to see where the next piece to be played could be found. It was only during the last rehearsals that I understood what an important role I would have as an interpreter in the success of this experimental performance and in offering a musical sensation to the festival audience. We only had enough practice time to go through everything once. Other countries also needed to get accustomed to the festival stage. The Finnish performance was first in the programme after the opening of the festival.

I have no recollection how everything went during the performance. The Danish sound technician was magnificent, he did everything he could and followed my instructions. The audience did not have any sense of what was happening behind the curtains on stage, which gave them the rhythm of the dances and music.

Our actors from Helsinki and Turku gave their best in the performance: the facial expressions had never been just so right and the movements as truthful in the practice sessions as they were in the festival performance. We received unconditional praise from the audience for our performance. We were still being thanked for our programme days after it. I was be proud to be Finnish.

That was what I wrote as the FAD information officer in the *Deaf Magazine*.

Still now, when I play the LPs that I was allowed to keep, this highlight in my interpreting career comes back to mind. I doubt if the deaf people in the performing group understood either then or afterwards how much

178

they had stretched the limits of an interpreter's job description without realising it – and I just stretched, but did not break.

Astronomy lecture

I had been asked to interpret the inaugural lecture of the new professor for general linguistics at Helsinki University in sign language. It might have been the first time that a lecture had been interpreted into sign language for some 300 people in that university lecture hall. I was well prepared. I had received the lecture beforehand and read it thoroughly. It dealt with sign language research as a part of linguistic research and sign language as a language among other languages. The new professor was familiar to me because I had interpreted his linguistic lectures before. It was with a calm mind that I came to the inauguration lecture. I knew that his rhythm would be slow and his way of speaking very clear. I was expecting to have a twenty minute pleasant session to interpret, which I was anticipating enjoying. It was also rewarding to know that the new professor felt it important to bring up sign language issues in his inaugural lecture.

Well in advance I arrived in the lecture hall, since I always wanted to check the place for interpreting and the seating for myself before anything started. Besides me, the deaf participants needed to see the lecturer and possibly needed audio-visual aids. The audience was seated in a half-circle in the auditorium. The speakers were behind a high table, in speaker's rostrum. I needed to find myself an extra chair, which could be placed under the speakers' table immediately below the stage. The deaf participants had already arrived early to reserve good seats where they could see well. I sat down on my chair to wait for the lecture to start. If people have not seen sign language interpreters before, they usually are interested in the person sitting in the front facing them, but the more interpreted situations there are, the more natural people find we interpreters. In a way, we sign language interpreters in front are an extra show. People like to watch how we handle difficult situations, keep up with a fast speaker, and understand difficult terminology or other challenges that might occur. We are different from the spoken language interpreters because we can be seen, are present in front of all the people.

The linguistic lecture was a pure pleasure to interpret, I could feel satisfaction rise within me. Everything went as planned. As an interpreter I felt that I had been able to convey not only the speaker's message, but also his way of expressing himself, how he highlighted matters and the reactions from the audience. It is not very common to have this kind of a feeling in an interpreting situation. But it is possible to reach, if the speaker takes the interpreter into consideration, the lecture materials are available in advance and the speaker cares about his message being translated into another language. I was proud of my achievement. I felt that maybe, after all, it is possible to succeed in this profession. I sat there waiting for the chairman to close the session and the event to be over.

The chairman thanked the linguistic professor for his interesting lecture. Then he introduced the next speaker who was the new astronomy professor at the Helsinki University. I interpreted what the chairman was saying and at the same time tried to catch the sight of the deaf participants to get assurance that the situation was over for us and we could leave as long as it was still somehow possible. Deaf people were interested in what was coming, in this unexpected new situation.

The chairman asked the astronomy professor to step forward and give his inaugural lecture. I gave a long look at the deaf people and asked them in signing:

– Do you want to stay and listen to this following lecture, too?

I expected to receive a head shake, after which I was prepared to get my things together and leave the room as quietly as it still was possible. But from the middle of the audience I only received anxious nods and big smiles.

– Of course we want to stay!

I felt all energy escape from my body, my head was empty. But I had to pull myself together in front of all those people and try to do my best in this impossible situation, although I already saw a complete disaster in front of me. I wanted to disappear under the floor.

The astronomy professor started his lecture. He also had 20 minutes reserved for him. I felt that he had planned to tell the audience everything he knew about astronomy within those 20 minutes. His speed was incredible. I hardly could distinguish his words from another, not to mention that I had no time to process into sign language what he was saying. The theme was completely unfamiliar to me. The lecture did not shed any more light on astronomy for me. Once in a while during that lecture, like giving me a break or extra strength to continue, the lecturer dropped a word or two, which I could make some sense of and which I grabbed into fingerspelling them or interpreting them into sign language. My head was numb, my neck and arms started to ache. I did not know any longer whom I was interpreting for because in my misery I was too ashamed even to look at the deaf people in the audience. They had wanted to see this astronomy lecture interpreted, they got a completely nonsensical and inferior performance. As suddenly as this unexpected situation had started for me, it also ended. 20 minutes might have been too short a time for the speaker to say everything he wanted to say, but for me it felt like eternity. I felt that I had been waving my hands desperately in the air without any purpose and that it would never end. The chairman thanked him for the interesting lecture. The occasion was over.

For me it actually only began then. Participants from the hall started streaming in my direction, not at all deaf people. Old astronomy professors from other universities and other people who had astronomy as their main hobby had followed my signing very closely, my hopeless hand waving in the wonderful world of astronomy. They wanted to come and thank me personally for this completely new experience. For the first time in their life they had seen the astronomy terminology expressed so well in sign language! From my interpreting they had picked out some single signs, for instance, MOON, STARS, and COPERNICUS. Some of them wanted me to show them some other terms. What I thought was failure had actually turned into triumph.

In the spotlights

Like a star on a concert stage. In the spotlights, centre of attention for all participants. Bringing positive experiences for people so that for a moment they can forget their problems and sorrows. This is usually offered in daydreams or fantasies. A man in the street usually has the role of a recipient, a seat in the audience as a listener or a spectator, an enthusiastic fan of a popular artist or an applauder. Once, in a passing moment, I was able to experience the fulfilment of my dreams in the spotlights.

In 1980 in Finlandia Hall there was a charity concert where numerous famous Finnish singers, including my favourite for many years, Anneli Saaristo, had agreed to perform for free for the Finnish Association of the Deaf. The singers had been asked to send information on the songs they were going to sing in the concert. Copies of the texts of the songs were distributed to the sign language interpreters beforehand. The singers were also asked to arrive well in advance to discuss with their interpreter the practical points of performing with a sign language interpreter. Of course, the singers were familiar with the different kinds of stage and spotlight, which were needed in a concert like this, but we sign language interpreters were not all that familiar in those days and needed some advice in advance about where they wanted us to stand and if there were any other special wishes they had for us. There was a list of six to seven top artists performing at this concert. We interpreters were given the chance to choose an artist whose songs we were familiar with and whom we felt most comfortable with.

We sign language interpreters had arrived nice and early in the artists' foyer in Finlandia Hall to wait for our artists to arrive. Some of us had been lucky enough to get the texts of the songs beforehand to be practised at home, but not all were that lucky. The singers dropped in one by one and we kept an eye open for the moment when our artist would arrive to agree upon our joint performance. Of course, there are always big stars among the artists in these charity concerts who do not want to waste any of their own time on this cause. Their record company had thought this to be important for publicity. These ones arrived at the last minute, thought that they could just go and sing their songs and leave having done their duty. All you can do is to feel sorry for the interpreter who had to interpret this kind of artist's performance "cold". It was almost like having to compose the signed performance from scratch, when they had no idea what and how it would come, what the words of the song were, not to mention the rhythm of the song. Luckily, we did not have any choirs performing that night because usually choral songs were the most difficult for making any sense of the words.

I had had a hard time deciding what to wear for that important, different kind of interpreting situation. It had to be something festive enough for the Finlandia Hall stage and for the 75th anniversary of the Deaf Association. But it could not be too glamorous and be something that would take attention away from the performing artist. We were only sign language interpreters whose task it was to convey the message and the feeling of the songs to the deaf audience in sign language. We did have an important role to play that evening. I had decided to wear a full-length, dark-rose, Indian cotton dress, which had sewn decorations in the front. Now that I think of my outfit, it might not have been the most appropriate for interpreting. But in those days we did not know better and deaf people were not that demanding over what interpreters wore. The outfit felt good, something I liked to wear. In it moving was easy and the best of all, the wet signs of my nervousness from below the armpits would not show right away.

A couple of singers had already performed and received big applause from an almost full house. It was not clear if the applause was meant for the big stars, or if the audience was thrilled to receive information in sign language about the songs, which were familiar to the hearing audience through radio programmes and even from performances on TV. Those had meant big, moving mouths and gestures, which had no meaning to the deaf audience. There had been only one TV programme which had had a few interpreted songs in sign language so far, which had left deaf viewers hungry for more.

I was standing behind the curtains with my singer, Anneli Saaristo, waiting for the announcement of our performance. We were standing side by side, two well-built, well-formed, big women. I had always liked Anneli's songs and her style in the records I had listened to at home. A short encounter before going to the stage gave me the assurance that she was a very straightforward, honest woman. We were to perform together. We were nothing without the other person. Hearing people wanted to listen to her singing, deaf people wanted to receive the content of her songs through my fingers. What could have been a better choice for our song together but her popular song called *I am a woman...*

All of a sudden, I found myself standing in the middle of the stage in the bright lights of the huge Finlandia Hall. I knew from before that the hall was almost fully sold-out, but I could not see a single face in those lights shining directly into my eyes. I got a bit nervous. Whom would I interpret for now? Who would give me feedback on my performance? I wanted to have a few faces in the audience at whom I could direct my interpreting, someone looking at me, smiling to me, nodding at me as a positive hint that I was doing OK, that I was being understood and that they wanted to receive more of it. The audience was in darkness behind the brightly shining spotlights. I had to pull myself together to continue. I tried to believe that they were there and happy with my performance. All I could do now was to trust my own judgement on the choice of signs in interpreting the content of the songs, to convey the music and rhythm to deaf ears. In the song, *I am a woman...* is repeated many times. I felt that it was my own song which I performed to the audience personally. I let the song to take me along: I was a woman!

For some reason the second song, although it was touching and beautiful, also one of her most popular, a song about a girl and a dancing bear, did not make such a deep impression on me. The audience just loved our performance. Applause did not seem to end at all. We had succeeded together and as each one of us. We were bowing to the audience and to each other. Still I could not see the reactions from the audience. I just had to believe that everything had gone well.

Hardly had I had time after the concert to get myself to the foyer of the hall, when the joy broke out. People came up to me to tell me how the audience had had such a grand time following my interpreting. They had had to keep themselves from laughing in order for Anneli Saaristo not to get the wrong impression of their reactions to her song. She would not understand the niceties and details of sign language anyhow. When her first song came to this line which was repeated numerous times during the song *I am a woman...* they had to put their hands over their mouths not to burst out laughing aloud. Laughter was bubbling up inside them. As the line kept coming up over and over again, I had innocently but determinedly stretched out the sign for a WOMAN to become long, stretched breasts following the rhythm of the song. And yet again it went *I am a W-O-O-O-M-A-A-A-N...* Although both Anneli and I had quite big breasts, the woman in my song must have had even bigger breasts, at least F or G size and the breasts pointing straight ahead.

It had been lucky that I had not been able to see the reactions of the audience, because if I had, I would have run away from the stage and disappeared because of the shame I was feeling from the audience's feedback. I had not even for a split second stopped to think how the choice of my signs and how I performed them on the stage could be perceived. I only had lived through the song as a woman in the song sung by Anneli. No matter how much afterwards I have tried to reanalyse my own performance, I could not or would not have done anything differently. The interpreter should follow the rhythm of the song. Full stop. It was impossible to sign a small breasted woman without breaking the rhythm of the song. It would have been completely impossible to keep repeating the sign for WOMAN as many times as the signing of that word took in the song. That way the rhythm of the song would have been seriously broken. When I in my memories years afterwards go back to my performance that evening and how I would interpret it now, I would sign it to look like a long balloon stretching out, when air is blown into it. The breast would grow towards the audience and would get longer and longer till it was time for the hand to return to its original position under the breast and for the repetition to come again: *I am a W-O-O-O-M-A-A-A-N...*

Partying with stars

On the phone, somebody was asking for a sign language teacher with English skills. The switchboard operator at the Deaf Association forwarded the call to me. The contact person of an American film crew introduced the subject: a group was coming to Helsinki to film *Gorky Park*. A Finnish deaf actor was needed to play a minor part. A few hours of sign language training also was needed for an American hearing actor.

In 1983, the American film makers could not get over the border to the Soviet Union to film Russian scenes there. Helsinki with its empire centre often got the part of playing Moscow. The Kaisaniemi Park became Gorky Park for a few weeks. We had snow and winter even here in the south. That year there was hardly any snow. In the film plot, according to the manuscript, snow played an important part, three frozen bodies were found buried under the snow in the park.

The American filming project started to be mentioned in the news. Volunteers were needed for minor roles and to walk on the streets of "Moscow". A picture of Lenin was painted in Union Street on the wall of an apartment house next to an empty lot. The stores along that street received Cyrillic signs for the filming. In letters to the editor columns in the newspapers, people kept discussing the plan to have a star at the top of our National Museum tower for it to play the part of one of the Kremlin towers. Some people felt that it was sacrilegious and an insult to the Finnish national spirit.

I passed on the message from the American crew to the Helsinki Deaf Club. I went there with the Finnish contact person from the crew to meet three deaf male actors. The final choice was to be made by the American director. Risto Rautanen, an albino pantomime performer, was finally chosen to play the part because of his skills, but maybe also for his appearance.

My task was to go and teach sign language to Brian Dennehy. He was playing the part of a policeman from New York who travels to Moscow to search for his missing brother. At the hotel reception I asked for the actor at the time we were supposed to meet. I was directed to his suite. At the door I was greeted by a fair-haired, robust actor. His face looked familiar from some films I had seen, but I could not locate him by any specific film. Brian seemed very easy-going and eager to learn a few signs. First we discussed the role of the deaf person and why he, as an American policeman, should know how to say something in sign language. Once again, I had to explain the basics about sign language: it is not international, every country has its own sign language, although the structure is quite similar in different sign languages. In an American film, there was no point in his learning Finnish Sign language, which I knew best. Maybe the use of American Sign Language would look odd because the deaf man whom he was to meet in a shady bar in Moscow certainly would not be using ASL. He was supposed to receive information from this deaf man about where to look for leads for the murder. In my opinion, the best solution was to use some kind of gestural language, which hearing people use, and to learn that for this role.

We went through the lines in the manuscript where sign language was needed. We practised gesturing and the use of facial expressions, which the deaf person would understand. A couple of hours of in the afternoon flew by merrily. I promised to pass on the results of our discussions to Risto who had been chosen for the deaf role. Risto could go through the lines using those signs with Brian before the filming began. We would meet again, but for the present the scene in the hotel room was over.

Because of a work trip, I did not make it to the actual filming as an interpreter. I heard afterwards that everything had gone smoothly and that they had been satisfied with the deaf man's performance as the *Jumping man*. In the film itself that scene would only be a few seconds long. That was what we were told. We were happy and proud that a deaf person had been chosen for the deaf man's role. This was what the American deaf actors had been demanding for years.

Brian Dennehy was just a small star in that film. The Finnish evening papers were trumpeting the arrival of the bigger star, William Hurt, in Helsinki. A marketing campaign of the Deaf Association coincided with the visit of the American film crew. Because we already had a natural connection with them through the role of the deaf actor, we sent an invitation to the director and actors to a cocktail party organised by the Deaf Association. We were excited to see if the Americans would accept the invitation.

When the party was well underway, someone came to tell us that the director and actors were on their way over. Risto greeted them like old friends. In passing, I had time to ask Brian how his signing had functioned during the filming day, before I was asked to interpret the introductions of William Hurt and director Michael Apted to the FAD executive director and other deaf people. We exchanged a few words with them, and had a drink together before they hurriedly had to leave for dinner after a long filming day.

We waited with excitement for the premier of *Gorky Park* in Finland. There was a group of us who went together to see it the first evening. In the darkness of the cinema we were waiting to see the scene where the deaf man gives a hint to the American policeman. The plot of the film progressed, the familiar scenery of Helsinki flashed by our eyes: Kaisaniemi Park where snow had to be loaded by lorries from out of town in order for the park to look wintery. The Russian names of shops on Union Street. The red star at the top of the National Museum tower. People walking on the grey and slushy streets of Moscow looking grim. An hour and a half had slipped by. The credits were already showing on the screen. The plot of the film had been changed. The scene with the deaf man had been cut out. Our pains had been in vain.

William Hurt would not have been recognised in the Finnish street scene because he looked so ordinary. He became a star in the deaf world in 1986, when he played the other main part in the film *Children of a Lesser God*. The deaf actress Marlee Matlin received an Oscar for her part in that film. For the role of a speech teacher in a deaf school Hurt had to study American Sign Language. In the film, he learned that from a deaf cleaning woman who refused to use her speech and voice. This actor couple also dated each other and lived together for a while. I am sure William Hurt's sign language skills developed fast with the help of his home teacher.

– Who lifts the cat's tail, if not cat himself? I thought when I was reading these stories about them.

I am sure that this big star got his first contact with sign language when he was visiting Helsinki.

Lost for words

I was born to be an interpreter. I grew up as a citizen of two worlds. Born bilingual. The choice of profession seems to have been clear to me since I was small. However, work among deaf people and sign language has not been self-evident. Career choice for me has merely been a series of coincidences, lucky right choices in different situations. Someone else might call it providence. Even wishes I have not expressed aloud have come true. A year away from home in the big world, listening to the values and opinions of hearing people, taught me to appreciate my deaf background, language and culture which I received from my deaf parents. In the process of balancing between two languages I gained a third language, English, and to date learning its fine tuning and numerous alternatives has burned into my life.

The sign language I learned at home and the general knowledge Jyväskylä Girls' School offered me were sufficient for interpreting for my parents, relatives and our small deaf community. Sometimes the specific terminology some professionals were using went high over my head. But being a hearing person I still had in my hands more concepts that hearing people were using than my deaf parents did. At least, that was the impression deaf people had in those days.

In my first job, when I interpreted morning and evening prayers, religious meetings and joint lessons for deaf students in the college, I often realised that the everyday sign language I had used at home was not sufficient for those interpreting situations. Every day in interpreting I drowned in the inefficiency of my language competence, all I had to offer were half-expressions of the source language. I translated only the trunk, when my sign language was not rich enough to describe and to paint the whole foliage of the message. While my language competence slowly improved, living every day with deaf people and following their lively language, I never felt that I was proficient enough. The whole time sign language lives and develops depending on the situations where it is used and needed. The forbidden everyday language of deaf people of my childhood times has nowadays become an accepted, desirable and interesting language even among hearing people.

It has not been enough that I have had to balance between two languages while constantly testing my own limits, but the Deaf Association soon noticed the hidden international interpreter potential in me. In those days, in the 1970's, there were not many sign language interpreters in Finland who could speak English. If my inefficiency in two languages took away my energy, I now was able to feed my low self-confidence by trying to learn and understand the subtleties of the mighty world of English. Eight years of school English and the everyday American English I had learned during my exchange year were not enough. The first years at the Deaf Association I interpreted alone at congresses, seminars and international meetings. There was no expectation at that time that the organisers of meetings and presenters would provide the materials beforehand for studying. Sometimes it was considered good enough if we had the programme for the event in our hands before it started.

From the late 1980's on I had the pleasure of being introduced to the jargon and fine nuances of the English language, when my interpreting field was enlarged to interpreting at the UN, its specialised agencies, and meetings of international organisations. Technology and the problems it can cause to interpreters, and also the other languages used at the meetings, came along. I often received source information that already had been processed by other interpreters. I had to try to make some sense of what people were saying no matter how much crackling the microphone caused when it picked up all the interference from the surroundings or when my earphones were also bringing through the other languages. Very few speakers had English as their mother tongue, my ears had to get used to understanding very strong accents. When formulating the documents, the participants had to come up with wording first in English, which everyone could accept, before they could be translated into other languages for final approval. It was no longer a question of AND and OR or AND/OR, which I had learned had much importance when I was studying social legislation.

Gradually when international co-operation and contacts started growing, we Finnish Sign Language interpreters also had to realise that interpreting alone was an impossible and too demanding task. Processing language at the speed of speech for long stretches at a time makes the brain grow tired and the interpreting is no longer of good quality. Working with an interpreting partner one had more energy to last through the whole day. The helping hand of a colleague was your support in difficult situations, when you did not hear, could not make sense of or did not understand the speaker. There have also been moments, when even good co-operation did not bring you glory.

There is a rule in the professional code for sign language interpreters, which states that one should estimate one's own skills in carrying out the assignment even before accepting it. I, as the pioneer in the field have had to break this rule many a time. Very often a better interpreter was not available, although I understood the limitations of my own skills and language competence. To this very day, hunting for lost words has been a constant battle in my life.

The world will teach you for sure

It is almost impossible to hide congenital talent! Woodstock in *Peanuts* sings on a tree branch in a card, which I years ago received from a friend of mine. As I have been patted on the head because I was so clever, handy, skillful and for all kinds of skills I was said to have, once in a while I started trusting myself for the praise I was getting from people around me. As a hearing child I was the fulfilment of the dreams and hopes of my deaf parents. Hearing people were considered to be clever and smart in the deaf world, because in addition to hearing, they also knew the written and spoken language. It was the key to information, contacts and services. I was expected to use my gift, not only to help my parents and make them happy, but also for the good of the deaf community we lived in.

Quite soon, as my information about the environment around me increased, I slowly learned that the reality and values of the deaf world were not always the same as the hard requirements of the hearing world. I wanted to become perfect, or at least to succeed in whatever I was doing. I soaked up the praise and acknowledgement. I always did well in school. I liked to accomplish all kinds of things and to succeed in tasks, tests and in doing something collaboratively. When I functioned as the hearing ear to my deaf parents and as their interpreter I was used, even in the adult world, to taking up the reins, it was customary for me to be the leader, organiser and promoter in other kinds of situations also.

Failure or the fact that I could not do something has always been difficult for me. I have been a bad loser. That is why I never liked playing cards or games. I am fast in my movements and everything should succeed and function right away. Conflicts and disappointments were waiting for me, when my own expectations were not met. It was difficult to show this to hearing outsiders. My mother must have been the only person to whom

I could show this side of myself. She must have been the only one who knew how to handle me in disappointing situations. I still can see those situations in front of my eyes as if they were happening today. The child in me came to the surface, I threw whatever I was knitting or crocheting in the corner when whatever I was doing was not as easy or the result did not turn out as I expected. Similar situations also took place in the kitchen, when the dough did not roll as I wanted and got stuck on the board, or the rice porridge I had made for the Karelian pasties was too runny, and I did not know how to make it thicker. My mother never started to scold nor comfort me in the situation itself. I could not have handled or taken it. After I had let most of the steam out I gave an indirect gaze in mother's direction. I saw how she had taken my knitting or handwork. She always had patience to undo the part done wrongly and even start from the beginning, if needed. She never finished anything for me, as many of the mothers of my schoolmates used to do, but just helped me over the difficult part. Mother quietly put the handwork in my basket, where I could take it up after the situation had calmed down and continue it with new enthusiasm. The same way she led me to the secrets of how to roll the crust for an apple-pie or for Karelian pasties.

This feature in me, reaching for perfection, has led to the most setbacks in my work as a sign language interpreter. The interpreting situation is the sum of many factors, which the interpreter has very little, if any, opportunity to influence. Other people might have thought that I had managed the interpreting situation, if not in a praiseworthy way, at least honourably, but very rarely I could be satisfied with it myself. The Little-Raili was always sitting on my shoulder and observing severely what I let out of my mouth or produced with my hands. With some lag time I started getting comments from her on what I actually should have said, what the speaker had meant, what certain concepts had meant. Once in a while to keep up with the speaker's or signer's speed, I have had to take shortcuts here and there, to cut corners or come up with something that was close, meaning almost the same, as I could not remember the exact word needed. By interrupting I would have shown that I did not understand, could not know or manage in the situation. It did not comfort me at all when in the interpreters' room afterwards we were discussing it, and I could see that the other interpreters, especially those of us who also were interpreting from a foreign language, had also had similar problems in understanding.

The world has taught me, if nothing else, at least to be kind to myself. Once in a while, I have even been able to laugh at myself and my own failures. I still do live on praise and thanks, but in the later years of interpreting I also have been able to find the thanks myself indirectly. I knew my own failures and I could feel them, but the praise I learned to find in between the lines. If the audience was giving thanks and praising the presentation of the deaf person I had been voicing for, I knew how to think that, without my successful interpreting, the listeners would not have received the message in the way they did. Especially those hearing people who could not understand Finnish Sign Language.

The real hardship for we interpreters has always been the short moment after the presentation when the audience asks questions. Each one of us must have wished that the time allotted to the presenter would have been used to the last minute with no time left for questions. If there was time, one or several hands were raised. Fear crept in to me. I hoped the listener had understood the facts correctly and asked the questions on the basis of the facts. However, once in a while, the listeners had understood the points wrongly or differently from the views of the presenter. When interpreting the question to the presenter, I could feel cold sweat rising on my forehead. I could see an angry wrinkle on the face of the presenter, when he directed an accusatory look toward me, his interpreter, before giving his answer. There is no point in trying to get out of the situation as being innocent. People have the right to misunderstand or understand differently, but why it always is the interpreter's fault? It might have been that the interpreting mistake was made by the other interpreter who interpreted from my production into another language. In those kinds of situations it has been difficult for me to accept making the mistake. Or it might be the case that even I make mistakes and am sometimes wrong.

A photo on the wall

On the wall of my bedroom, at the end of my bed, for some time there has been a black and white photo in a brown wooden frame. For years this photo was in the bottom of a drawer, when my modesty somehow had prevented me from having it on show. But for a while, every time there was a need to raise my self-confidence in a new job where everything was new to me, to show that there was at least something I knew how to do, or at least have known how to do, the photo was on the top of a cabinet during my short-lived career as a librarian.

In a Finnish home, guests rarely find their way to the bedroom, but once in a while when someone has, they have certainly noticed my valued photo.

– Is it really her in the photo? Who's that on the left side of the photo, it cannot be, can it? Quite common questions are expressed by our guests, when they have happened to stop by this photo.

I still remember smiling and how I felt when I first received this photo in a smaller version from my friend and colleague Liz from Scotland. I laughed out loud, when I realised how I am the biggest and most central person in the photo. That is how a sign language interpreter usually is in a discussion where interaction between the partners cannot function without the interpreter conveying the message between two persons with two different languages. When I think who the two other people in the photo are, maybe the photographer could have focused and framed the photo a little differently. I was not the VIP person in this event by any means, in this set-up the main characters are close to falling out of the sides of the picture.

It is difficult to forget this interpreting event, it was so important, effective, and a once in a lifetime experience. The significance of the situation has been emphasised by the way other people have reacted to it when seeing the photo:

– What, is it you in the middle of that picture? Have you really met her in real life? What was she like?

It is over thirty years since that event, but the memory of meeting her does not fade from my memory. Maybe one reason might also be that since 1981, she has been portrayed such a lot in different kinds of media, she and her family have been followed and had their lives disturbed, during her life as well as after her death. Based on a momentary meeting, a few minutes' encounter, I have been trying to pick out and find my own truth in these stories, something that I can believe was how she actually was when she was alive.

She came into my life as an important person for the first time in 1981. Unfortunately, only through television, when I was in Bristol, England and we were following the royal wedding of her and Prince Charles televised directly with live subtitling. It was the last day of the meeting for sign language interpreters and sign language researchers, we gathered around the television to witness this unique event, how an ordinary girl gets the prince. For us foreign watchers, this remarkable event became even more so because for it the BBC was trying out live subtitling, which in a moment changed spoken English into a written form on the bottom of the screen. Everyone knows that English is not spoken as it is written. The attention of us foreigners was geared too often to the mistakes the machine translation was making, and making us laugh. Once in a while, the text was complete gibberish and deaf watchers could not make any sense of the commentary.

On the evening of the same day, I continued my journey from Bristol to London to visit my friend Sidney for a few days there. In London I was invited to join the party as the royal wedding day there was a party for everyone. The inhabitants of Chiswick had moved out into the streets for the whole day to celebrate the crown prince's wedding. The tables and chairs had been carried outside, food and drinks were shared with the neighbours, music was playing and people were dancing in the streets. I experienced a completely new side of the staid Brits who were well aware of their own value. At the same time, I also heard interesting background information on this girl who became the princess, the focus of the whole nation's and the world's interest. Sidney showed me pictures of rich girls like her who had gone to private school, were dressed in plaid skirts, white shirts and cardigans, wearing pearl necklaces, pearl earrings, and whose only goal in life was to get married to a suitable man.

I followed the international deaf news at my work in the Deaf Association from different countries' deaf magazines. I found a piece of news, which announced that Princess Diana had agreed to function as the patron of the British Deaf Association. Once in a while I also saw other photos of Diana, of her family and children, which were different from those I saw in Finnish magazines. Princess Di started to study British Sign Language. My colleague, Liz Scott Gibson, who was in charge of sign language work in the BDA, was her first teacher, but after a while a deaf teacher started teaching her. I also saw photos of Diana visiting deaf schools, old people's homes for deaf people, and launching a BDA campaign.

The British Deaf Association was celebrating its centenary in 1990 in Brighton. The highlight of the celebrations would be the visit by Princess Diana. When I packed my suitcase for this working trip, I did not know what to expect. The English weather had always been grim, rainy and cold, when I had visited there previously. I had packed mainly long-sleeved outfits and rain clothes. As soon as I got to Brighton, I had to go shopping for more suitable clothes. The couple of previous days I had spent in London had shown that I had brought completely the wrong clothes with me, the heat wave of the century had hit England just then.

When we arrived at the conference place with the WFD General Secretary, we were informed that a rare honour was waiting for her: meeting Princess Diana at a luncheon served in her honour. The security guards from the palace had carried out an inspection of the conference venue many times and after a certain time no one was let into the building. A very minutely-detailed programme had been made for the Princess and her planned visit. It was agreed clearly who could address her and with whom she would spend a passing moment. We were not native users of English, had no previous experience of talking with the royals, we received guidance from Liz who was working as interpreter co-ordinator for the conference. When addressing her we always had to start the sentence with words Your Royal Highness Princess Diana! So formal, not to say frozen English I had never used before. I really had to sharpen up my skills for the forthcoming moment.

We saw Diana for the first time, when she arrived in the conference venue and was guided to her place. I could not have missed how tall she was, how beautiful she was with graceful posture. At some point in the anniversary programme, Diana stood on the platform to accept the BDA's 100th anniversary history book. In her short speech she used some sign language in the beginning just to show that she wanted to speak directly to the deaf participants in their own language.

The luncheon had been organised in a cocktail form, my skills in cocktail interpreting for once got a chance to be used. I had often taught young interpreters how to function as a sign language interpreter in situations, where you have a wine glass or drink in one hand and a plate of food in the other. I was surprised to see in the photo that my hands were bare and free for interpreting. Usually when food was being served, I have always taken the opportunity, since as an interpreter you never know when you get something to eat or drink.

Because of my professional secrecy rules, I at once forgot what we talked about with Diana. The photo does reveal how intensely and with what deep interest Diana looks at me, when my hands are resting and I am concentrating in getting the signing of the WFD General Secretary, Liisa Kauppinen, into as high a level of English as possible. Diana is wearing a white sleeveless blouse, a skirt with a high waistline, a genuine pearl necklace and pearl earrings in her ears. My little wrinkled, green linen shirt and long skirt with African animals on it might not quite have been up to the level of the occasion, but at that time I just did not happen to have any other summer clothes to wear, we did not know of this encounter till we arrived at the conference venue.

After the light luncheon, there was a clearly-planned exit route for Diana through the audience. Diana must have been a headache for the security guards as she was constantly stepping away from that route, when she saw deaf people in the audience she had met before and wanted to greet. She seemed to have a warm conversation with her deaf sign language teacher. During some of her visits she had met a deaf AIDS patient and at the event she wanted to exchange a few words with him, too. Her interest in and contact with people were always genuine. She knew how to take her discussion partner into consideration with her warm gaze, genuine interest and shy humility.

A few years after the Brighton conference I visited Liz's home in Edinburgh. Diana and Charles had divorced. The newspapers were full of stories of the couple's affairs, new and old relationships. Liz showed me her Christmas card collection, which she had received through the years from Diana. Since she had started teaching sign language to her, she had received her personally signed Christmas card. In the beginning there was a happy young couple, later with one, then with two little boys. In the last card there were just the sons William and Harry alone. The parents were divorced that spring, when cruel revelations of Charles and his relationship with Camilla, that had started even before his wedding to Diana, became public.

My sympathy has always been on Diana's side. Her work among the deaf, disabled, AIDS-patients and landmine victims cannot be forgotten. After Diana's death every person who has met her personally has become important to the media. One reporter did not want to leave my friend Liz alone when she learned that Liz had taught sign language to Diana and even visited her home. No matter how hard Liz tried to make the reporter to ask for more detailed information from the BDA about Diana's work among deaf people, Liz's personal views, experiences and thoughts about Diana would have been of more interest to the readers. I am waiting for someone to give me a call any day. I am greatly surprised that the Finnish tabloid press has not yet contacted me and asked my views on what Diana actually was like and what I think of the accident, which has been claimed to be organised by Charles, and if I knew if Diana was pregnant when she died or not. I have met Diana in person and even talked to her.

Christmas alone

I had decided to carry out my long-time dream of spending Christmas all alone in my Helsinki Street flat. After all those Christmases which I had spent in my childhood home or with my brother's family, I finally was ready to get my own Christmas traditions started. I had made the preparations well in advance and the schedule for my different kind of Christmas was ready. It felt good to think of easing off and settling down to Christmas in my own home, in my own rhythm after the busy autumn, which had been full of travel. I did not have the energy to start packing again and get on a bus to travel to my home district in congested Christmas traffic.

In Finland, we eat our festive meal on Christmas Eve. Hardly had I had time to make and eat my Christmas rice porridge, when the telephone rang. A call from the Espoo police. They apologised for disturbing my Christmas, but it was a question of an emergency situation. They had been calling up dozen or so sign language interpreters, but no one seemed to be willing to take an interpreting assignment on Christmas Eve. It was an urgent case because the young man who had been arrested had to be interviewed that very day. Three days after the arrest, he either had to be released or imprisoned. Thus far, I had been trying to avoid taking everyday interpreting assignments in my work, I had enough interpreting to do. Neither did I have any previous experiences of interpreting in police interviews or in court. The policeman at the other end sounded so desperate and so in need for help that I decided to let my principles go this time. It would only take a couple of hours with the travel.

I did not know the arrested young man. He seemed to be happy to get some company who communicated in sign language. He was an ordinary deaf person who expressed himself well and fluently in his own language. Using Finnish in spoken, written or reading form seemed to function poorly for him. Now I remembered why I had not liked to take police interviews as interpreting assignments before.

The responsibility of the interpreter is enormous: You must get the terminology of bureaucracy and legal terms interpreted so that the deaf client can feel that he is an equal participant in the interrogation. You have to be impartial and neutral. You should not lead or explain the questions. How to choose the signs in order not to point directly to the incident in question? How to interpret the question with difficult umbrella terms to a person who still might not understand that the question is about his involvement in the crime?

Of course, as an interpreter I was not primarily responsible, but I could not but worry about the destination of this young man. How much better chances in life would he have had, if his parents had used sign language from very early on and if at kindergarten and school the interaction and information had been given to him in sign language? Because of not doing too well in school and because of his poor skills in Finnish, the young man had become unemployed when still quite young, had become dependent on social benefits, and had been in bad company. His hearing mates had escaped from the crime scene before the police had arrived. The degree of friendship is well described by the fact that the deaf young man did not even know the names of his mates. He only could describe what they looked like, but could not even tell where they lived.

After the interrogation the policemen in Espoo offered me Christmas coffee with gingerbread cookies. Although a working Christmas had not been part of my plans, somehow sitting there among the grateful policemen at the Christmas table, the Christmas spirit took me over. I had done a good deed, a service to society. At the coffee table the policemen told me how, later on as the Christmas Eve evening grew later, their telephones would start ringing nonstop. Not only would family violence cases due to too many Christmas drinks bring work to them, but also many people spending Christmas alone would call the police after emptying their bottles, when loneliness filled them. All those who work at Christmastime, hospitals and police, are familiar with how they are the only human contact for lonely people. When I told them about my own plans of spending my first Christmas alone, they laughed and said that they would like to see at which point I would grab the telephone and call them up after I had emptied my red wine bottle.

The Espoo police station was so far away and with such bad transport connections, especially on Christmas Eve, that the police gave me a ride home in a police car as reciprocal service for my interpreting. That way I would get home to continue my interrupted Christmas programme as soon as possible.

The winter evening had started to dim. I wanted to visit the Hieta-niemi cemetery for the first time in my life to see all the candles burning in the lanterns on the graves. I had witnessed that scene many times on TV. After that walk, and tired from the demanding task of the day, I returned to my flat. Finally I would have time to settle down and start celebrating my quiet Christmas alone. Luckily, I had made my Christmas dinner preparations in advance so that only the casseroles needed to be heated up in the oven. My hands were numb from cold and shaking from being hungry, when I lit the fire in the gas-oven and started to set the Christmas dinner table for myself.

Whatever might it have been that made me glance in the oven after a while? The gas was burning there without a flame. My hands started shaking from fright. I turned the oven off. I opened up the window towards the park. I had to get a proper airing for the room. I wondered how much gas must have escaped into the room. During my fifteen years in Helsinki I had read news of gas explosions in flats. In the newspaper I had read of an "accident" that had taken place not too long ago on the other side of the park, opposite my window, which had reminded me of the dangers of gas. In the police investigations it had been revealed that the young man in that flat had blown himself and his flat up with gas.

That Christmas I had a cold Christmas dinner. The whole evening I did not dare to light the candles to bring some spirit to the flat not to mention turning the radio on. The smallest spark might have lit the gas. I sat in darkness all alone through the Christmas Eve. I could see in my imagination the news headlines in the newspapers that came out after Christmas about a flat blowing up on Helsinki Street. At least the Espoo policemen would have drawn their own conclusions from that.

I have to

I should be on my way already. My suitcase is still open and empty on the living room floor. I have been collecting and piling up clothes and things on the sofa in my study for my working trip, but when it is time to put them in the suitcase, I cannot find them anywhere. I have taken them off the hangers in the closet. But they are nowhere to be found. I run frantically from one room to another. They are not in the dirty clothes basket, nor on the clothes line. Maybe I had decided to take along the other suitcase and put the clothes piles in there? I should already be on my way. Otherwise I will miss my flight.

I sit in the train, which is late. The train just stands in the middle of nowhere and no information is given about the reason for the stop or how long it will last. I glance at my watch. The minutes fly by too fast. Only ten minutes till the transfer to the other train. I wonder if that train will wait for this connection. No one to ask. The conductor has not been around for a long while. I keep thinking feverishly of other possibilities for continuing my journey. I cannot be late. I am being waited for. There are no other interpreters present. I will have to make that train, otherwise I will be late.

I run breathlessly and in a sweat along the never ending tube at the arrival hall of an international airport. My flight is late because of a thunderstorm. I know where I should go, it is just too far away and my transfer time is running out. When running I am trying to pass slower passengers and people coming towards me in huge groups blocking my way. My winter coat is just too much to have on, but there is no time to take it off. I have too much to carry. The cheap bottles I bought from the tax free are so heavy and the handle of the plastic carrier bag presses deeply into my flesh. No time for stopping and changing hands. The numbers on the gates do not seem to get any smaller. My flight is at the other end of the wing. I am trying to add some speed, otherwise I will miss it.

I am interpreting at a UN meeting. We have received the meeting papers beforehand for preparation. The secretariat is constantly producing additional materials to be dealt with and for approval. I have studied the documents with my dictionary till late at night. I did not get much sleep. I did not wake up when the alarm went off. I wake up into a nightmare, where I cannot make any sense of the strong Indian accent of the chairman. I should already have had breakfast, now I will have to skip it otherwise I will be late.

For once, I had made it to an international conference of the deaf as a participant myself. I am among the audience enjoying listening to the presentations. I did not need to understand every word that was uttered, nor did I need to follow every presenter's line of thought to every dot. For a change it was wonderful to let my own thoughts fly to different associations, memories and experiences of my own. Lovely to be able to think of all the coffee and lunch breaks and free evenings, possibilities and time for being free to discuss and have fun with the other participants. There were so many old friends and acquaintances from past years and conferences. Wherever I glanced among the audience, my eyes met a meaningful smile and look: let's talk more later!

It was time for a break in the programme. I followed the crowd down the stairs to the lobby. The interpreter co-ordinator met me there and grabbed my sleeve worriedly.

– Raili, we are one interpreter short in the team. The interpreters are having big problems in voicing. You have to come to the rescue!

– No, I do not!

It was then that I woke up. I felt light and relieved. I had jumped off the treadmill at speed and made it. No longer was there the demand coming from outside to hurry, stress, meet tight schedules and deadlines. This was when my nightmares ended. I started to have lighter dreams, most of which are usually so light that I cannot capture them put on paper.

At a summer camp for deaf people organised by the church in Äänekoski.

In 1975 in Washington D.C., the sign language interpreter did not yet have an idea of a proper interpreting outfit.

Leading a sign language choir at the inauguration of the Turku Christian College in 1974; Archbishop Simojoki following with his eyes.

The sleeves were still flying in Tallinn in 1976.

Interpreting at Fred Karlsson's lecture on general linguistics.

First time interpreting with an interpreting pair at the meeting of sign language researchers in Rome in 1983.

Interpreters at the WFD Congress in Palermo in 1983.

At the World Conference on Deaf Education in Manchester in 1985.

In an interpreting uniform for the first and last time in Lillehammer in 1982.

Elina Lehtomäki as my interpreting pair at a sign language seminar in Arusha in 1988.

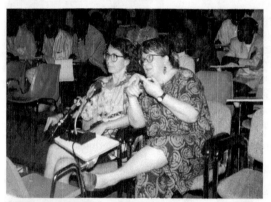

With Raija Moustgaard in Brazzaville Congo in 1993.

Unfailing concentration.

Kati Marjanen voicing at an Arab countries' conference in 1995.

With a twinkle in the eye.

Can you hear anything, is my hair good?

207

At the Deaf Way -conference in Washington 1989.

Interpreters at a wedding of an interpreting colleague in 2003.

Interpreting my brother's speech at the Kopola Course Centre.

Special outfits were demanded for the interpreters in Iran in 1996.

Using many languages with my interpreting colleague Anna in Alma Ata.

Working with Virpi Thurén in Jordan in 2003.

V
Once an information officer, always an information officer

Me and my many tasks

– I thought that there was something familiar about you. I looked at your colours. You often wear orange, do you not? Were you not the mute interpreter?

A friend of my writer colleague, whom I had met a few times in passing when we had sat in the corner café and whose attention I had attracted in the corridor of a flea market, succeeded in poking directly into my sore spot. I thought I had lost it during my working years in the field of deafness. The pain and irritation rose slowly to the surface, I only had a moment to realise it before the woman had disappeared again behind the shelves.

– I would not have remembered your profession otherwise, but I remembered how exciting that combination was, to be MUTE and however an INTERPRETER.

The woman appeared once again in front of me from behind the corner and continued on her way so that I did not have time to say anything from behind my frozen smile.

The angry child of the "mutes" arose from inside me as I took in this expression, which I had heard uttered many times by unthinking and foolish hearing adults. They used these far from flattering expressions about my parents in their presence, and on top of that laughed at their joke. It did not matter to them that I could hear what they were saying. I was only a child. I could not interpret all that cruelty to my parents. My father might have been very angry about it.

Hearing this name-calling did not hurt so much when it came from the mouths of children. They were only repeating the stupid and uncomprehending attitudes of their parents. Mute-Eero often played a part in the stories of his relatives and neighbours, when they described the heroic acts of his youth in the home farm or on the country road. Those were easier to bear. The users of these words did not know anything else, as they did not have a common language with my father apart from gesticulating and making faces. Father-Eero was respected for his carpentry and sporting achievements. It was obvious that my father's speech was unclear and his voice very harsh. My cousins always had a new game after our visit, when they could play *Eero and Terttu* by imitating them and producing strange sounds, making faces and waving their hands.

In the 1960's, deaf people themselves were still ashamed of their own language, their poor command of Finnish and writing skills, and the fact that unknown hearing people could hardly understand their speech. Sign language had been a forbidden language for decades and deaf people had to learn to speak in school – even at the cost of learning Finnish properly. This shame of using sign language in public, when unknown people were present, also had its effect on we hearing children in deaf families. However, little hearing ears always were put to good use in situations where the parents did not for one reason or another understand the speech of a hearing person.

For my whole life, I had functioned as a conveyor between two worlds, so naturally, if not inevitably, I would start working in the deaf field. In the beginning, the term used was deaf interpreters/interpreters for the deaf. The terminology clearly showed where the emphasis was: the interpreter was on the deaf people's side, was an advocate for the deaf. This someone, this more knowledgeable person with more language skills, even gave guidance and advice to deaf people, if needed. When in the 1970's sign language was slowly accepted in rehabilitation and education, sign language also started to be taught to hearing people. We interpreters also began to understand that in the interpreting situation we were functioning between two different languages. When formal training was established for interpreters who had long functioned in the field, the professional term "sign language interpreter" started to be used.

Sign language research brought new information on the structure of the language and how it functioned. This strengthened the self-esteem of deaf people. Services were demanded in their own language. The term bilingualism started to be used as the objective of rehabilitation and education of the deaf. In the middle of the 1990's, Finnish Sign Language was accepted in the Constitution of Finland as one of the national languages, a minority language alongside Sami and Romany. The Constitution obliged changes to be made to the legislation in order for the sign language minority to better receive services in their language. The professional term for their interpreters was brought up once again. Our working languages are Finnish and Finnish Sign Language. The interpreters were expected to convey information impartially between the deaf and hearing client.

The terminology in the field undergoes changes all the time. We used to comment that *the deaf-mutes died out in the 1950's* because deaf people themselves realised that it was wrong and unfair to call them mutes.

For decades they had been denied the use of their own language at the risk of punishment and they had been forced to learn to speak. The fact that the speech of a born deaf person might never be completely understandable by outsiders did not reflect a lack of will or effort. A deaf child cannot learn the Finnish language in the normal way through hearing and interaction with his environment, nor can he hear the production of his own voice. The term hearing-impaired was brought up as an umbrella term in official contexts, but deaf people wanted to be called deaf. As sign language was now regarded as an official minority language, deaf people were also referred to as sign language users.

The unknowing and unintentional choice of words by the acquaintance in the flea market triggered the old response in me again. How does a dog get rid of his fur? In other words, once an information officer, always an information officer. The hurtful experiences came back during the night as glimpses of my former life as a hearing child of deaf parents, from my career as a sign language interpreter, and as the advocacy worker and information officer in the deaf organisation. I could not get my mouth open in the flea market because of my dismay, but the pain came out as this story.

How I became a fighter?

I am not sure whether my lifetime career was set as I sucked my mother's milk. Or, if after listening to all the stories my parents and other deaf people told me, I woke up one day to being the advocate for deaf people, the fighter for the rights of deaf people. Maybe as a little child I had already noticed the wickedness, wrongful information, beliefs coloured by prejudices about my deaf parents or deaf people in general, that hearing people were expressing around me. To become "the Che Guevara of deaf people" has never been my conscious choice, but fixing injustices and removing unfairness started first as a tickle and then as a flame inside me, and in my first job it changed into practical action.

Since I was small I have felt bad when hearing people have spoken in an ugly way and given false information about deaf people, especially when their deaf ears were present. Our landlady in Muuratsalo constantly kept moaning *how those mutes never remember to turn off the light on the staircase, they even walk so that the whole house wakes up or that they have no understanding of the rules of society, when they keep clattering and mak-ing noise upstairs.* I guess it was from somewhere there that my interpret-ing career began, when I had to interpret for my parents those untruths thrown against them. It must have been then, although unconsciously, that I started to reformulate the message, not only into another lan-guage, but changing it to suit the other culture and their understanding. When, ever since I was little, I knew that whatever was said or whatever I had to interpret to my parents was untrue or wrong, I just could not translate it as directly as the stupid hearing adults had expressed it in their anger. I already knew what my father was like with his temper from the north-western part of Finland and that he would not have wasted a second to make his response. His ferocious and heated jagged signing would have been accompanied with a monotonous growl and roar. Who would have had to put that all into words?

Stories in the deaf world interested me, for example how someone had to learn to utter words throughout his entire school days. How hour after hour he had to produce words that did not mean anything to him until the teacher was satisfied. How you were hit by a pointer on your hands if you were caught signing, all those injustices, which had prevent-ed deaf people from learning and becoming equal and active members in society, were of interest to me. I could see daily how even brighter deaf people had to be satisfied with low-status, hard and monotonous manual factory work, when all their school time had been spent in learning to speak. Speech, which unfamiliar hearing people would not have under-stood anyhow. I have had to interpret into sign language difficult writ-ten language, letters from municipalities or other authorities, and news from the newspaper, first at home to my parents, then to the members of the small Deaf Club and later on in my work with deaf people. For them, with their limited Finnish vocabulary, the complicated written language and difficult words were impossible to understand.

Through my own hurtful experiences I must have learned that no matter how right I knew I was, it was not proper to say it aloud. Attack was never the best way to get people to listen to you and to understand. For decades as an interpreter, information officer and advocate for deaf issues, I have had to keep my boiling feelings inside me, hide my anger against the lack of understanding among hearing people and how they were oppressing and subordinating deaf people. I have understood what is best for deaf people, how problems could so easily be solved by using sign language. But I have had to work to formulate statements, participate in seminar discussions, and listen to the goodhearted professionals in the field who, all enthusiastic from their own viewpoint, wanted to help deaf people.

Dozens of times we Deaf Association representatives had an appointment with the director of the Finnish Broadcasting Corporation to discuss how deaf people could receive news in sign language on television. The director always pointed out how expensive the technical solutions would be for this small language minority and how little money was available. Until at the party after one of the press conferences we organised, a hearing newscaster encapsulated the issue simply caused by people's negative attitude: *People do not want to be reminded when they are watching the evening news on their living room sofa that disabled people exist!*

I have been lucky to have worked as a flag bearer for the long-time visionary of the deaf world from my early years as the information officer and as her personal interpreter. It was grand to get to channel my own experiences and know-how in our joint fight to improve the situation of deaf people, first in Finland, and later on internationally. For almost thirty years we have walked together to clear new paths, overcoming resistance. I have been fortunate to live and work beside a fighter who believed in her cause. As her interpreter I got to share the progress of our issues and how the rights of deaf people were improving all over the world. My boss was, and still is, a charismatic person and speaker. When interpreting her manifesto into spoken languages, I have shared her glow and been able to share all the glory she has received. However, without my internal fire, I perhaps might not have found the right words to address the audience nor been able to sow her words deep into the souls of the listeners, where change can begin. I have been fortunate to be able to take my own part of the praise she has received. Of course, she has also always remembered to thank me for conveying our joint issues to the audience.

There have always been hearing so-called experts in the deaf world, who in their opinion always have known what is best for deaf people. No mention that one might have learned something from past mistakes and tried to correct the anomaly. Instead they always have the motivation and money to invent some kind of a better technical solution to make deaf people more like hearing people. After speech training, it became time for hearing aids. According to the experts, these could make deaf people almost like hearing people. How enthusiastic these people were when a new invention was introduced which could 'remove' deafness. Deaf people have always stated that they are happy and content with being deaf as long as they are offered services and information in sign language. After decades of fighting, we succeeded in getting Finnish Sign Language accepted in the Constitution of Finland as one of our national languages. Then cochlear implants arrived as a new invention and a 'solution' against deafness. At that point I did not have any energy left to sharpen my word tools and to collect a new arsenal to change people's minds to see deaf people more favourably. It was time for new, younger and more enthusiastic Don Quixotes to step into the arena, I was going to step down to reminisce about the good old times and all the fights we won.

It would be so useful

Is sign language international? This must be one of the most asked questions by people who have not had previous contacts with the deaf world, and who are dealing for the first time with sign language or interpreting. Usually their disappointment is great when we have to tell them that every country has its own national sign language which has been born in the deaf community of that country and is based on the culture of that country. Usually the person asking the question is surprised to learn that sign languages have not been standardised to be like international Esperanto. That would be so useful.

Since I was a child I knew the name of Gallaudet College. The American National Theatre for the Deaf became known to me from the *Deaf Magazine* pages. I could not have guessed, when I started my AFS-exchange year in Virginia, that I could also familiarise myself with these two important institutions in the deaf world. My first contact with international signing happened in 1967. I was scared stiff to meet the Director of Gallaudet Drama Department, Gil Eastman. How far would my Finnish signing suffice with English lip movements, if there was no American Sign Language interpreter present? Eastman either knew many sign languages or was an excellent lip-reader. Our discussion functioned without problems without a local interpreter. Once in a while, I was opening my mouth so wide that I must have looked like a fish on dry land. I could not be sure how well English pronunciation was functioning on my lips. I already understood how useless it was to use pure Finnish Sign Language. Signs, movement of hands are different in different sign languages. My expressive face, and taking my whole body along, maybe helped him to understand me.

I probably did not understand much more than an average American hearing person would have understood of the play performed by the NTD, without voice-interpreting into English. The hands of the actors seemed to fly in the air much faster than in the signing familiar to me. I had never before seen such fast finger spelling. It was used more than in our Finnish signing. It was impossible to distinguish who in the cast was deaf, who hearing. The sign language interpreters were also acting in the play and were dressed accordingly. They certainly had multiple roles to play: besides signing their own lines they also spoke for the roles of the deaf actors. Without the interpreting, Shakespeare's *Midsummer Night's Dream* would never have opened up to me, because the American Sign Language was so different.

In the summer of 1975, I had the chance, as one of the Finnish Sign Language interpreters at the WFD Congress in Washington DC, to witness how sign language functions as an international language. The official programme of the Congress, with its presentations and scientific papers, were interpreted into each country's sign language, in other words, in the languages of those countries which had sign language interpreters and which had been able to afford to send their interpreters to the Congress. It was wonderful to experience how sign language functioned so well as a language of communication between deaf people from different parts of the world. In those days I did not yet know what made sign language international. Around me I could see how deaf people and workers in the field were discussing everything possible with each other in some kind of a gestural language.

After this congress I was able to tell as a warning example, a story about a Finnish pastor for the deaf who, in his own Finnish Sign Language, told the Americans about the many deaf friends he had back home in Finland. At that time the pastor did not know that the sign in Finnish Sign Language for FRIEND is exactly the same as the American sign for TO BE MARRIED. No wonder the local deaf people were rolling their eyes in disbelief, especially because the man in question was of the church.

For myself, the completely different meaning of this same sign caused confusion, when I arrived in Colombia with a female colleague of mine.

We had already been warned before our trip by a Colombian deaf person who lives in Finland to avoid the Finnish sign for "a friend". To the deaf people who met us at the airport I accidentally introduced my colleague Anne while telling them with Finnish signs that we were LESBIANS. People usually clarify these kinds of issues in the first handshake, do they not? When using international signing and mixing it with signs from your own sign language you should be very alert to the reactions of your discussion partner in order for the communication not to go down the wrong track. That is something I often experienced during my career.

In the summer of 1979, I first saw international sign language interpreting at a WFD Conference in Copenhagen. Beside the national sign language interpreters, there were three American so-called international sign interpreters present. I was so sorry that for most of the conference I had to have my back to these interpreters. Only during my own breaks or from the side of my eye could I follow their work, which looked unbelievably wonderful. One of the male interpreters was called Bill Moody, who was fantastic. He could change a complicated message with his facial expressions and pantomime to be understood by all deaf people. Of course, the factual content could not be very detailed, but the presentation could be followed from his interpreting.

Later on, when I got to know Bill better, I learned that American Sign Language was not even his first language, but that he had learned it when doing volunteer work in a deaf church. Bill's first career had been as an actor, which explained the richness of expression in his face and body, how he could move his body during the interpreting. Later on, he spent a few years in France, where he was involved in setting up the deaf theatre there and developing French Sign Language teaching and teaching materials. For decades he has functioned as the top international sign language interpreter at the conferences and seminars of the World Federation of the Deaf.

When I was working at the Finnish Deaf Association I was fortunate to not only work in national activities, but also in Nordic and international activities as a sign language interpreter and expert in interpreting. The efforts of the WFD to develop so-called international sign language, which is better known as *Gestuno*, also became familiar to me. I learned that a language cannot be created by sitting at a desk or in working groups. Language will grow and develop among people, based on their interactions and needs. A working group had collected approximately 1500 signs from European and American Sign Languages into a Gestuno dictionary. Some of these signs are still being used, especially at the WFD meetings. As you can guess, the vocabulary of this Esperanto in sign language has not been sufficient even for use in meetings. The Deaf Associations in some countries have organised training courses in Gestuno signs for deaf people and sign language interpreters before important international meetings in order for them to manage communication better with deaf people from other countries.

The more Asian and African countries have joined in the international activities of the deaf, the more poorly this European-American based artificial language has served its purpose. The interesting point is that in some Asian countries, timelines in signing are produced differently from the way we in Western countries do them. One could not trust that the future is ahead of us and the past is behind us, as we understand it. For some Asians the past is in front of them, in other words it is known and can be seen. For them the future is behind the head and still unknown.

On a smaller scale this development of international language began in the Nordic countries in the 70's, when it was proposed that a common Nordic sign language be developed. The problem was that none of the five countries was willing to give up its own sign language and to sacrifice time and money to teach a joint new language to the deaf and hearing people who worked in the field. When this attempt came to a dead-end, new signs for fields which seemed to have more in common and were felt to be easier to develop were proposed. It was decided to begin with months, weekdays and numbers. Again a brick wall was hit. These concepts, if any, are based on the culture and customs of each country. A good example of this is a loan sign from Denmark for AUGUST, which is based on apples ripening in August as they do in Denmark. The old Finnish sign for August, GRAIN CUTTING, defended its position better and still was used by many deaf people. Many seminars and meetings ended with no result as the sign languages in all Nordic countries were developing so fast and signs were created for use as they were needed. A decision was taken that a Nordic sign for new global phenomena and concepts would be created and agreed upon. Of these almost the only one still in use in Finnish Sign Language is the sign for UFO.

One could imagine that numbers are simple and so much used that it would be easy to get international agreement on them. That has not happened. Different countries have numerous combinations of how ten fingers can be used to show numbers from one to ten. Many hearing people from the street often are mistaken in this, when they, for instance, describe number three with their fingers. Three fingers from the middle finger towards the little finger do not mean three, at least not in Finnish Sign Language, but number eight. Not to mention other sign languages. When we move to numbers beyond ten, hundreds and thousands, heaven is the only limit to how they can be described with ten fingers. At the WFD Conferences and meetings a decision has been taken that the fingers of both hands will be used, when numbers under ten are shown. In international contexts, drawing the number in the air is also a safe way of showing it.

However, with my little under forty years of experience, I can state with a strong voice that it does function 'internationally'. In other words, if you know one sign language, it is relatively easy to learn expressions in another sign language. In many sign languages the grammatical structures are similar. Localisation, use of expressions and the face, pointing, use of the body when showing who the person referred to is, as well as the size of signs, how big or small they are, or showing the form of something, does function internationally. Generally it is important that you first state the main subject and after that the details. When you add pantomime and borrow important signs from your partner's different sign language, the communication starts to flow. With these skills and my experience, I have functioned for years as the secretary for the WFD Board and Management Committee and as an international interpreter. When you take a moment to follow the signing of the foreign deaf person, it slowly starts to acquire form and linguistic content. If you do not understand right away, you only need to wrinkle your eyebrows, push your head forward a bit and squint your eyes to stop your discussion partner in full flow and get him to express what he was saying more clearly. In other words, it does function after all – internationally.

Crisis

Father and Mother of the family are deaf. Both of their parents are also deaf. The grandparents of the Father had also been deaf. Sign language had been passed on from the parents to the children and again to their own deaf children. Deafness was a natural thing for this family, a part of normal life. They were used to using sign language in discussions with their relatives, friends and acquaintances. Once in a while they came across a hearing person who did not understand their signing, that was when a paper and pen were needed.

The circle of friends of this family was formed of deaf friends, sign language interpreters and some hearing people who had learned to sign for one reason or another. The hobbies of the family were based around those possibilities offered by the local Deaf Club. Father was a fisherman, but also a member of the bridge and chess club. Mother participated in the women's activities, but was active also in the educational committee of the club. The Deaf Club offered a plentiful variety of hobbies, its members did not need to seek hobbies and stimuli from elsewhere. Friends were met at the club, but visits were also made to each other's homes and picnics were also popular. The Deaf Club organised interesting trips to the festivals and courses organised by the Deaf Association in different parts of Finland, but also a trip abroad once a year.

The family had been waiting and hoping for a Child for a long time. The subject had been discussed and the parents were ready to welcome the Child as soon as it was the right time. Mother became pregnant with the Child. Father participated in the anticipation with enthusiasm, as did the whole family and the relatives. Because deafness was dominant in the family, it was only natural that everyone expected the Child to be like them – deaf, a sign language user as were the others. The parents were planning the Child's future in their mind. Which day-care centre or which school for deaf children, where sign language is used, would the Child go to, which job possibilities were there for the Child in twenty years, what kind of a deaf spouse would the Child marry.

The time was ripe. Father took Mother to the hospital. The parents were well prepared for the delivery because they had taken the course with a sign language interpreter, even the Father was ready for the exertion. The Child entered the world with speed, crying out with a flame-red face. The doctors and the midwife seemed to have a discussion going on which the interpreter present could not quite make sense of. The Child received top points, was active and reactive from the very beginning. The nursing team tried to find out at this point already, if the Child was hearing or not. Their expectations were just the opposite to those of the parents of the Child.

The Child did hear, and well. The deaf parents were desperate. How could they bring up a hearing Child? They had no previous experience of the hearing world. There was something strange about the Child. The Child was different from them. The Child would learn sign language at home, but she would live her life in the hearing world, which was alien to them. The parents already started to worry about the forthcoming encounters as a problem: meetings and discussions with the hearing personnel at the day-care centre or future teachers of their Daughter, none of whom would, unfortunately, know how to sign. In the sign language day-care centre and school they would not have had these kinds of communication problems. More and more they would have to turn to sign language interpreters for help in issues concerning their own Child.

Another big sorrow the parents had was worrying about how they could offer their hearing Daughter stimulus from the hearing world. They were only familiar with deaf culture, fairy tales in sign language, and stories from the deaf world. Who could help them to give guidance about getting hearing stimulus to their Daughter? Where could they find information on what the children's voice- and video cassettes included? What was being said or sung? What were the children's programmes like on the radio or on TV? Who could accompany their Daughter to the children's theatre performances? Where would they get their information? Until now, everything had been so simple, for everything the address had been the Deaf Club.

The parents did not yet even dare think about what kind of a world their Daughter would meet when playing with the children in the neighbourhood. There had been no need to get to know any hearing neighbours yet. The neighbourhood they lived in was a normal middle-class town-house district, but they had read many stories about youth crime and drug problems. They became depressed thinking of the future awaiting their Daughter. They had a feeling that they had been given a strange Child whom they should get adjusted to. Everything that had been familiar and secure in their life was wiped away. They had to build completely new contacts with the hearing world to get information and services for their Daughter. Their Daughter should not and could not be the bridge between them and the hearing world, but they had to find that help and support within the hearing world.

At some point they had read in the *Deaf Magazine* that hearing children of deaf parents had set up their own organisation. At that time they had not paid any further attention to that piece of news because they were sure that their Child would be deaf. Now it was time for them to find out more about the activities of this organisation. Maybe they could get the information and the support they needed about how it was to live as a hearing child of deaf parents. Maybe they could assign their Daughter a support person who could guide their Daughter to the hearing world.

When the time was right, the parents also contacted the Sign Language interpreter at the Deaf Club, who also had deaf parents. She calmed them down by saying that the problem was not as big as they felt. The hearing child would adjust both to the hearing and deaf world quite naturally without needing special advice or guidance. The important thing was that the deaf parents should give their hearing Child a strong sign language base and background in deaf culture. The day-care centre, school, neighbours, friends and hobbies would lead their Daughter to the hearing world for sure, to the hearing culture and to the Finnish language. The hearing Child should not be considered as a problem, but as a new possibility which would also enrich the life of the parents with her new life-experiences. The hearing Child would grow up to be bilingual and bi-cultural. So being different would not be a loss, but a gain, a gateway to something new, and to growth.

The world in my story is upside down, all invented, but it is a reality in the mind of many deaf people, for whom deafness is something that they do not want to change. Many deaf adults who accept their own deafness and are proud of their own language and culture, hope that they can continue as deaf people by having a deaf child with whom everything will be so much simpler for them. When deaf mothers are expecting a child, they often say that they do not care if the child is deaf or hearing. The most important thing is that the child is healthy.

Deaf people have often dreamed of setting up their own Deafland a bit like the Vatican, which decides on its citizenship. The two basic criteria for being a citizen of this Deafland would be deafness and the use of sign language. That country would be open to tourists, students of sign language courses to come in and learn sign language and deaf culture in its natural environment. Quite soon there would be a problem: what to do with all the hearing children of deaf parents born in that country, because less than 5% of deafness is hereditary. Would the hearing children be accepted as citizens of that country, especially when they would probably marry a hearing person and have hearing children? This is how far this utopia got.

Appointment with the teacher

The winter evening was getting darker outside. Teacher Ahola lit the lamps in the classroom in order to continue preparing the next day's lessons for a little longer. She did not want to go home for the short time before a meeting she had agreed to with the mother of a problem child in the class after the mother's work was over. The boy had taken a note home to his mother, and no reply had been received. The teacher could only presume that the mother was on her way to meet her this evening. Ville had nodded, mumbling, when the teacher had asked about the note. Ville could not say more about his mother's more detailed timetable:

– She will be here after work.

Ville was in the third grade at elementary school. Problems started as soon as the first weeks, with a lighter timetable, were over in this combined third and fourth class. The first-second class teacher had only good things to say about this boy. He had been very alert, active and co-operative during those two years. The first grade teacher had mentioned in passing that Ville's parents were deaf and that the parents never came to any school or parents' events. There was no sign language interpreter available in the region. All notes from school had been sent with Ville to his home. No problems had occurred before.

Because the teacher did not have any previous experiences of talking with the deaf, she had asked Ville to stay in class after the last lesson for a moment. When Ahola asked Ville how one talked to his mother, the boy stated:

– She does not understand speech at all, you have to use sign language with her.

After that, the teacher was so worried that she asked Ville to come along and interpret for her at the meeting. Ville's behavioural problems had to be discussed with his mother and measures to be taken needed to be thought through in order to bring back peace to the class.

She heard footsteps from outside and went to meet the visitors at the door. Nodding, smiling and indicating the coat stand in the hallway, the teacher invited them to take their outdoor clothes off before coming in. Ville took his jacket off rapidly and slipped into the classroom by the teacher. The teacher watched the mother while she was taking her winter coat off and noted that the mother was surprisingly old to be the mother of a third grader. She thought that the official papers of the pupils did not reveal everything for sure.

Ville sat in his own place in front of the class. The boy had to be moved there right under the teacher's eyes, although he would have preferred to sit further back. There he would have had more possibilities to create a disturbance. His mother sat beside him in the double desk and the teacher climbed up behind the teacher's desk. Ahola had had a different arrangement in mind, sitting closer by, but did not want to change anything any longer. Mother looked at her son, wrinkling her eyebrows and after that posed a questioning look at the teacher.

– It certainly was nice that you could come to meet me today here in the school, Mrs Pikkarainen. Ville promised me that he would function as a sign language interpreter for you, didn't you, Ville?

– Yeah! Ville noted as his mother's head kept turning around looking at the fast moving lips of the teacher and then again to her son.

– TEACHER SAYS NICE YOU CAME HERE.

Ville's hands flew swiftly in the air and he kept producing words with his mouth to his mother. Now the teacher was not sure, if this arrangement had been wise after all. She could not control the situation from behind her desk as Ville's mother's gaze was constantly on her son, not the teacher.

– FIRST TIME HERE IN SCHOOL. REASON WHAT? WHY COME HERE TODAY?

– Mother is here for the first time and wants to know why she was asked to come here?

– Ville, could you please tell your mother that we have had some problems with you here in the class this autumn. I asked your mother to come here to see what might have changed in your home in the past few months or what could have be the reason for these changes in your behaviour. Or has the homework become so much more difficult after second grade that it has caused you to become so restless and inattentive...

The teacher realised that she had spoken far too long for Ville to be able to interpret it. She cut off in the middle of the sentence and turned her gaze from the mother to Ville waiting for him to start interpreting. Ville had been concentrating on listening to what the teacher was saying, the wrinkles in his forehead showed that the boy was thinking how to get that all interpreted for his mother. Mother was pushing the boy with her hand with a questioning expression.

– TEACHER SAY NOW NEW CLASS LOT HOMEWORK ME DOING

DILIGENTLY GETTING ON WELL.

– NICE TO HEAR. VILLE NICE DILIGENT BOY. READ MANY BOOKS AT HOME.

– Mother says that I do my homework at home diligently.

The mother noticed an expression of frustration on teacher's face the same time as she was waiting to get an answer to why she was asked to come to this meeting in the school after a heavy day at work. Ville was the apple of the mother's eye, a great help and joy to his parents. Maybe the teacher wants to tell her how clever a boy Ville is.

– Ville, could you ask your mother if I could write to her without your interpreting, so that we adults could talk at the same level.

– TEACHER DOES NOT WANT ME INTERPRET. WANTS TO WRITE TO YOU.

– NO, NO, VILLE GOOD INTERPRETER. FINNISH LANGUAGE DIF-FICULT TO UNDERSTAND. SIGNING EASY FOR ME TO FOLLOW.

– Mother does not want to write as she does not understand everything then. She wants me to be her interpreter.

Ahola feels that she has lost this battle. She has never before been in this kind of situation. At once the troublemaker of the class has become the master of the situation and has all the winning cards in his hands. This is no way to solve Ville's problems. The teacher tries to smile to the mother and points to her watch. It is time to end this meeting and go home. She just has to try to find out where the mother could get a professional interpreter for another meeting in order to start talking about the problem. Ville will continue his playing-up in class until the ultimate reason for his behaviour could be found in discussions with the mother. Ville slips from the desk into the hall as soon as he notices that the teacher has given up. He won this round.

Marriage no-noes for deaf people

In my older years, when I have nothing else to do, I have started to play the IF-game. My own existence has depended on such minor coincidences. My grandmother had to make the journey back home over the Atlantic one more time to meet my grandfather, a young man who lived in the neighbouring village. My mother's artist boyfriend had to die of tuberculosis before she got interested in her classmate from the Oulu Deaf

School. There were also other obstacles in their way to getting married to each other in the 1940's. Getting married was not straightforward and simple in those days, especially if there was hereditary deafness in the family.

At the end of the 19th century, the eugenics movement, which had started in Germany where they wanted to improve the quality of the human race, also arrived in Finland. With Darwin's theories the authorities tried to prevent the transfer of useless or bad traits to any offspring. This movement also typified the oralists, whose intention was to reduce the number of deaf people. Alexander Graham Bell, who invented the telephone, saw deafness as a curse. He also wanted to deny deaf people the right to marry each other in order to prevent hereditary deafness.

Oralism in deaf education had developed in Germany. Sign language was no longer allowed to be used in teaching deaf children, the oralist method was used instead. All teaching took place in speech, signing was forbidden. Oralism did not only mean teaching by speech, but it also prohibited the significance of sign language in a deaf person's life. The spreading of oralism was also connected with nationalism. Its progress in Europe added to the pressure to standardise minority groups, such as the deaf community. Deaf people should not be different from the majority population. Sign language, as many other minority languages, became "culturally wrong". Oralism was a part of the eugenics' way of thinking, whose goal was to improve the quality of the human race by preventing the transmission of undesirable qualities. Deafness was seen as hereditary, of bad quality. Accepting sign language meant that even more deaf people would be born in society. The abnormality was seen to be harmful to society. The oralists thought that it was important to eliminate deafness. On a practical level this meant that marriage between people with hereditary deafness was forbidden.

In 1924, a proposal for a new marriage act was approved in Finland. The rights of deaf-mutes to marry each other were made more difficult. Such deaf-mutes had to ask for permission from the President of the Republic to marry. The marriage between two born deaf-mutes was subject to a license, although according to the medical experts, getting this permission was not even necessary. This act was based on the heredity of deaf-muteness. It was considered that idiotism and other deficiencies were connected to it and that the deaf-mutes had a low intellectual level.

Deaf people reacted very strongly through their organisations to the justification for these changes. A questionnaire was sent to the membership. From the results it could be seen that deafness at birth and deafness appearing later in childhood were difficult to distinguish from each other. It was impossible to detect deafness in new-born children. Only some 15–20% of deaf people had inherited deafness from their parents or grandparents. In spite of the opposition from deaf people, the marriage law was passed in Parliament in 1929. Deaf people were also included in the law of sterilisation. Accordingly, only deaf-mutes who had been sterilised could marry each other. Deaf people were not directly mentioned in the law, but the authorities interpreted the law as meaning that deaf people were required to have their capacity for reproduction removed before they could receive a license to marry.

According to the Deaf Association, the legal text was mixing the terms of born deaf and hereditary deafness. A deaf couple who wanted to get married had to provide the authorities with a certificate that they were not born deaf. According to the Deaf Association, they should instead have made clear whether there was hereditary deafness in the family. The couple who wanted to get married had to go from one doctor to another in order to receive a certificate for the license to marry. Often pastors refused to marry deaf people, citing this law. In addition, doctors could not clearly say when the person in question had lost his hearing. Many deaf people lost their chance to marry each other.

The limitations on the marriage of deaf people described here clearly contravened the human rights of deaf people. Deaf people have always married each other. Usually they have hearing children. If in those days the pastors for the deaf refused to marry a deaf couple, both of whom had hereditary deafness in the family, deaf people often found a way around it. Some decided to live together without being married, some ended up getting pregnant. In those days it was a smaller crime to let them marry than to have a child born out of wedlock. Living together without marrying was not taken well. Such couples experienced discrimination and scorn in the deaf community.

I have lived in the deaf community for decades and listened to these stories. I have met many unhappy deaf people because they were not allowed to marry the person they loved, because of this family burden. Some deaf people stayed single because their parents or authorities forbad them from setting up a family with a person of their choice, with whom their heart was bonded. There is also clear evidence that the birth of the first deaf child to a deaf couple led to sterilisation or the abortion of the next pregnancy. In some cases, it was thought that deaf people were not capable enough to raise their own children as parents, and the children were taken into custody.

After a change in legislation in 1944, the marriage law applied only to hereditary deafness, as the deaf community had suggested earlier. This section in the law, which disgracefully limited a person's freedom, was finally removed for deaf people in its 1969 amendment.

I can only imagine how difficult it must have been for my parents to get married in the summer of 1945. In my mother's family deafness was plentiful, four out of eight children were deaf. Father had had meningitis at the age of two-three months, which in those days was difficult to prove as the cause of his deafness. The pastor for the deaf refused to wed my parents. According to my mother, the vicar of her home church saw that there were no grounds for them not to be allowed to marry. In those days people did not travel long distances, 170 kilometres to a wedding, especially when there was plenty of work in the fields. My parents' second wedding was arranged in my father's home village in Pohjanmaa.

It is quite probable that my brother and I carry a latent gene, which we have received from our mother's side of the family. In our families there has not yet emerged another latent gene. This is why we have not been able "to breed this gene of the family for future generations".

A trip I will never forget

It was November some twenty years ago. I was going to Sweden by the Silja Line ferry with two deaf colleagues of mine to a seminar on deafness. In those days we used the cheapest means for travelling, although it was more time consuming. Travelling was considered to be fun, as a social benefit. We had reserved one cabin for the women and another for the man.

As we got on the ferry, my travelling companions wanted to go right away to the first seating of the buffet-dinner. I had had enough of those buffet-dinners on my trips, I decided to enjoy the selections of the à la carte restaurant menu, although I had to eat there alone. We agreed to meet in a couple of hours at our cabin to make further plans for the evening.

When I was sitting alone at my table I was regretting the missing company. I knew what the buffet had to offer and I wanted to enjoy some new tastes with good wine. I ended up ordering a fancy pasta dish with salad and white wine. I was not sure what I would be getting, but at least it would be a new experience to tickle my taste buds. Red wine might have been more suitable with the pasta, but in those days my head did not like red wine and our further plans were still open, I did not want to take the risk of having a headache, so white wine had to do.

A young, important looking, male waiter brought my wine in no time. I felt stupid sitting on my own in a full restaurant, but I had hopes that the dish I had ordered would compensate for the missing company. The boat had started rocking a bit after we left the harbour and entered the open sea. I had not read or listened to the weather forecast, I did not pay much attention to the rocking boat. My pasta arrived. I was hungry enough to enjoy it. After a couple of forkfuls my eating started to slow down. There was an herb that tasted strange in the sauce, which just was not agreeing with my taste buds. Had come to this à la carte restaurant for this?

On my travels I had learned that the client is always right. Especially because of the expensive price you paid in the restaurant, you really should get what you had ordered. When I got the waiter's attention, I told him that the dish had not been what I expected and there was a strange herb in it, which was not to my taste. The waiter listened to me and suggested that perhaps I was getting seasick as the storm was rising. I completely disagreed with him, I had never been seasick on my previous trips on a ferry. It could not be that this time either. The food just was not what I expected. The waiter brought the menu to me again. When I did not know what to order instead, he suggested that maybe I should order something plain and less spicy. He recommended a minute steak with herb butter and French fries. When I could not find anything that would have interested me on the menu, I settled for his recommendation.

The storm kept rising and the waves grew bigger. Every time the bow of the boat hit a huge wave, the whole boat started shaking, dishes and glasses were jingling. The thump was as if it had hit a wall. The swaying grew bigger. I received my new plainer meal and started to cut pieces of my steak. After a couple of bites I could not eat any more. It was not the taste or the spices. My stomach started to go down and up and I felt sick. The waiter might have been right after all, the seasickness had hit me. I signalled the waiter to my table:

– Could I have the bill and fast?

I staggered out of the restaurant with a white face, holding on to my stomach and keeping my hand over my mouth. I hurried through the long corridors towards my cabin. I had hardly got the door open when I dived in to the tiny toilet. Out came both the spicy and less spicy food and drinks I had had. I held on to the walls and then fell on my bed. My stomach was still rolling, but as I lay still on my bed with closed eyes, I felt quite good. Once in a while I had to get up and go to the toilet to throw up again. Even a lifting my head slightly from the pillow made the world spin around. This it is what being seasick feels like? Luckily we were not in the Atlantic or Pacific!

Weary, in a half-stupor lying on my bunk I heard the captain's message on the radio:

– Attention, attention, passengers are strictly forbidden to go to the deck in the storm! The deck is icy and slippery!

My travelling companions, who were deaf and would not have heard this announcement, flickered into my mind. Should I get up and go to warn them? However, my miserable condition won over the sense of responsibility, and I dropped back into my stupor.

After some time I woke up to a rustling as the cabin door was being opened. My cabin mate tried to sneak in as quietly as possible and get her coat from the rack, as she thought that I had already gone to bed. I noticed her intention of going out on the deck, jumped up and told her about the captain's warning. Both of my travelling pals were deafened people, they did not sense the swaying of the boat at all, nor did they get seasick in the storm. Being visual persons they enjoyed nature's phenomena, big waves, and harsh wind and wanted to go to the deck to enjoy the storm.

The mere thought that, if they had been travelling on their own as deaf people, not knowing anything of the dangers awaiting them on deck, they might have been washed off the deck, gave me the shivers. This time they stayed indoors.

Once an information officer, always an information officer I noted when we got home from that trip. I called the Silja Line and told them how badly they serve and inform their clients who cannot hear the announcements. They promised in the future to pay more attention to this. The problem according to the company is that deafness does not show in person's appearance, nor do the staff know about having deaf passengers on the boat. That was the only bad storm I have encountered on my trips in order for me to test the promise of the company to improve their information systems, or how easily I might become seasick in a storm.

Visual radio and deaf people

All my life I have had difficulties with the media, first with the auditory ones, then the visual ones. It was not an obvious thing to buy a radio in a deaf family. We did not even have electricity in our house for the first few years. The power line went close by, but getting the lines to our and our neighbour's house would have been too expensive. My brother and I did our homework first under the dim light of an oil lamp and later on by gaslight. If we wanted to hear the popular radio plays of those days, we had to go to our neighbour's to listen to them.

We got a radio in the early 1960's. Listening to the radio was kind of difficult because once in a while we had to interpret the radio news to mother and father. It was difficult for our parents to understand that a hearing person could listen to the radio without hearing it, in other words without clearly registering what was being said. In order to interpret the news, one had to concentrate on listening to it, but of course it would have been good to have more information on the news background. The words and names flew by so fast and did not stay in the mind. Father and mother had difficulties in understanding that. Since those early days I have had a bad conscience and felt guilty because I did not interpret the auditory information into a visual form every time it was possible.

When we started hearing about the arrival of television, deaf people began waiting impatiently for the arrival of this visual radio, when they would finally be able to receive the news and information in a visual form that would mean something to them. Deaf families were the first ones to purchase this new piece of furniture in the corner of their living room. Their disappointment was huge when they soon realised that the programmes in television mainly consisted of talking heads. The movements of the mouths were too fast, faces were hidden behind a thick beard and moustache, and the speakers were too far from the camera or in bad light. Not even a good lip reader could make any sense out of their speech. For decades the TV news and Finnish culture remained incom-

234

prehensible for deaf people. Luckily here in Finland, dubbing of foreign films and series never was the tradition, Finnish deaf people could follow foreign programmes with subtitles.

After these disappointments the Deaf Association started to put pressure on the Finnish Broadcasting Corporation. The first demand was that the requirement to pay for a radio license should be removed from deaf television viewers. At the same time, a wish was expressed that more subtitles in Finnish programmes and programmes in sign language should be produced. In 1966, visits to the director of the broadcasting company led to news in sign language starting twice a week on the Tesvision-channel for four months. This channel in those old days was broadcast from Tampere and did not serve the whole country; later it became TV2. Most often deaf people received church services and religious programmes interpreted in sign language.

The difficulties I had had with the radio now moved to the television. Every evening my parents watched the TV. They developed sheer mastery in guessing and combining. They read the morning paper very carefully, although their Finnish vocabulary was limited and the complicated way of expressing matters distorted the information. Father and mother could name all the politicians, sportsmen and celebrities who were shown on TV, although their names were not in text on the screen. For my father, a former active athlete, all track and field and skiing competitions were a matter of life and death. If we children happened to be in the same room, we had to interpret metres, centimetres, minutes and seconds, before digital technology was provided in the TV sports programmes.

When I moved away from home to live my own independent life, via Tampere and Turku to Helsinki, I did not have a television in my household. It must have been due to the constant bad conscience I had for years about our television set at home. I did not miss any of the TV programmes. In the 1980's the television license inspectors came door to door to check those households whose name was not in the license register. Once the inspector showed up at my doorstep to ask for my license. I let him in, although that was not necessary. I got worried. Where on earth had I put my radio license receipt, which I was sure I had paid. The inspector calmed me down with a smile noting that the requirement for a radio license had been removed a few years back.

As the Deaf Association information officer and interpreter for the executive director, I was involved in the preparation of the statement from the annual meeting. For years it always stated how poorly television served deaf people, how more subtitling for Finnish programmes was required, as well as the need for news and current programmes to be interpreted into sign language. I was usually the interpreter when the statement was taken to the director of the broadcasting company and the programme director.

Almost always, when I met a hearing person who was interested in deaf people, the discussion moved to the problems of accessing information experienced by deaf people and how little deaf people could understand and follow the TV programmes. A very effective demonstration was to tell these hearing people to turn the volume of the television off during the news, try to understand what had happened in the world. The hearing people had the advantage that they usually did have more background information on the world.

Through personal contacts with people working in the broadcasting corporation, we got a few reporters interested in subtitling their own programmes in Finnish and we started making teaching programmes. Vesa Saarinen, who had a deaf son himself, became our agent in the company. Irja Hämäläinen in the adult education programmes fought for years for there to be regular sign language teaching programmes in the same way as other language teaching programmes were made. Her programmes *Hearing impaired – one of us* and *Say it with your hands*, and the teaching materials connected with them, got many hearing work colleagues in deaf people's work places to make contact with them for the first time. There were a few programmes interpreted into sign language over the years. *We wish, we wish* programme also collected money for the Deaf Association. The songs in that programme were interpreted into sign language, attracting hearing people to admire the beauty of sign language expression.

Previously, the two channels produced the main TV news at the same time. The Deaf Association tried to get the news interpreted into sign language even on channel two, although this channel could not be seen everywhere in Finland. When we visited the leaders of the broadcasting corporation, they tried to reason that the population of deaf people was too small to allocate funding to, or that getting the sign language interpreter placed in the corner of the screen would have been too difficult to organise technically. However, this already functioned well in some European countries, and in some developing countries it had been possible to arrange, so it was in use before Finland. The real reason was revealed at a party the Deaf Association arranged, when I talked with one of the main newscasters. As I mentioned earlier, he stated straight away that people do not want to be reminded during their leisure time and in their living rooms that disabled people exist. It was not a question of money after all, but negative attitudes in the company.

In the 1980's deaf people started getting a programme in sign language once a week called *In this sign*. It offered news from the deaf world. Then commercial television made a breakthrough. To celebrate their receiving their own news broadcast they hired a sign language interpreter to interpret the morning news. I do not know if it was because of this living language or the pretty interpreter, but these news broadcasts in sign language became really popular even among hearing people. Many hearing people realised that sign language is as rich and nuanced as any other language and with it, that it was possible to express complicated issues just as in the spoken language. Because sign language had been forbidden for so long and in use only in the everyday communication of deaf people, the interpreters had a hard time searching for sign language equivalents for new expressions. They had to ask deaf people for help.

My husband Pärre had experienced my mother's enthusiasm for watching television news in practice. My mother knew exactly what time and which channel was providing the news service. She had to watch each and every one of them in order to keep up what was happening in the world. The most important news for her was the TV1 sign language news at 5.30PM and then the main news at 8.30 with captions. Other news programmes for her were mainly a picture cavalcade or bits from foreign news with subtitles, which offered information on what had happened elsewhere in the world. Once my husband happened to change the channels to watch his own popular series on TV in the middle of my mother watching the daily news service.

– NEWS! she cried out signing to me at the same time.

Pärre solved this problem by walking into a store the next day and buying a second television for our household. The same solution functioned well when, a few years later, our granddaughter kept watching the *Barbababa*-videos for the tenth time in a row. Her grandfather wanted to watch his favourite programme on TV. After that we had a second video recorder attached to our bedroom TV. For some reason the whole crowd always ended up on the bed by the grandfather to watch whatever he was watching, the TV in the living room unused.

TV captions, which arrived in Finland in 1981 during the UN Year for Disabled Persons, brought a new way for deaf people to receive information from television. This service was developed for the hearing-impaired together with the captioning crew. On those pages the organisations of the hearing impaired could send in their latest news, information about different events, and possible changes in the appointment times of the workers for the deaf, deafblind, deafened and hard of hearing people. The number of captioned programmes increased every year. There have not been funds for real-time captioning, it has been used only as an experiment in some sports events and the releasing of election results. The Finnish language functioned better in this context than English, whose funny translation mistakes I followed in Bristol during Charles' and Diana's wedding. The text was such gibberish that it had nothing to do with the announcer's speech. The reason for that was that English written and spoken languages are so different.

Being able to watch the Finnish Broadcasting Corporation's programmes has required a license for over 80 years. This always has paid for the activities of the corporation in Finland. The Deaf Association had discussed getting its own channel for a long time. The whole FAD video production could be shown there. That is how they could avoid the twice monthly posting of their videos. Where could funding for this sign language channel come from?

I had time to think of my own relationship with the "bubble gum for the eye", as Pärre used to call it. I watch very little TV. I am still annoyed at how little television is visual and how poorly it serves deaf people who do not have hearing and who use sign language as their first language. The new tax that took effect in 2013 probably will not change the situation for deaf people very much.

Square root versus beetroot

Her arrival as a teacher in the Jyväskylä School for the Hearing Disabled was expected. The reputation of the last oralist in Finland, almost a relic or a fossil, had flown from the Kuopio Deaf School all the way to Jyväskylä. In 1973, in the education of the hearing impaired, a new system of municipal school had been adopted where children could go to school each day from home. The Turku and Kuopio government-owned deaf boarding schools were discontinued. In the autumn of 1974, their staff were transferred to the remaining Finnish-speaking schools in Jyväskylä, Mikkeli and Oulu. Before retirement, this teacher would do her couple of remaining teaching years in our school in Jyväskylä.

The first school day in the autumn was starting and people who were interested in the newcomers were hanging from the windows to spot them among all the people getting out of the bus. The new teacher could easily be seen from the crowd because of her proud posture and determined walk. Her grey hair was twisted into a tight bun on her head. The tall woman had a light stylish autumn trench coat on and was carrying a thin brown leather briefcase in her hand. Her authority could be felt. I am sure I would have dropped a curtsey upon meeting her from pure respect.

For my 24 years I had lived with the damage that oralism had caused, repairing the marks of speech training. First I had helped my parents, with their limited Finnish language, restricted vocabulary, and inadequate choice of words. Later on, I had worked as a sign language interpreter with deaf people in the community. Daily I had seen and experienced how even the most common words in our language can change, when deaf people were reading them in the newspaper or information booklets, when an ending was added to the stem or when the meaning was expressed in the passive tense or if the sentences were too long. New expressions and words are constantly born in a living language, the meaning of which no one explained to deaf people. There were no Finnish dictionaries in those days which would have explained the difficult words with multiple meanings to deaf people in an easily understandable language and with examples. Not to mention that all the words in the dictionary would have to have been explained in sign language.

I had heard from my parents and other deaf people of the strict teaching methods which had been used in the deaf schools. The pupils were hit by a pointer on their hands if they used sign language during the lessons. Sometimes those dormitory staff members who believed in strict oralism gave punishments for using sign language, even during the students' free time. However, sign language lived among the students as a secret language and was passed on from the older students to the younger ones. Publicly it could not be used. At the end of the 1970's, the use of signs to support speech became the new method in deaf education. In 1973, the first sign language dictionary with photos was finalised by the Deaf Association. A study among deaf students who had finished school had shown that their active vocabulary was only 1500 words. Usually these words were known only in their basic form. The educational authorities realised that radical rapid changes were needed in deaf education.

In the autumn of 1974, I started my work as the first school social worker at the Jyväskylä School for the Hearing Disabled. I was especially interested in how deaf education had changed since my parents' time and how the use of sign language could also change the results of education. Unfortunately, quite soon I had to realise that Rome was not built in a day. The inclusion of sign language into deaf education could not succeed in one or even two generations. It was not merely a question of offering the teachers and other staff working in the school the opportunity to learn sign language. The most difficult part was to change of old attitudes and to turn away from the old practices.

Hardly had the warm winds of sign language started to blow in the Jyväskylä school, when the harsh winds, in the form of the new teacher, started to blow in the teachers' room in the deaf unit. It was hard to imagine how one single person could have such a huge effect on opinion forming. Hardly had the discussions started on the positive effects of sign language and signs in the study of the Finnish language and learning results, when the presence of one oralist stymied the whole discussion in the teachers' room. Her views, a mere sniff in the direction of a speaker with a different opinion, or just a glance directed from top to toe at such an individual, stopped the discussion short. The sign language supporters moved somewhere else to continue their conversations. It was interesting to note how the arrival of this strong supporter of the speech method provoked a few teachers who had been quiet and retiring to show their true colours. There had been surprisingly many hidden-oralists among the teachers. When the guru in the field had arrived they started having the backbone to express their own views against sign language. These views had previously only been expressed by complaining, keeping conversations going in the back seats during the teachers' training days, when the executive director of the Deaf Association *once again kept on talking about the same old stuff on sign language.*

One teacher who had befriended this oralist, and who unfortunately had a class of her own to teach where she had five or six completely deaf and quite intellectually challenged pupils, was once on a long sick-leave. Her substitute teacher was the director of the school, who was in favour of using sign language in teaching. On his first day in the job he stormed into the teachers' room during the break and protested with puffs of anger:

– What kind of work ethic does a teacher have who has recorded in the class journal that last week she taught this group square roots, when they hardly know what a beetroot means?

It was customary in the school that the same teacher would take the group from kindergarten to the secondary grades. The classroom was almost the teacher's sacred space where no one was allowed to visit without permission from him or her. Everyone knew that this teacher did not use sign language with her pupils, but that she wrote everything she taught on the blackboard. Diligently the pupils copied every word from the board in their notebooks without understanding what it meant or how it was said. At that time, these pupils were in the fifth and sixth grade and after a couple of years they would leave the safe environment of the school to go into the big world. They did not even know the answers to questions about their home address or their parents' names, not to mention more difficult issues which concerned them.

Luckily, the career of this oralist teacher at the Jyväskylä school was for only a couple of years until her retirement years began. I was able to follow from the side lines how the oralists functioned and think about when the winds from the Kuopio speech school had momentarily blown into Jyväskylä.

I wish I could have been there – Milan 1880

My Spanish interpreter colleague, Esther, invited to me to give a presentation at a conference in Madrid and to have one week holiday at her home in Barcelona. She had been able to "sell" me as an expert in sign language interpreting to the symposium organisers, FIAPAS, The Spanish Confederation of Families of Deaf Persons. I was expected to present a half an hour paper on the second day of the symposium. My theme was how sign language interpreting can move barriers in communication. My work at the WFD Secretariat and involvement in the EFSLI activities made it possible for me to include a worldwide perspective in my presentation. I was prepared for an anodyne, restful holiday and being together with friends in a new environment.

Half an hour can sometimes feel like a long time. When you try to compress everything that is essential on the importance of sign language interpreting in the lives of deaf people, the time is ruthlessly too short. My intention was to get the listeners to understand that, with the help of sign language, deaf people could reach equality and participate in situations where spoken language is used. For all this half an hour was not enough. I had drafted the outline for my presentation before I left for Madrid. My intention was that after the first symposium day, I would make the necessary adjustments to it. By then I would have a personal involvement with the symposium participants to whom I would direct my thoughts.

At the end of July Madrid welcomed me with a heat wave and humidity. The glowing streets of a city in plus forty centigrade did not tempt me to do any sightseeing. I had reserved my flights so that I would have one whole day free in Madrid. However, I could not feel free. At the back of my mind, the challenge waiting for me was bothersome. How to convince the symposium participants of the rights of deaf people to sign language interpreting services, or at least to get them to understand its importance in functioning communication? In my work I had heard that this European parents' organisation still favoured oralism. Its member organisations in many countries were advocating Cochlear Implant operations for deaf children. Would my statement be just like fighting against windmills?

When I finally received the final symposium programme in my hands, after listening to the presentations on the first day with the questions and comments from the participants, I realised that my half an hour was the only time in the whole three day symposium where sign language would be mentioned. The representative of the Australian Cochlear Implant firm had been given more than two hours in the symposium. What could not be cured with all kinds of technical equipment, at the end they would be helped with speech therapy? The parents and the experts believed in equipment. It was thought to repair the deficiency, the disability, the "broken" part in a human being. Very few hearing parents were able to see their deaf child as an unbroken entity who should be offered the chance to learn a visual language. The vision of this symposium was to have "speaking deaf children". We in Finland had believed in sign language for over twenty years. We had noted what wonderful results the use of sign language could have. Back home in Finland, we had seen how bilingual deaf children could acquire information better and grow up to be more equal citizens in society.

A day of agony! At the end of the first day I had written in my diary. The outline of my presentation needed to be completely changed. In half an hour I had to fit the whole ideology of bilingualism and the results which could already be seen. From the 1970's, in my work as the information officer, I knew how difficult it would be to change people's obsessive convictions. Attack was not the best approach here. What kind of facts would I have to offer to support my own convictions and views? I only had one night available to reformulate my presentation and I only had my own experiences from my life and my work with deaf people to base it on. Only a brief mention would be left this time for interpreting. It was more important to get the audience to understand the significance of sign language as a key to the learning of a second language, access to information, and participation.

Some deaf people from the UK, Uruguay and a couple of Spaniards who attended the symposium were seated in the first row to support me. I was speaking for them about the importance of sign language. The chair for the morning session seemed quite strict when he told me that in my half an hour I also should reserve time for a few questions and comments from the audience. I had to compress still more what I planned to say. My speech could not be too fast in order for the interpreting into many spoken and sign languages to function well. Without that interpreting, my thoughts expressed in English would be left incomprehensible for most of the audience.

I could feel the pressure of time, as I progressed clearly point by point in my argument, but believing strongly in my own views. From the nodding of the deaf people in the first row, I received positive feedback. They agreed completely with what I was saying. The cold looks and inscrutable expressions behind the deaf row did not encourage me as a speaker. I could not get any confirmation that my argument had been understood or that it had any effect on them. When not glancing at my notes, I let my gaze move around the audience, it was them I was talking to. I received encouragement from the deaf people to continue. The chair informed me that my time was running out. I was asked to conclude. So much was left unsaid, but I could be quite happy with my input. The wild applause from the front row was evidence of that.

Unfortunately, there was time left only for one question from the audience. The chair of the morning gave it to an Italian older deaf gentleman. He did not sit among the other deaf people, but with his own folks. It took time to find an interpreter who could understand his speech. The man did not use sign language, but wanted to express his views in spoken Italian. The symposium interpreters could not help him as his speech needed to be translated first into one of the official languages of the symposium. Only after that could it be interpreted for both the hearing and the deaf audience. One speech therapist among the Italians volunteered to interpret the views of the deaf man into English. After some hassle the matter was resolved.

The old deaf man gave overflowing praise to his school teachers, who had taught him to speak. By speaking he had done well in life. I was astounded to listen to his views interpreted into my earphones in English. The whole hall gave massive applause to his comments. The chair thanked me and the deaf man for his input by noting that it was good to end the morning session with this comment.

The eyes of the deaf people in the front row were glowing with disbelief and anger towards the deaf traitor. If looks could have killed, the Italian deaf man would have been dead. This comment from that Italian deaf man sucked all the energy out of me, my head was spinning and I could not say anything. When that kind of an opinion had been expressed by a deaf person, it completely undermined my presentation, no matter what the listeners thought about it. I started to wonder how the Italian deaf man was able to participate in the symposium at all only by lip-reading, without his own interpreter, when at the symposium there was no interpreting into Italian provided. He would have had to follow the international interpreting. I started to wonder if this intervention had been organised to undermine the credibility of sign language.

During the break, the deaf people and a few hearing parents of deaf children came to thank me for my presentation. The deaf man from Uruguay came to tell me that the deaf group had condemned the Italian man for deceiving the deaf community. The man had told them that he had not said what was translated and that the volunteer interpreter had put those words in his mouth. When he was told how his views had been expressed, the man had got frightened. That had not been his message at all. Whatever the truth had been, the harm had already been done. My presentation had lost its credibility and its foundation, when just one single deaf person had given an opposite view.

I felt that I had been in the same shoes as that one American deaf person who was the only deaf person participating in the Milan Congress in 1880. The congress was organised to resolve the fight between the supporters of the speech method and those of the sign language method. The supporters of these two methods had fought for years about the right way to teach deaf children. Of the 164 participants of the congress most were from Italy and France. Apart from the deaf person from the United States, all the other participants were hearing. After twelve presentations, the only issue to be resolved was the dispute over the teaching method. The Italian chairman gave a presentation against sign language that took two days. At the end of the congress a vote was taken over a statement that had eight points. There sign language was banned. The speech method was defined as the only correct method in deaf education.

Both the deaf and their hearing children have had to suffer a long time from the consequences of that Milan congress. The speech method did not guarantee the learning of a language for deaf children. Speech is only a part of a language and the learning of a language. Acquiring a language is a much wider issue than simply knowing and producing single words. A small vocabulary is not enough to acquire information, or to be able to communicate with unfamiliar hearing people. I wish I could have been there to support the deaf participant then. Probably we would have been overruled anyhow.

Ideologies in war: the fight over deaf people

The front seats at the Conference on Education for the Deaf had been reserved only for invited guests. It was impossible to rearrange the immovable seats in the auditorium so that as a sign language interpreter, I would have been able to sit opposite my deaf client. We could have moved an extra chair to the side of the aisle, but then the deaf people would not have seen either the presenters, the audio-visuals they might have used, and me as their sign language interpreter. Once we had registered for the conference, we decided to confront the organisers. We took over a couple of seats in the front row and moved the interpreter's chair into the empty space in front of the stage.

Many deaf teachers and representatives of deaf organisations had gathered in Manchester, where, for decades, the university had been the cradle of oralism. Through its effective exchange student programme, for years the university had been able to distribute "the good news about speech training for deaf people" widely in developing countries. Four years earlier in Cologne at the previous conference, there had been only a few deaf participants. In 1985, the deaf participants had formulated a plan to raise the views of deaf people, sign language, and to begin a dialogue with the teachers. As there were amongst them deaf people who were teachers of the deaf themselves, they wanted to be regarded as not only being the target of deaf education, but as having, from their own experience and training, something positive to contribute to developing deaf education at all levels. They wanted to be equal partners in the field.

As well as many influential hearing people who were invited guests, there were deaf oralists who had been invited who were dependent on lip-reading in their communication. The conference organisers had reserved them for the Lip speaker interpreters. The previous year on my study trip to the States I had met a few of these lip speakers. They highlighted their lips with dark red lipstick and by opening their mouth wide repeated every word the presenter expressed. I was sorry that I could not follow that method to amuse myself. It was not used in Finland at all. Their clients asked me to kindly move away from their seats and field of vision. Before the opening of the conference, my signing with my client had disturbed their eyes and mental balance. When my deaf clients refused to move from their seats, the party moved further back away from the contaminating radiation of sign language. We had the whole front row all to ourselves.

The deaf participants of the conference were using the breaks and the evenings to develop their own strategies. By being active and being seen, they wanted to demonstrate the existence of deaf teachers, and the significance of sign language which enables equal participation. Deaf people organised press conferences for the local media and a protest march where they brought up the importance of sign language as the first language for the deaf, its significance in deaf education and in accessing information. They emphasised that deaf people should have the chance to have a say in the content and development of deaf education. From their own experience as the recipients of deaf education, they were experts in the field, they knew what would be most helpful. They wanted to make sure that every session in the conference programme was attended by a deaf participant with a sign language interpreter.

We Finns were given the task of following the presentation of the great guru in oralism, Father van Uden. I had already heard van Uden's name, when working in the Jyväskylä Deaf School. My friend, who at that time was working as a guidance counsellor for deafblind children had made a study trip to Holland to the rehabilitation and resource centre Sint-Michielsgestel, where van Uden was the director. I had heard of the fixed views of this churchman about how deaf children had to be taught to speak and how they should be adjusted to hearing society as speaking persons. We had read his abstract in the conference book beforehand, knew the important concepts he would be using: long-time diagnostic therapy for children, which starts when they are born and lasts till they turn five. That is when the children start school in Holland. The presentation also included the use of the manual alphabet with deafblind, multiply-disabled and deaf children who could not benefit from monolingual teaching. I was really looking forward to the encounter with this master who was highly appreciated in these circles.

The organisers of the conference had made a serious miscalculation when they had assigned a room for Father van Uden's presentation which was far too small. We were there well in advance. We were able to reserve the front row seats right under the eyes of the presenter. As a sign language interpreter I had to put my chair on the stage right next to the podium. The room filled up in record time. Even before the presenter arrived, the steps at the side of the room were fully occupied by people sitting on them. A huge flock of disciples was left outside the room. The conference organisers were contacted. There was a rapid decision to move van Uden's presentation into the big auditorium, which had been in use for the opening ceremonies. Following the great oralist guru like sheep following a shepherd, the flock moved there. I could not believe what I saw: the followers had bright shining eyes and a happy smile on their lips, like "disciples" they moved to the auditorium following their master. Everyone who "needed strengthening of their belief" would be given the opportunity to listen to the great leader. There were only a few of us doubting Pharisees. We wanted to be present to prove that most of his theses were wrong and heretic.

When Father van Uden's speech finally started, I was unfortunately unable to see his reactions to my beginning to move my hands to the speed of his presentation. My chair was next to his podium and I was physically under his spell. He could not have missed my swiftly moving hands, the changing of expressions on my face, and the key words of his presentation which I formulated on my lips. The Finnish deaf participants received the exact translation of his words and concepts he used. He must have noticed from the corner of his eyes that I was following every word he expressed, although he did not understand Finnish nor any other sign language.

I did not have the chance within my intensive and demanding interpreting to follow the facial expressions or reactions of his true disciples when they saw me using sign language in front of them. I wonder what went on in their heads, when they were trying to avoid seeing me, the distraction. Did any one of them happen to think during the presentation how it might be possible to convey Father van Uden's thoughts in "this language of apes", which was said just to be poor, inadequate gesturing? The oralists had mostly justified the prohibition of sign language in the rehabilitation and education of deaf children exactly with these words. According to their view, the use of sign language would close deaf people into a sign language ghetto where they could not get out to hearing society.

My signing must have interested the presenter, as after the lecture he came to stand by me and asked me which method I had been using. Had it possibly been *SimCom* (simultaneous communication where signs support the spoken text produced by the lips)? I told him that in my interpreting I had been using Finnish Sign Language. I wonder if the great master had the slightest idea or understood how much that conveyed about the effectiveness of sign language.

The conference in Manchester was a great breakthrough for deaf people and for sign language at future meetings in the field of deaf education. There was no going back any longer to the old ways. Information about and understanding of sign language as the first language of deaf people started to grow. With the help of sign language, it is easier for deaf people to learn the language of the environment as their second language and after that, even other languages. Other industrialised countries gradually gave up the idea of total communication and started to follow the countries in the vanguard, the Nordic countries and United States, using bilingualism in deaf education. Unfortunately, this new ideology has not yet reached many developing countries. Every country has to follow its own path with different phases. The slogan used in the placards in the Manchester protest march has continued to live among deaf people: THE ONLY PLACE FOR ORALISM IS IN THE BEDROOM!

At the 21st international conference in deaf education in Vancouver in 2010, a public apology was given for the wrong decisions made at the Milan Congress in 1880, which put aside the use of sign language as a language in which to educate deaf children, and permitted teaching to be carried out only through the use of speech. The period of oralism started in Milan and sign language was displaced in deaf education for almost a hundred years. The public apology at this conference is seen as a milestone in a new era in deaf education. It is based on the UN Convention on the Rights of Persons with Disabilities and on the statement of the 2007 WFD Congress, both of which emphasise multilingual and multicultural education. Basic rights for deaf children can be reached through their own linguistic and cultural identity.

Wedding photo of my parents.

Deaf people at the Säynätsalo Deaf Club wanted to hear about my experiences in the U.S. in 1968.

Preparing the 75th Anniversary exhibition of the Deaf Association in 1980.

In front of the FAD office in Kuitinmäki.

The FAD office was in Kuitinmäki, Espoo 1977–1987

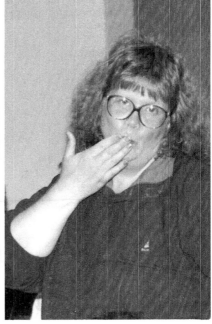

The information officer visiting the Deaf Clubs around Finland.

Someone caught me signing GOOD.

As a lecturer at a symposium in Madrid in 1993.

Had to fit everything about sign language in a half an hour lecture.

My lecture was interpreted into three sign languages.

The Dangers-of-Smoking -lecture in Oulu.

My first contact with international signing in Copenhagen in 1977, Bill Moody interpreting.

Professor Harlan Lane's lecture is interpreted into European sign languages in Manchester in 1985.

Training with Anna Komarova in Kirgizstan in 2005.

The administrative officer at the WFD office.

Handing over the book of *The Presidents of Finland* published by FAD to President Urho Kekkonen in 1980.

Tarja Halonen, The President of Finland, Patron of the FAD 100th anniversary, arriving at the Fair Centre in 2005.

VI
My career beside Liisa Kauppinen

Liisa – my friend, boss and the visionary of the deaf world

I met Liisa Kauppinen for the first time at a course for sign language instructors in the summer of 1973 in Malminharju, the Course Centre of the Deaf Association. Afterwards Liisa told me that she had already noticed we Ojala children a couple of years earlier at the annual meeting of the Finnish Association of the Deaf in Jyväskylä. Both my brother and I had turned heads because of the way we were dressed and because we had long fair hair. The next summer, at the Nordic Congress of the Deaf in Turku, I worked in the office. During this Turku congress I got to know Liisa better. There we became friends. Liisa had already by then decided that she wanted me to come and work at FAD. She wanted me there to keep throwing my long fair hair off my face with a slight hand movement.

Liisa was born in Koura, in Pohjanmaa, the north-western part of Finland. She lost her hearing at the age of five after meningitis. She already had a rich Finnish language when she lost her hearing. She was sent to the Oulu School for Deaf-mutes, where she met signing deaf people for the first time. It did not take long for this gifted and socially clever child to learn this language of hands from her schoolmates. Because Liisa already knew the language of the environment, she quickly learned how to read and find information in that language. Already during her school years she had become a conveyor of information and a leader among the deaf pupils. Of course, Liisa was also hit on her hands with a ruler, if she made the mistake of using what in those days was the forbidden language in the classroom or in public. She has often told me how her school years, and sharing the experiences of other deaf children, were the best education for her later work in the field of deafness and her becoming the leader of the Deaf Association.

As well as her certificate of graduation from the deaf school on her CV, Liisa also has a certificate for completing the Nikkarila School in Home Economics. Beside these, she has privately accomplished middle school and, over the years, different university courses. Liisa's secret weapon is the fact that she has an exceptionally good memory. Sometimes when listening to her I have felt that she has memorised everything she has ever read. When needed she is able to quote word for word, in her comments or presentations, almost any text she has read.

In her early years Liisa moved from Pohjanmaa to Helsinki to work as a seamstress in spite of her family's opposition to it. She found accommodation as a subtenant with the family of Runo Savisaari in Espoo. In those years she must have acquired a lot of knowledge and useful contacts which she needed later in her future career, as during that time Runo was the President of the Finnish Deaf Association. Liisa married her fiancé Esa quite early and had two children, Susanna and Jukka. After she studied to become a punch card operator she found a new job in the forestry ministry, then later in a bank, where she worked in the computer department as a line manager of hearing workers. After working for a few years in a computer company, then as an operator in 1973, she was asked to work as an information and training officer in the Deaf Association.

At the beginning of 1976, she was elected as the executive director of the Finnish Deaf Association. Quite soon she realised that, as a deaf executive, it would be difficult for her to make contact with hearing people and authorities if she did not have a sign language interpreter available. In the autumn of 1976 I could not have guessed what Liisa had in mind when she asked me to join her and her children on the 80 kilometre Bear Trail in Lapland. After eight days of sloshing through marshes with our heavy backpacks, sleeping together in the huts and sharing every hour of the day, she asked me if I would come and work at FAD as an information officer and interpreter for her.

In November 1976, when I came to work at the FAD office, which at that time was located in Elizabeth Street in Helsinki, it had three rooms and a kitchen while there were ten of us working there. My good friend Aune from Jyväskylä had been employed earlier as the chief social worker. There were three strong Taurus women taking care of matters in those days, Liisa, Aune and me. FAD was a very small and invisible organisation back then. It was mainly the confederation for the local Deaf Clubs. Compared to many other organisations of people with disabilities, the funding received by FAD from the Slot Machine Association was very meagre. FAD had a part time person who took care of the finances. I can still remember how worried we workers would be about whether we were going to receive our monthly salary on time, because the financial situation of the association was so poor. In the beginning of 1977, FAD moved to new bigger office quarters in Kuitinmäki, Espoo, after the organisation had received greater funding from the Slot Machine Association for the first time.

In Liisa's hands FAD started a completely new phase. Authorities had thought that it was not possible to contact FAD by phone because of the deaf leader. Of course, there had been hearing people answering phones in the office before and interpreting for deaf staff members, but borrowing Liisa's words "the change came in the form of Raili". Soon after my arrival and at the start of our cooperation, Liisa began to notice how important it was that the sign language interpreter had a well-rounded education and good educational base. Later on she often referred to this fact, when in the late 1970's sign language interpreter training started in Finland. As an example of the earlier problems, she often mentioned how difficult it had been for her to respond to phone messages from authorities, when the person who had taken the message had not understood the facts correctly and could not write the request down properly for making further contact.

With Liisa in place, the FAD started to be visible and to be represented at different meetings and seminars together with the other organisations of people with disabilities. When Liisa had her personal interpreter with her, hearing people were freer to contact her, to start a conversation, to ask questions they had wanted to ask for so long, but never had dared to ask. Liisa's speed was unbelievable. She never accepted "NO" for an answer from authorities or other bodies. If the matter did not progress with one request, Liisa found a new way until the often reasonable and long awaited wishes and needs of deaf people were met.

Since the 1950's there had been regular cooperation between the Nordic Deaf Associations through the Nordic Deaf Council, where the presidents and executives met twice a year to exchange their experiences and information. Sweden had always been the model country in providing services for deaf people. They had money for all kinds of new experiments and services, which the other countries heard about with jealousy. Liisa used Sweden's advancement to our benefit when she advocated for deaf issues in Finland. When it could be shown that a service functioned well for deaf people in Sweden or sometimes in the Danish model, it had to be made available for Finnish deaf people in an even better form. By the end of the 1970's and 1980's, Finnish deaf people received sign language interpreting services provided by the government, FAD social workers were available in every district to provide social services to deaf people in sign language, and there was also sign language production in video in order for deaf people to receive information in their own language, just to mention a few of the new services.

The office in Kuitinmäki had been sufficient both for the number of personnel and the needed office space when FAD moved there, but in a few years the number of workers had grown so much that the organisation had to rent office space nearby. When in the middle of 1980's the FAD was operating in at least five different premises, it was time to apply for further funding from the Slot Machine Association to build a new office building. Liisa did not lack ideas about what was needed in the new building. Deaf people needed a high school for their own community, a video production centre, a deaf theatre in its own space, a library and a museum. When the Hard of Hearing Association, the advocacy organisation for the hard of hearing and deafened people, happened to apply for funding for a new office building at the same time, the funder forced the two organisations in the field of hearing impairment under the same roof. Unfortunately, FAD had to cut quite a lot from its plans for its future needs in the new building in order that the most important activities of both organisations could be fitted in. Beside the two main organisations in the field of hearing impairment there were also other organisations, which moved into the Light House, as it was called: The Service Foundation for the Deaf, the Parent organisation, the Deaf Mission, the Deaf Sports Federation and the Helsinki Deaf Club. Liisa was the promoter and motivator behind this huge project.

Work grows to be worldwide

In 1983 Liisa was elected on to the WFD Bureau and at the same time became its Vice-President. With the help of advocacy work from the Nordic Deaf Associations, Liisa was elected as the WFD General Secretary in 1987, after which the WFD Secretariat moved from Rome to Helsinki. The Nordic countries had started to think that the status of deaf people in these countries was relatively good, that was why we should start helping other countries by sharing our knowhow. Thereafter the FAD development cooperation work started, which has included some twenty countries. After Liisa Kauppinen served as WFD General Secretary for two terms she was elected as the WFD President in 1995. In this role she served two four-year terms until 2004, after which she was nominated as the WFD Honorary President.

Although the World Federation of the Deaf had been in existence since 1956, its visibility and activities had been quite slight until Liisa started her work. She persuaded the Finnish Slot Machine Association to grant funding for the WFD Secretariat for two terms. A 4-6 person staff was working together with the General Secretary to build better connections with its member organisations, the UN and its agencies. Until then the part-time General Secretary had for over 30 years been an Italian hearing doctor. During Liisa's term the participants at different meetings in the UN and its agencies started to better understand deafness and the rights of deaf people to participate with a sign language interpreter. Liisa would not be Liisa, if the activities of the WFD had not also improved, grown and strengthened during her terms. The number of member countries increased rapidly, functioning regional secretariats were formed to support the members, and expert networks were developed to help the General Secretary in her work. If the work of the WFD before had been mainly to organise the WFD Congress and General Assembly every four years, now it also started to work between those Congresses.

It was impossible to keep up with Liisa's pace. Her motivation, enthusiasm, energy and resources seemed to be endless. She always stayed late and was often the last one in the office, formulating a statement, a letter or a presentation and in the morning was the first there, energetic, ready to grasp new challenges. Liisa never had regular working hours. Her calendar was booked so full of meetings and engagements that she rarely had time to get prepared for anything. Everything seemed to be accomplished by her at the last minute, but at meetings and other events she was always 110% present. She always had new ideas, views, standpoints and she was especially good in making summaries of discussions. Liisa is a fabulous and popular speaker. She knows how to engage her audience. She always has something new as a seed for thought. Because she reads a lot, and follows what is happening in the world and in research, she has always been a visionary in deaf matters. For years now, Finland has not needed to follow the Swedish models, but through Liisa's leadership, has become a model country in deaf issues for the rest of the world. Liisa is a very popular trainer and consultant in training events in many countries.

In travels with Liisa, my world has also grown greatly. As Liisa's interpreter I have been able to travel to many countries and places which

I never could have dreamt of before. When I started my work at FAD, I promised her that I would stand and fall with her and that I would be available to her as an interpreter whenever she needed me. Liisa has often mentioned, when referring to our cooperation, that I was her Annie Sullivan, Helen Keller's truthful teacher. Especially in the beginning, the work days were limitlessly long because in those days I was working alone as the interpreter. Between and after the official programme of a meeting or a seminar, interpreting was needed during breaks, dinners and during unofficial gatherings late at night. I was young then and functioned well, I was also eager and burning for this good cause. As long as Liisa wanted to continue and participate and make contact with hearing people, I felt that it was my responsibility to interpret to the boundaries of my capacity, because the issue was usually important, a once in a lifetime possibility, or it might have just been the very discussion that would advance the deaf cause. I do not think I could have stretched so much for any other deaf person, because I received back enormously from Liisa myself.

Liisa was the first deaf person in my life with whom I worked on equal terms and who was my true peer. She led me gently deeper into the deaf world, to the experiences of deaf people. With her help I learned to understand deaf people better, although I had grown up in the deaf community, but after all, I was a hearing person. She knew both languages well, she had had better opportunities for acquiring information and adapting it to the situation of deaf people than grassroots level deaf people among whom I had grown up. If Liisa taught me to understand deafness better, I, as a hearing person had the opportunity to share with her our hearing ways of thinking, our experiences and also, as her interpreter, the auditory world which surrounded us. Many auditory experience were completely new for Liisa. What one does not hear, the eyes might not see. Together we had wonderful discussions, travelling to distant countries and cultures.

If Liisa's working tempo in the office was tireless, the pace accelerated during her travels. Because Liisa's calendar was fully booked, she often left for her work trips at the last minute, barely making it to the meeting, seminar or conference she was going to. To organise and change Liisa's travel plans, even at the last minute, was an art in itself. Luckily I never had to do it, but her assistant had that task to do. At some point the FAD travel agent tried to suggest that it would be possible to link Liisa's many flights together in order to get cheaper tickets. But because of Liisa's ever accelerating speed at work, her calendar had to be flexible, even to have a last minute meeting or important appointment fitted into it, which was why her flight tickets could be produced only at the last minute.

Usually Liisa does not travel alone. For most of her meetings and events abroad she needs at least two interpreters along. Nowadays when the interpreters have learned to keep a closer look at their working hours and their capacity, Liisa's participation in some UN meetings has demanded even three Finnish interpreters to fly over. Interpreting is not only needed during the meetings, but during breaks, meal times and get-togethers in the evenings, which are the best kind of preparation and advocacy time for the participants. When I was more actively involved as an interpreter, and was not yet married, I tried to book my flights so that I had enough time to settle down, adjust to the surroundings, get over jetlag, and get used to the language I was going to interpret from.

Liisa does not suffer from jetlag at all. Right after arrival she is ready to roll up her sleeves and start working. When she returns home from her working trips, she often has another suitcase already packed for another trip either in Finland or abroad. Many a story could be told about Liisa's leaving for a trip, which her whole work team is committed to. Presentations and papers were often being prepared late at night before the trip or even with the taxi waiting at the door to take her to the airport. The last minute scrambles are hard to describe, but a nice peace falls over the whole office and its workers, when once again Liisa has been escorted to one of her trips. For Liisa, everything is got ready at the last minute. She has never yet missed her flights, but for that the helpful taxi drivers can be thanked, who to avoid the rush-hour traffic to get Liisa to the terminal and gate the fastest way, have taken minor roads, travelled along ditches or even have speeded to get her there.

When I started work as Liisa's interpreter, I told her that one of us had to change our habits in order for me not to get ulcers. As a country girl I was used to being wherever I needed to be well in advance, rather a quarter before than a quarter after. Because I was the interpreter, I wanted to arrive in good time to check the place and the seating for myself and Liisa in order to have the best view of the speakers and enable us to follow the participants. Often I needed to organise an extra chair for the room and drinking water for myself. (I often wondered why there always was a jug of water for the speakers, but very rarely for the interpreters, although they had been registered for the meeting, too.)

Besides being a sign language interpreter for Liisa, I also worked as the WFD President's Assistant for a few years. The task suited me well because I knew her and the WFD matters well. Her WFD correspondence went through me. Because Liisa was so busy, as her assistant I could help her workload by preparing documents and letters as far as possible before our meetings. I created standard letter templates, where necessary details could be added so that Liisa only needed to approve the letter or email message with her signature before it could be sent out to the world as her response. For me, both as an interpreter and assistant, Liisa approved quite a lot that she would not have approved for any other person. That was because she trusted me. My work has always been very independent. I was able to organise my own timetable and what needed to be done and when. Although there always was more work than I could accomplish, whatever I was doing did progress matters.

Liisa continues working and receives awards

In the past few years Liisa's life has been full of awards and achievements. She has received all the possible awards and medals FAD and WFD has had to offer. The Federation of Social Security has given her the title of Organisational Counsellor for all her work in the Finnish social security field. She received the Golden Cross of Finland's Order of the White Rose in 1989. In 1991 she received the American Edward Miner Gallaudet award for international and national leaders for promoting deaf issues in the world. The Nordic deaf organisations have taken turns in giving her recognition. She was made an Honorary Doctor in Law in 1998 by Gallaudet University, an Honorary Doctor in Pedagogy in 2004 by the University of Jyväskylä and an Honorary Doctor in Law by Trinity College, Ireland in 2013. This has all been recognition of her enormous contribution to promoting and advocating for deaf issues in Finland and in the world, improving the status of sign language, and promoting the human rights of people with disabilities.

In 2013 Liisa Kauppinen was awarded the UN Human Rights Award for her work in improving the human rights of deaf people, the first person in Finland to receive it. This award, which is given out every five years has previously been given, for instance, to Martin Luther King and

Nelson Mandela.

When receiving these awards, Liisa has always remembered to mention that she has not been alone in doing her work, but has always had good and trustworthy colleagues doing the work with her. Luckily my self-esteem has been good enough that I have understood that I should also take these thanks from Liisa's success for myself. If a presentation of Liisa's has been praised, I have realised that it would not have been given to the hearing audience in those words if I had not been there to interpret it. If Liisa's discussions with hearing parties have gone well, I have known how to enjoy the situation as the interpreter, for it was I who had been conveying this discussion from one language to another. If I did not have this skill and attitude, I probably would not have been able to work in that position so long, so intensively and so much.

During the past few years Liisa has been actively involved in drafting the UN document on the human rights of people with disabilities. Always at her best, Liisa has been in these negotiations with the representatives of governments and other organisations. Over the last few years, Liisa has also become the spokesperson for other disabled people and their organisations. Very often it has been she who has been asked to present the joint statement or address from all the international organisations of people with disabilities. Liisa is respected and listened to in the UN, all its member countries and agencies, as an expert in the field of deafness.

Although Liisa is at home in international circles, when she is at home she always has time to listen to grassroots deaf people. One of her most important achievements has been how she supported the studies of a gifted deaf young man. This deaf man's Finnish skills were very inadequate and he had hardly any knowledge of other languages, but was very skilled in pantomime and dancing. With the help of a sign language interpreter he made it to the dance department of the Theatre University. Liisa and her friends supported his studies by providing him a support network, which interpreted all the theory texts for him connected with his studies. The exams were taken in sign language and he received his MA in dancing, although he hardly knew much Finnish at all.

For years Liisa kept telling us what she would like to do after she retired at the age of 65. She had plans to study cultural anthropology at university. She also wanted to spend more time with her four grandchildren. Liisa turned 65 in 2004. It was no surprise to us that Liisa decided to continue for two more years in her position because in 2005 FAD was celebrating its 100th anniversary. Liisa could not step down before that event where it would be possible to highlight all that the Finnish Association of the Deaf had accomplished in Finland and around the world. The highlights of the celebrations were the Human Rights Conference in Finlandia Hall, a protest march and a petition from deaf people that was given to the spokesman of the Parliament, and the actual 100th anniversary celebration in the Fair Centre where the President of Finland, Tarja Halonen, who was the patron of the FAD's 100th anniversary event, participated.

Because Liisa's work history also includes my own work history so much, I wanted to write this memoir of our journey together. It has not been easy to live, to work, to grow and to suffer in the shadow of this great person. It has not been easy to accept my own role as 'just' an interpreter. Everyone wants to be herself, not only the interpreter, conveyor, bridge between two worlds. Walking at the side of a visionary like Liisa has been educational, rewarding, but also demanding and onerous. In my role I have often felt little, insufficient, empty, stupid and unaccomplished. Luckily I learned quite early that at Liisa's pace I would not last long. We others who work in the deaf field to earn our living have a completely different starting point for our work. For Liisa, who is deaf herself, who grew up in the deaf community, work has always been part of her own life. I have been tired at times, I have rebelled and left my task, but Liisa and FAD as an employer have been wonderful because I have always been welcomed back with open arms, usually into a new position, a new task, and new challenges.

Liisa has always been a hopeless correspondent. She has the will, but no time. Now I am waiting to see if our friendship will continue after she has retired, now that I have already left my work to find out who I am as a hearing person.

Three Tauruses: Aune, Liisa, and me at the Elizabeth Street office in 1976.

With Liisa in Tallinn in 1976.

Interpreting for the sport teams of deaf schools in Tallinn.

At the East-African sign language seminar in Ethiopia in 1990.

In Lebanon at the Arab countries' conference for deaf people in 1995.

At the annual development co-operation negotiations in Zambia in 1997.

Interpreting for the representatives of the Ministry of Social and Health Affairs at the Light House.

The speaker and interpreter received flowers in Iran in 1996.

The scarfs stayed on.

With WFD President Yerker Andersson and General Secretary Liisa Kauppinen in Vienna 1990.

In Kanazawa, Japan. The interpreter also had to learn ikebana.

I lay a wreath on the Hiroshima memorial.

Leaders of the international organisations of people with disabilities met the UN Secretary General Kofi Annan in New York.

Signing Kaubamaja.

In Slovakia with Liisa.

Interpreting with Kati Marjanen for the WFD delegation at the Great Wall of China.

The support interpreter sits beside Liisa.

Conquering the world with Liisa.

Epilogue

Was it coincidence, or did I just happen to grasp the opportunity that was meant for me? Not everything went as planned, when I was starting my study leave in autumn 2000. My intention was to improve my foreign language skills for my work at the WFD Secretariat. My German and French were rusty from secondary school days, Spanish I wanted to start all over again, and I also wanted to finally study the basics of Russian. Two weeks before the one-year course was supposed to start, I was informed that the course had been cancelled. There had not been enough applicants for it. On my way to work in the train I noticed an advertisement in the free paper, that the University of Helsinki was organising a writing course for unemployed academics. I contacted the organisers, explained my situation and was invited to a group interview. I was one of the lucky sixteen people who were elected for this free pilot course, *Life books into order – IT skills into hand*.

During my exchange year in the States my English teacher, Peggy Sange, awoke the writer in me. My senior high school teacher, Pentti Nuorti, encouraged me into creative writing. For ten years I had been producing information texts while working as the information officer at the Finnish Association of the Deaf. Throughout my whole career I wrote newspaper articles, press releases and minutes of meetings. Verbose and detailed descriptions have always been my besetting sins, on which I have continuously been given negative feedback. Luckily I have been free to empty my plentiful word chest into postcards filled with scribble, many-paged letters, and overflowing email messages, when keeping in touch with my friends all over the world without anybody complaining about it.

During my first ten-week writing course, reminiscences of incidents from my childhood became unplugged. These images from events and experiences had to be hurriedly noted down in bullet points to mature and to be written down later as stories. It was important to get the chance to tell stories about my own experiences, from growing up as a hearing child in a deaf family to working as a sign language interpreter in the deaf world, and about my life as a bridge between two worlds.

During my study leave I also started a creative writing course at the Järvenpää Adult Education Centre, led by Seija Viitaniemi, where I have continued and which I still attend. In autumn 2005, a new *Lifeline writ-*

ing course started at the Centre, first led by Eeva Lehtovuori, and after a couple of years by Riitta Riihonen. During the last year of the course we gathered all our stories into manuscript form. In autumn 2010, at the *Write a Book* course led by Pauliina Susi, I was encouraged, and received tips on how to make my stories work better as a book.

I would like to warmly thank Timo Montonen and Heli Hulmi who in the beginning guided me into the wonderful world of story writing. Seija Viitaniemi has continuously encouraged and supported me, both in my writing and in getting my stories published to open up hearing eyes. Eeva Lehtovuori guided us on the seven-year phases in a person's life. Inspiring writing tasks from Riitta Riihonen led us into our memories. My course mates from different courses have encouraged me to continue my writing with their feedback and enthusiasm about the marvellous deaf world. I have also found great friends in my writing circles, a few of whom I would like to mention separately. Ritva Romero, Riitta Habes, Tarja Mattila and Salme Saarikoski, you have made my baroness-like everyday life these days much richer. From those circles I have also found winter swimming company.

My mother and father would have been so happy about this book of mine and would been so proud of me once again. I also would like to thank my late husband Per-Olof (Pärre) Signell for the years I had with him. He was one in a million for me.

My brother Risto and his whole family, Anita, Solja, Suvi-Tuuli and Ilja, have been an important part of my life and shared both my joys and sorrows and have been there for me at my moments of loss, too. I would like to express special thanks to my sister-in-law Anita who as early as the 1980's designed this logo ✌ for me to express my spirit and career as a sign language interpreter.

Without my friend Aune and her support, my life would have been much more difficult and also poorer. With Ritva Sandelin and other overexhausted workers in the field of sensory impairments I have experienced many hilarious moments together. In addition, without all my friends my life would not have been worth living.

I would like to express special thanks to Liisa Kauppinen and Markku Jokinen, my friends, colleagues and bosses during my working life at the Finnish Association of the Deaf and the World Federation of the Deaf, for reading my manuscript and giving their comments on it, and especially for their agreement to get these stories published. I would like to also thank Markku for the recommendation he wrote in support of an application I made for a publishing grant and for his subsequent permission to include it as the prologue to my book.

I would like to thank my sign language interpreter colleagues for our joint learning experience. By working together we have achieved appreciation for our work, have found professionalism in it and hopefully been able to develop better practices and services for deaf people's participation and access to information. With longing I remember my interpreter colleague Raija Moustgaard. Special thanks to my support interpreters/interpreting partners for many years, Susanna Söderlund, Elina Lehtomäki, Kati Marjanen and Virpi Thurén. I often received support and help from you uphill, not downhill. I also would like to thank my international interpreter colleagues Bill Moody, Anna Komarova and Liz Scott Gibson for their friendship for many years and for our very rewarding and educational interpreting trips together.

I would like to thank the hearing children of deaf parents for providing me with a reference group and some hilarious moments at the CODA get-togethers. We CODAs are not completely hearing, but not deaf either. Eino and Runo Savisaari have been great role models for me to follow.

But my story would probably have never come out in book form, if my partner Markus Wahlberg, together with his dog Ettan, had not appeared in my life. He has helped me to find this final form for my stories with his enthusiasm, questions, support and with his red pen. With his sharp researcher's eyes and patience he has also gone through my English translation and compared it with the already printed Finnish book and found quite a few shortcuts I had made in my translation work. For all of this, and for his positive outlook on life, I would like to express my loving thanks to him.

I also would like to warmly thank my graphic designer Eeva-Liisa Bahnaan for her tips, skillful layout and also for getting this English version of my memoirs ready for printing. She has also been my support person in all technical details, in getting the materials in the right form for the Book on Demand format, and in setting up a user account for me to get my book distributed internationally.

Although English has been my working language throughout my career and I have translated these stories of mine into English myself, they never could have been published without getting help from my native

English speaker friends Liz Scott Gibson, Carol Norris, AFS-sister Janet Daugherty and Sidney Smith, my AFS-friend from New Zealand. All have reviewed sections of my English text and given me advice for improving it, and I greatly appreciate the time they have spent doing so. I would like to give my warmest thanks especially to Sidney who has thoroughly and speedily proofread the latest English manuscript and put it all in good English for publishing.

In Järvenpää 7th of November, 2018
Raili Ojala-Signell